FOREWORD
BY DAVID MAY

Hi to all you United Fans,

I bet you are all looking forward to the start of another premiership season, In which we will get our title back from Stamford Bridge.

I played for the world's biggest club for nearly 10 years, I was involved in a lot of very big games which I played at centre back but occasionally filled in at right back. The season before I came to Old Trafford I was in a Blackburn Rovers team that finished runners-up to United in the 1993/94 season, then in that July I eventually signed for United for £1.2 Million.

In my first season we actually finished 2nd to my old team, what a reversal! I played a lot in the 1995/96 season and I scored the first goal on the way to us winning the title on the last day of the season v Middlesbrough, We won 3-0. I was a starter also in the FA Cup Final v Liverpool, where I'm sure you can all remember the King got the winner.

In 1996/97 I made over 40 appearances as we retained the League Title and we finished semi finalists in the European Cup. I also started in the 1999 Fa Cup Final.

My final competitive appearance was against Burnley in in the League Cup in 2002, which was the team I ended up joining after United.

I had a wonderful time at United and was involved in winning a lot of the silverware, what a great period it was with some great players.

I think this is a very well written book and a lot of details has gone into it, it brings back a hell of a lot of great memories and

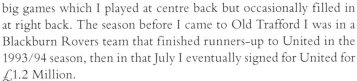

some of the great players I played with.

I am still involved a lot with United with a number of things as I'm sure a lot of you are aware.

Hope you enjoy the book and I will always carry on following United's results.

All the Best

Maysie

THE MANCHESTER UNITED PREMIER YEARS

STEVE BROOKES

EMPIRE
PUBLICATIONS

First published in 2010

EMPIRE PUBLICATIONS
1 Newton Street, Manchester M1 1HW
© Steve Brookes 2010

ISBN: 1901746 704 - 9781901746709

Cover design and layout: Ashley Shaw

Printed in Great Britain by KnowledgePoint Ltd.

CONTENTS PAGE

ACKNOWLEDGEMENTS

Hello, To all you Millions of United Fans ..

Manchester United have obviously been the best team in the Premiership over the last 18 years, so many titles have ended up at Old Trafford that even though this book is based on United's Premier League years I have also included a section of all the trophies Manchester united have won in that time also.

A lot of supporters of other teams secretly admire United and are envious even though they openly say they hate them. Manchester United have a great history, they have had great players and improved Old Trafford massively, I hope you enjoy reading this book and relive all those famous memories and look forward to the years ahead.

I would like to say a massive thanks to Ashley Shaw for helping with this publication, Charlotte Montgomery, Neil Brookes, Sue and Phil Montgomery, Stacey Fellows, Teigan Bailey Brookes and Izzy-Mai Brookes.

I hope you enjoy this book,

Kind Regards

Steve

RECORDS
(as at end of 2009/10 season)

Attendance: 82,771: vs Bradford PA - FAC4 -29/1/1949 (Maine Road)
76,098: vs Blackburn - Premiership - 17/9/2006 (OT)

Best league win: 10-1: vs Wolves 15/10/1892 - Division 1

Worst league loss: 0-7: vs Blackburn R. 10/04/1926 - Division 1

Best cup win: 10-0: vs Anderlecht 26/09/1956 EC Preliminary

Worst cup loss: 1-7: vs Burnley 13/02/1901 FA Cup R1

Most capped player: Bobby Charlton: 106 England

All-time appearances: Ryan Giggs 838 - 1990/2010

League appearances: Bobby Charlton: 606 - 1956/73

Hisghest goalscorer: Bobby Charlton: 249 - 1956/73

Highest League goalscorer:
Bobby Charlton: 199 - 1956/73

Most goals in a season:
Denis Law: 46 - 1963/64

Most League goals in a season:
Dennis Viollet: 32 - 1959/60 Division 1

Largest Transfer fee received :
£80m - Cristiano Ronaldo from Real Madrid - 1/7/2009

Largest Transfer fee paid:
£30.75m - Dimitar Berbatov to Tottenham - 1/9/2008

HISTORY

Manchester United Football Club's size and popularity on the world stage is nothing short of colossal. Nearly every decade football gifts have been established and encouraged at the club before being let loose for the world to see. However, this has not always been the case.

In 1878 at Newton Heath, Manchester, at the height of the industrial revolution, railwaymen from the Lancashire and Yorkshire Railway started their own football team. Newton Heath Lancashire and Yorkshire Railway FC or Newton Heath LandYR FC was the beginning of a rather special moment in English football history. Their first playing ground was nothing more than a field on North Road that they shared with the firm's cricketers and leased off the railway. After a decade or so the club dropped the 'Lancashire and Yorkshire Railway' moniker and went forth as Newton Heath FC - thus no longer a work's team the LandYR withdrew the ground, the nascent team moving to Bank Street, Clayton in 1894.

By now a Football League club Newton Heath yo-yoed between the two divisions of the league weighed down by debts. By 1901, the club stood on the brink of closure. Football at this time saw many clubs come and go and it seemed Heath would join this long list. Fortunately, Heath's captain, Harry Stafford, was unusually determined to make ensure the club's survival. The birth of Manchester United owes much to serendipity - the following (probably apocyrphal) story has gone down in legend.

After much thought, a Grand Bazaar was set-up to raise funds to save Heath and pay off its debts. Stafford attended the bazaar with his St. Bernard dog to whom he attached a barrel so people could donate a few shillings as it wandered around. Unfortunately, Harry left his dog, 'Major', at the hall where the fundraiser was being held overnight and when it was disturbed by a nightwatchmen the dog escaped and ended up at a local pub. The pub happened to be owned by brewing magnate John Henry Davies whose daughter took a shine to 'Major'. When Stafford eventually discovered the whereabouts of his pet he was asked by Davies if he cared to sell the animal. Stafford refused the offer but then took the conversation to the subject of Newton Heath and the problems it faced.

Regardless of the truth of the tale the fact was that Davies was persuaded to become chairman and, after making a large financial donation and clearing the debt, he changed the colours of Newton Heath from green and gold to red and white and, after much discussion, decided on a new name - Manchester United. Also, as part of the deal, 'Major' ended up at the Davies' household.

The club's first few seasons were spent in Division 2 but they always managed to finish in the tables top half. In 1904 and for a record transfer fee at the time, United signed Charlie Roberts for £750 from Grimsby Town. Roberts had an instant impact the following season as United finished second and gained promotion to Division 1.

At this time, United were definitely the junior team in Manchester. However when FA Cup holders Manchester City ran into trouble with the FA for paying their players 'under the counter' they were fined and forced to sell their best players. United got wind of this before the competition and snapped up centre-half Sandy Turnbull and winger Billy Meredith, then the greatest player in the country (which in Edwardian times meant the world). United also poached City's manager Ernest Mangnall and sowing the seeds of a century-long rivalry.

In 1907/08 United finished 9 points clear of Aston Villa to win the League. The next season saw the club lift two trophies – the Charity Shield and the FA Cup, then the most important trophy available. After winning the League title again in 1910/11 season, following the club's move across the city to Old Trafford, United embarked on a barren period, failing to trouble the Brasso until after the Second World War. During this time the vast Old Trafford ground (capacity 70,000) frequently echoed to home crowds of less than 5,000. The death of chairman Davies and the economic depression of the 1930s didn't help and United nearly went under in 1930 when players' wages were not paid and the few supporters left threatened to boycott.

Things reached breaking point in Autumn 1931 following a record run of defeats. Eventually, local businessman James Gibson stepped forward promising that if supporters rallied round the team and attendances improved, he would wipe off the club's debts and take-over. A crowd of over 33,000 (29,000 more than the previous home gate) turned up on Christmas Day 1931 to watch United beat Wolves 3-2 and Gibson took control soon after. Nevertheless the era between the wars was characterised by more yo-yoing between the divisions and further success for rivals City.

By the end of the Second World War, United had been effectively managerless since 1937. Old Trafford had also been bombed meaning that the club were without a ground and with no immediate means of repairing it with all government funds pressed into more vital matters.

Amid this apparently hopeless situation a letter sent to then Liverpool player Matt Busby was the catalyst for resurrection. Busby, then serving with the army in Italy, was offered and accepted the manager's job on condition that he was given complete control of all playing matters at the club including training, selections and most importantly signings - this was unheard of back then.

Busby's first signing and in his own words 'his most important' was former Welsh international Jimmy Murphy as assistant manager. Busby, impressed at the Welshman's oratory while giving a speech to a group of soldiers at a PE talk in Bari, Italy, thought Murphy would be the ideal man to train and motivate his players.

Although Matt was unfortunate to inherit a club with little or no facilities, he was fortunate in that the club had already started its own youth system before the war (MUJAC) with the ideal of one day selecting a club based entirely on local players. As a result United had already signed the likes of Jack Rowley, Charlie Mitten and Stan Pearson who helped United finish runners-up in the First Division in the first three years after the war before, while in 1948 Busby led United to FA Cup victory beating Blackpool 4-2. And all this while United played 'home' games at Maine Road as Old Trafford still stood in ruins.

Yet it wasn't just the success of the club that attracted the crowds. United played open, attacking football - typical of this was their defeat of Aston Villa 6-4 at Villa Park on their way to lifting the cup. After the grim monotony of the war years, United played a brand of football with universal appeal. A league title followed in 1951/52 as the players of the immediate post-war era bowed out.

One of Busby's successful guiding principles (which may also have come about as United were using any spare funds to repair their ground) was to get more youth players on board and even though this took time, the rewards were beneficial in the long run. By the time United returned home to Old Trafford in 1951 younger players were starting to emerge. Given the tag 'The Busby Babes' the likes of Eddie Colman, Duncan Edwards, Dennis Viollet, Bobby Charlton, Liam Whelan and Roger Byrne formed a formidable team that won the league in 1955/56 and retained it the following season, missing out on the double when they lost 0-2 to Aston Villa in the 1957 FA Cup Final.

In addition, they were the first English team to take part in the European Cup reaching the semi-final (where they lost to Real Madrid) having beaten Belgian club Anderlecht 10-0 in one of the early rounds. This is still a United record in competition football.

By 1958 the team seemed to be on the brink of greatness. However upon their return from Belgrade following a 3-3 draw that saw them progress to the European Cup semi-finals, their plane stopped at Munich to re-fuel but crashed on take-off. 23 people died - 8 of these were members of the Busby Babes. Duncan Edwards was one of the fatalities; he died 14 days later in hospital through his injuries. Many hold the belief that given the chance, Edwards would have been the best footballer in the world. The other players along with him were Liam Whelan, Tommy Taylor, David Pegg, Mark Jones, Eddie Colman, Roger Byrne and Geoff

Bent.

With Busby recovering from his injuries, Jimmy Murphy became acting manager. Harnessing what remained of the club, mainly youth players and hurried signings from other clubs, Murphy guided United on perhaps the most remarkable cup run ever as United defeated Sheffield Wednesday, West Bromwich Albion and Fulham to reach the 1958 Final amid often hysterical scenes. Cheered on by a nation inspired by Murphy's miraculous achievements, United lost the final 0-2 to Bolton before being defeated 5-2 by AC Milan in the European Cup semi-final. There is little doubt however that Jimmy Murphy saved United.

When Busby returned to the club the following season United performed yet more miracles, finishing runners-up to a very good Wolves side in the 1958/59 Division One table. Yet the losses from Munich gradually took their toll - mid-table finishes in three successive seasons forced Busby into the transfer market.

In the summer of 1962 Busby spent £115,000 acquiring Denis Law from Torino. Later the same season he bought Pat Crerand for £65,000 from Celtic and, the season after, gave a debut to a young Irish lad named George Best. The latter was discovered by United scout Bob Bishop when he was just 15 years old. Bishop sent Busby a telegram from Northern Ireland, in it, it read, "I think I've found you a genius." Football gifts like Best do not come along too often. He had it all in terms of pace, skill and the ability to out-manoeuvre the finest defenders – one way then another with the ball glued to his feet - he was a joy to watch.

1962/63 proved to be a critical season. United only avoided relegation following a controversial Maine Road derby thanks to a last minute Denis Law penalty equaliser. A fortnight later they defeated Leicester City 3-1 in the FA Cup Final at Wembley to secure United's first trophy since the Munich Air Disaster.

The following season Denis Law sent records tumbling as he plundered 46 goals in all competitions while George Best made his debut the same season. Then in 1965 and 1967, Busby's United won the League Title before lifting the European Cup in 1968, making the United the first English club to win the competition.

Having finally accomplished what he had set out to do in 1955, Busby stepped down as United's manager the following season, appointing reserve coach Wilf McGuinness as his replacement.

Unfortunately the new manager failed to adapt to being the boss. He lacked authority, being the same age, or younger, than some of his players and his hands were tied in the transfer market by Busby who had stayed on as General Manager (which is something of an irony given Busby's initial demands when he became United boss). By Christmas 1970 McGuinness has gone, Busby taking over the reigns in the short-term before the relatively unknown Frank O'Farrell was surprisingly given the job.

His spell in charge coincided with the growing disenchantment with football of George Best. Now a pale imitation of what he had been, Best turned to drink, frustrated at the lack of quality signings and struggling to come to terms with life at a mid-table club. Having taken to United to the top of Division One by November 1971, Best 'retired' from football in January 1972 and United embarked on a disastrous run of defeats. Despite Best's return that summer, O'Farrell was sacked in December following a 0-5 humiliation at Crystal Palace and replaced by Tommy Docherty.

'The Doc' quickly got to grips with the glaring problems at the club - Denis Law was sold to rivals Manchester City, Bobby Charlton retired and Paddy Crerand was appointed assistant manager. Other members of the European Cup winning squad were sold off, while George Best was invited back in October 1973, when he was clearly struggling to regain full fitness. George played a dozen games under the Doc finishing with a 0-3 New Year's Day defeat at QPR, his last game for United. The following Saturday he turned up at Old Trafford and was informed he had been dropped, this time Best walked away from United for good.

To add insult to injury, United were struggling at the foot of the table and needed a win at home to Manchester City to stay in with a hope of surviving the drop. A 0-1 defeat, thanks to a backheeled goal from, of all people, Denis Law, helped to condemn United, although results elsewhere meant they would have gone down anyway. That game was abandoned following a pitch invasion and the following season saw Tommy Doc's Red Army storm the Second Division as United's travelling support (often numbering over 20,000) toured the country seemingly hell-bent on destruction. Incidents at Cardiff, Norwich and Blackpool became infamous and questions were asked in parliament.

Fortunately for police forces up and down the land, United were promoted as champions that season and The Doc's wing wizards, Gordon Hill and Steve Coppell blazed a trail in the First Division as United finished third in 1975/76 and lost a controversial FA Cup Final 0-1 to a goal that most supporters felt was at least three yards offside...

The following season, United's great cup form continued as they met Liverpool in the 1977 final. The Merseysiders were attempting an unprecedented treble of League, FA Cup and European Cup and having already secured the league comfortably, they were red-hot favourites. However a 2-1 win, all three goals coming in a ten-minute spell early in the second half, made good The Doc's promise after the previous season's defeat to 'come back and win it'. It also ended Liverpool's treble ambitions.

Within days however United were plunged into crisis once more as newspaper revelations about Tommy Docherty's private life resulted in his dismissal. Having rescued the club from near oblivion, most supporters felt that he had been poorly treated, albeit that the woman in question was the wife of the club physiotherapist. Dave Sexton was appointed as The Doc's replacement .

Sexton was a very different animal to the exuberant 'Doc' and unfortunately his teams failed to inspire as his predeccessors had. Despite this, Sexton's team came as close as any before the arrival of Alex Ferguson to winning the coveted league title. In 1980 United went into the final game needing a win away at Leeds to win the league provided Liverpool failed to win their final home game. Unsurprisingly Liverpool won at Anfield and United lost 0-2 at Elland Road. The season previously United had battled their way to Wembley once more, disposing of Liverpool in a semi-final replay before succumbing to Arsenal in the most dramatic circumstances. The Gunners dominated the game and led 2-0 with just 5 minutes remaining when first Gordon McQueen and then Sammy McIlroy scored to level the tie. Incredibly, United then allowed Alan Sunderland to make it 3-2 at the other end as thoughts turned to extra-time.

By the summer of 1981 Sexton had gone, replaced by Ron Atkinson, a larger than life character more in the 'Tommy Doc' mould. Big Ron wasted no time in acquiring West Brom's Bryan Robson, one of the best midfielders English football has ever seen and later added the likes of Norman Whiteside, Mark Hughes and Paul McGrath from the youth set-up. Atkinson soon established a new stronger United and the club returned to form, winning the FA Cup in 1983 and 1985 and finishing in the top four in every season he was the club.

The following term (1985/86) United were front-runners in the league following a stirring start to the season that saw them win ten games on the trot. But January 1986 proved to be disastrous for Ron. United were hit first by injuries and then by the proposed sale of crowd favourite Mark Hughes to Barcelona. What made the story all the more bizarre was the allegation that Chairman Martin Edwards took a cut of all transfer fees going in and out of the club, suggesting that Ron had little say in the matter. In the event United crumbled under the expectation as Liverpool completed the Double. By October 1986 Ron's days were numbered as United sought a saviour who could turn them into a team capable of rivalling Liverpool.

The arrival of Alex Ferguson was not unexpected. During his time in Scotland he had become perhaps the only manager in the modern era to have successfully broken the duopoly of the Old Firm, winning the league title three times, the Scottish Cup four times and adding the European Cup Winners' Cup in 1983.

Yet if Ferguson hoped for the best of starts managing United, he certainly did not get it. For the first 3½ years, Ferguson produced nothing special and by Christmas 1989 many supporters felt that he had had his chance and failed. Yet a surprise 1-0 win away at Nottingham Forest in the third round of that season's FA Cup changed all that. United battled their way to Wembley

THE MANCHESTER UNITED PREMIER YEARS

beating Hereford, Newcastle, Sheffield United and Oldham before
overcoming Crystal Palace 1-0 in the final replay (after a 3-3 draw)
at Wembley. The following season United brought the European
Cup Winners' Cup to Old Trafford after a sensational 2-1 win in
Rotterdam against Johann Cruyff's Barcelona.

The following season however was disappointing despite the
club's first League Cup victory. United were odds-on favourites
to win the league at Christmas and continued to lead going into
Easter but nerves and a fast-finishing Leeds United inspired by
a certain Eric Cantona left them runners-up. The final straw
was a 0-2 defeat at an hysterical Anfield that confirmed Leeds as
champions.

Meanwhile behind the scenes, the club needed to generate
cash and the board decided to float United on the stock market,
which raised £47 million. United began the first Premiership
season (1992/93) uncertainly. A lack of goals had cost them the
title the previous term and Ferguson had acquired Cambridge
United striker Dion Dublin in an attempt to put it right but he had
broken his leg within weeks of his arrival. A chance phone-call
by the Leeds chairman enquiring about the availablity of Dennis
Irwin led to the signature of Eric Cantona for a bargain £1m.

Eric's arrival finally unleashed United's attacking potential.
Going into Easter 1993 they were level with rivals Aston Villa and
Norwich. Yet United trailed 0-1 at home to Sheffield Wednesday
as the game entered injury-time. Captain Steve Bruce however
proved to be the hero of the hour scoring twice to turn the game
around. After that there was no stopping United, as they pipped
Aston Villa to the title on the penultimate Sunday of the season to
end 26 years without the league title.

United's all-conquering form continued into the following
season which saw them win the league and cup double. However
a controversial defeat at the hands of Turkish team Galatasaray left
the club some way short in Europe.

The following season saw United pipped to the title by
Blackburn but only after one of the most notorious events in
English football history. Playing at Selhurst Park in a midweek

league match Eric Cantona was red carded following an altercation with Eagles centre-half Richard Shaw. On his way to the dressing room, amid the abuse of the home crowd, the French striker leapt in to the stands and assaulted a Palace supporter, Matthew Simmonds. The fall-out meant Eric was banned for 9 months and as a result United lost the title by a point and the FA Cup final 0-1 to Everton.

That summer Alex Ferguson shocked football with the sale of Mark Hughes, Paul Ince and Andrei Kanchelskis. Their replacements – the likes of David Beckham, Nicky Butt, Paul Scholes and the Neville brothers were still young and, when United lost the first game of the following season 1-3 at Aston Villa, Match of the Day pundit Alan Hansen wrote the new United team off saying "you'll never win anything with kids".

Eric's return on first October proved the catalyst for the new, young team. A 2-2 draw against Liverpool, in which Eric set up one and scored another from the spot, was followed by indifferent form until New Year by which time United were 12 points behind leaders Newcastle. Yet a 1-0 win at St. James' Park saw them embark on a title charge that overhauled the Geordies to win the league on the final day at Middlesbrough. Progress in the FA Cup also saw United seal the double with a last minute Cantona winner against Liverpool at Wembley. Most agreed that the Frenchman had changed his ways during his enforced absence from the game and returned a stronger, wiser player – he won both the PFA and the Football Writers' Player of the Year Awards.

After a further championship triumph in 1997, after which Eric Cantona shocked fans by announcing his retirement, United lost out the following season to Arsenal as Arsene Wenger's team secured the double.

By 1999 United were in a tight tussle with Arsenal for domestic honours. The pair met in an FA Cup semi-final replay at Villa Park that has gone down as one of the competition's greatest ever matches. The teams were level at 1-1 when Roy Keane was dismissed with only a few minutes to go, before Nicolas Anelka had a goal controversially disallowed for offside. Then, in injury-time, Phil Neville brought down Ray Parlour and the ref pointed to the spot. Dennis Bergkamp's shot was then miraculously saved by Peter Schmeichel and the game went into extra-time. With United down to 10 men, Arsenal were still favourites but when Patrick Viera misplaced a pass to Ryan Giggs the Welsh winger went on a jinking, dazzling run from half-way and slalomed his way through the entire Arsenal defence, his finishing shot gave United a 2-1 win to keep the club on course for the treble.

United then embarked on 10 days of glory. First they wrapped up the league with a 2-1 win at home to Spurs. Then with goals from Scholes and Sheringham they added the FA Cup beating Newcastle United 2-0. To complete the treble they were up against Bayern Munich in the Champions League final in Barcelona. To get there, United had disposed of Inter Milan (3-1 on aggregate) before somehow getting past Juventus in the semi-finals. Following a 1-1 draw in the home leg, United trailed 2-0 in Italy before goals from Keane, Yorke and Cole turned the game around.

Yet United were a poor second best for much of the final. The Germans deservedly led through a Mario Basler free-kick and should have added more goals in the second half. As the game drifted towards injury time United's amazing run seemed to be at an end. However a late flurry saw Teddy Sheringham equalise following a Giggs flick before a last minute corner, flicked on again by Teddy, was volleyed in by Ole Gunnar Solksjaer at the far post to complete the most unbelievable comeback. The Munich players could do nothing but sob on the pitch. Not many clubs in the world could have pulled that out of the bag at exactly the right time. Later and deservedly so, Ferguson was knighted for his services to the game of football.

After that triumph, United were always going to struggle to go one better than the treble. Nevertheless they became the first English club to be crowned world champions that December following a 1-0 win against Brazilians Palmeiras. Yet even with the club topping the Premier League in 2000 and 2001 there were disappointments in Europe following defeats in the quarter-finals to Real Madrid and Bayern Munich. Alex Ferguson announced he was retiring from football in May 2001 before changing his mind in February 2002 and agreeing a new contract. Unfortunately Arsenal romped away with the double that season and The Gunners great form continued well into the next. Going into what the manager described as 'squeaky bum time', the Londoners held an 8 point advantage. Yet United, inspired by van Nistlerooy, Scholes, Solksjaer and Keane, went on a fantastic run to clinch the title on the penultimate weekend of the season. However this was to be David Beckham's final season at United, Real Madrid snapping him up for a bargain £25m that summer.

2003/04 proved to be difficult for United as Arsenal won the league without defeat. There was now also a new threat in the shape of Chelsea to consider who had been bought by billionaire Roman Abramovic. With the arrival in 2004 of Jose Mourinho, the Pensioners won the next two league titles at a canter, consigning United to the minor placings.

During this period it seemed that Sir Alex Ferguson had met his match. The dismay within United ranks was highlighted with the effective sacking of captain Roy Keane following an outburst on MUTV and, later that season, the sale of van Nistlerooy to Real Madrid following some half-hearted performances.

To cap it all, in May 2005 American businessman Malcolm Glazer completed a hostile takeover of the club that led to despair among supporters. Many vowed never to return to Old Trafford and used that season's FA Cup final appearance (which United lost on penalties to Arsenal despite dominating) to mourn for the club they had supported all their lives. A breakaway club (FC United of Manchester) was formed and many die-hards have never returned.

Nevertheless there were some reasons for optimism. In 2003 United had paid Sporting Lisbon £12.24m for winger Cristiano Ronaldo after he had tortured John O'Shea in a pre-season friendly. A season later United paid £25m to Everton for Wayne Rooney. Thus the club had signed two players who would be instrumental in United's re-emergence as a European power.

Ronaldo, arrogant and cocky at times, was an instant sensation at United with his ability and skill while Rooney's commitment left few in any doubt of his value. Victory in the 2006 League Cup, while seen at the time as being little more than a poor consolation for a terrible season (United had failed to make it out of the Champions League knock-out stages and trailed Chelsea by a distance in the league) proved the catalyst for a title charge the following season.

The 2006/07 season saw a clash of the managerial titans as Ferguson and Mourinho went head to head for the title. United started the season in blistering form and led Chelsea every step of the way with Rooney, Saha, Ronaldo and a revitalised Giggs and Scholes guiding United to the title. The reds clinched the title with three games to go but then lost the FA Cup final to Mourinho's men a fortnight later.

United were odds on to retain their title following the early season departure of Mourinho from Chelsea (which they did comfortably) but Europe was where most supporters hoped the club would succeed. Most seemed to agree that a solitary European Cup was a poor return for Ferguson and, following some impressive performances the previous season, most notably a 7-1 thrashing of Roma at Old Trafford, United were one of the favourites to win it.

United cruised through the group stages before beating Lyon, Roma and Barcelona to reach the final in Moscow against Chelsea. United dominated the early stages in Russia, taking a goal lead and missing three or four good chances before Frank Lampard equalised. Then the Londoners dominated, hitting the woodwork several times. With the game heading to penalties however Didier Drogba became involved in an altercation with Carlos Tevez and was sent-off - this proved crucial in the ensuing shoot-out as first Ronaldo missed giving Chelsea captain John Terry the chance to win the cup. Terry slipped as he took the kick, hitting the post - had Drogba not been dismissed, he would surely have taken the winning spot-kick. United seemed destined to win it now and when Nicolas Anelka's half hearted penalty was saved by Edwin van der Sar United had secured their third European Cup.

Ryan Giggs was also honoured in Moscow by breaking Bobby Charlton's record in the final, Sir Bobby went forward with the team to accept the trophy. That December, United also won the FIFA Club World Cup trophy thanks to a solitary Wayne Rooney strike. United also retained the Premiership despite a late surge from Liverpool who won 1-4 at Old Trafford. A win at Wigan and a goalless draw at home to Arsenal secured Ferguson's second championship hat-trick, quite a feat for a manager who had been a 'spent force' just four years previously.

United's continued good form in Europe took them to a second successive Champions League final. Unfortunately United failed at the final hurdle, going down 0-2 to an outstanding Barcelona side. In the weeks following the defeat the news was dominated by the news that Cristiano Ronaldo had agreed terms with Real Madrid. His £80m transfer fee was a new record.

2009/10 saw United initially struggle without the Portuguese. However United still carried off the League Cup and lost the title by just a point to double winners Chelsea. Perhaps the most prominent aspect of the season however was the renewed anti-Glazer protests in the shape of the new 'Green and Gold' campaign that took the colours of the original club Newton Heath. As you will recall, that club was on the brink of folding because of its debts, let's hope the same fate does not befall the current club.

CHAIRMEN

MARTIN EDWARDS

Charles Martin Edwards was born on 24th July 1945, he was the chairman of Manchester United from 1980 until 2002. He is now the honorary life president at the club.

He was elected to the United board in March 1970. He became chairman in March 1980 following the death of his father Louis, the previous chairman When the FA voted to allow football clubs to have one paid director, Martin became Chief Executive and paid himself an annual salary of £30k.

The season when Edwards took over as chairman, we finished runners-up to Liverpool in the First Division but we had not won the league since 1967 and had not won a major trophy at all in 3 seasons of Dave Sexton's management. At the end of 1980-81 season, we finished 8th in the league after 7 successive wins at the end of the season. Sexton looked set to be offered a new 3-year contract, but the deal was never signed and Edwards sacked him after 4 seasons as manager without a trophy.

Martin then began the hunt for a new manager. There was talk that he would appoint Lawrie McMenemy, who had guided Southampton to a shock win in the FA Cup final 5 years earlier, as successor to Dave Sexton. It was also rumoured that we were interested in recruiting Brian Clough, once a league champion and twice a European Cup winner with Nottingham Forest, but Martin insisted that he would not be approaching Cloughie about the job vacancy. He instead turned to Ron Atkinson, whose impressive West Brom side had qualified for the UEFA Cup 3 times in 4 seasons with top 5 league finishes, reaching the quarter-finals on one occasion. Big Ron accepted the offer, and soon after this appointment, Martin made the funds available for him to bring in Albion's midfielder Bryan Robson for a national record fee of £1.5million. This national record would remain unbroken by English clubs for 6 years, and Bryan went on to be one of our greatest ever players.

Ron guided us to two FA Cup victories (in 1983 and 1985) but in the 1985-86 we faded away to finish 4th after a 10-match winning start to the season and speculation about his future as manager was mounting.

In 1982, Martin had begun looking for younger personnel to introduce to the board. Sir Matt Busby had been appointed president of the club and Michael Edelson was appointed to replace him, followed in 1983 by the addition of solicitor Maurice Watkins and a certain Bobby Charlton.

In the summer of 1986, Martin bought in £2.3million (a record fee involving a British club, though Robson's record set in 1981 had yet to be broken by a British club) from the sale of striker Mark Hughes to FC Barcelona.

On 3 November 1986, we were floundering in the bottom half of the top division and that night were eliminated from the League Cup with a 4-1 defeat at Southampton.

The following day, the four man board convened in Edwards Old Trafford office and decided a change of manager had to be made. The unanimous decision was to see if Alex Ferguson, then manager of Aberdeen FC in the Scottish league was available.

According to Alex's auto-biography, he received a call in his office at Pittodrie from a man with a Scottish accent. He subsequently discovered that this was Michael Edelson who asked if he would be interested in meeting Martin.

Following a short discussion, Martin made contact with Aberdeen chairman Dick Donald and the United board drove immediately to meet Alex halfway between the two cities in Glasgow. Negotiations were quickly concluded and 72 hours later Alex was installed as manager of Manchester United, What an amazing day in the history of our club. Alex has gone on to become the most successful British football manager in history.

Edwards had never shown much interest in football before

inheriting the club, He tried to sell United to Robert Maxwell in 1984 and to the property developer Michael Knighton in 1989. The sale for £10m collapsed when, after being given access to the United's books, Knighton was unable to raise sufficient funds. However, He was still given a seat on the board, and sources at the time suggested that this was in exchange for keeping quiet about what he had seen in the books...

After the failed sale, United's other directors persuaded Martin to float the club on the stock market. This raised significant funds for the existing shareholders such as Edwards. Being a public company did not have the stabilising effect that was originally hoped for. The club has been subject to takeover proposals by Rupert Murdoch's BSkyB with Martin reportedly agreeing to sell his stake for £98 million. He gradually disposed of his equity in the club and resigned as Chief Exec in 2000, appointing Peter Kenyon as his successor.

Meanwhile, his efforts helped us enjoy some of the finest moments in our history during the 1990s and 2000s. The appointment of Sir Alex as manager in 1986 was indeed the turning point in our history after two decades of relative mediocrity, but it took time for things to improve.

We finished second in the league in 1987-88 (Sir Alex's first full season as manager), and around this time Martin had made millions of pounds available to strengthen the squad with the reacquisition of Mark Hughes as well as the signing of high profile players including Brian McClair, Gary Pallister, Paul Ince, Neil Webb and Danny Wallace. However, an 11th place finish in 1988-89 tested the patience of our supporters and as 1989 drew to a close, our form was so bad (we occupied 15th place in the league on Christmas Day) that there were continued calls from the fans for Sir Alex to be sacked. However, Edwards stood by Sir Alex and insisted that the issue of him being sacked was never up for debate. While Edwards, naturally, admitted that he was disappointing with the lack of progress in the league, he understood the reasons for the disappointment, which was largely down to a series of injuries to key players, and said that he was pleased with Sir Alex for his reorganisation of the squad.

The decision by Martin to remain loyal to Sir Alex paid off in 1989-90 as we lifted the FA Cup to end our 5-year wait for a major trophy. A year later, we won the European Cup Winners' Cup. 1992 saw us win our first-ever Football League Cup, and a year later ended our 26-year wait for the league title when crowned champions of the inaugural Premier League. The double followed a year later. 1994-95 was a relative disappointment for Edwards and indeed everyone else connected to us as we were pipped to both the league title and the FA Cup and left without a trophy, but United bounced back the following year to win a unique second double. By this stage, Edwards had been able to raise the funds for us to break the national transfer record on 2 occasions in the space of 18 months - the £3.75million move for Keano in the 1993 close season, and the £6million move for Coley in January 1995. The success continued for the rest of the decade with another league title in 1997 and a unique league title/FA Cup/European Cup treble in 1999. By the end of the decade, Edwards had made available the cash for us to buy the first 2 eight-figure signings of our history - defender Jaap Stam and striker Dwight Yorke.

In the 1998-99 he had accepted a £623million bid from Rupert Murdoch's BSkyB corporation to take over Man United, but the takeover was blocked by the Mergers and Monopolies Commission.

The Irish duo J.P. McManus and John Magnier also built a stake in the club. However, the club continued to have unprecedented success on the football pitch despite an uneasy relationship between Sir Alex and Martin Edwards. The success continued into the 2first century, as we retained the Premier League title in 2000 with a record 18-point margin and gained our 3rd successive title the following year.

Edwards enabled us to break the national transfer record twice in 2001 when we signed Dutch striker Ruud Van Nistelrooy and Argentine midfielder Juan Sebastian Veron, but he was forced to resign as Chairman in 2002, after allegations of using a prostitute on an official club business trip to Switzerland. Despite this, he continued to represent the club at FA and UEFA meetings.

He still remains at Old Trafford as honorary life president and sits on the club's football board alongside Sir Bobby Charlton. He sold his 6.7% share in the club to new investor Harry Dobson in 2003.

SIR ROY GARDNER

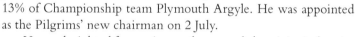

Sir Roy was born on 20th August 1945, in Brentford. He resigned soon after Malcolm Glazer took over control of the club and made the club private, as chairmen are not required in private limited companies. The other independent non-executive directors also resigned, for the same reason.

In July 2009, Gardner and business partner Keith Todd secured ownership of 13% of Championship team Plymouth Argyle. He was appointed as the Pilgrims' new chairman on 2 July.

He was knighted for services to the gas and electricity industries in June 2002.

MALCOLM GLAZER

Malcolm was born May 25th, 1928. He is an American businessman and sports-team owner. He is the president and chief executive officer of First Allied Corporation, a holding company for his varied business interests, most notably in the food processing industry. He holds controlling stakes in Manchester United Football Club, and owns the Tampa Bay Buccaneers, a National Football League team in Tampa, Florida, United States.

Between 2003 and 2005, he gradually bought out other United shareholders in a deal that valued the club at around $1.47 billion. The takeover was fiercely opposed by many fans, who organised ourselves in the form of the independent Manchester United Supporters' Trust (formerly Shareholders United), partly because the takeover saddled the club with a large debt (over $850m) and the interest that comes with it (approx £60 million a year). The mainly match-going fans object to the escalating ticket prices at a time when the club receives more money than ever from TV and sponsorship deals. In anger at the takeover, thousands didn't renew their season tickets. Many of these got together to set up a new club called F.C. United of Manchester. The new protest club has had great success which includes three successive promotions in three years while attracting gates of well over 2000 fans each week, with a record attendance of 6023. Anti-Glazer songs and chants are still regularly heard at away games across the country. Since 2005 the ticket prices have been increased by over 42% (12.3% then 14% then 11%).

The protests were re-invigorated in January 2010 following publication of a bond prospectus. Of particular note was the section detailing where the money from the sale of Cristiano Ronaldo had gone (it appeared to be mostly on interest payments). As a result the supporters began wearing the colours of the original Newton Heath club (green and gold) at matches. The success of this initiative culminated in former United star David Beckham wearing one of the scarves after the AC Milan Champions League tie at Old Trafford in March. Joel and Avi Glazer were in attendance at Old Trafford at the time and they were left in no doubt about the strength of feeling against their regime as the protests swept around the ground. Although David subsequently denied that his action had any significance, it was taken by many to indicate that he was in support of the anti-Glazer protest and was described as "an iconic moment" by the Manchester United Supporters Trust.

In March 2010, a group called the Red Knights led by Goldman Sachs' chief economist Jim O'Neill, announced it was preparing a bid to buy the club from the Glazer family. However, a spokesperson for the club said that the Glazers were not interested in selling.

As of August 2010 the club remains under the control of the Glazer family.

MANAGER

Sir Alex Ferguson

Full name:Alexander Chapman Ferguson
Date of birth:31 December 1941
Place of birth:Glasgow
Playing position:Striker
Current club: Manchester United (manager)

Senior career

Years	Team	Apps	(Gls)
1957–1960	Queen's Park	31	(15)
1960–1964	St. Johnstone	37	(19)
1964–1967	Dunfermline Athletic	89	(66)
1967–1969	Rangers	41	(25)
1969–1973	Falkirk	95	(36)
1973–1974	Ayr United	24	(9)
TOTAL		317	(170)

Teams managed

1974   East Stirlingshire
1974–1978 St. Mirren
1978–1986 Aberdeen
1985–1986 Scotland
1986–   Manchester United

After an unexceptional playing career, Alex Ferguson began his managerial career in June 1974 at East Stirlingshire, aged 32. This was a part-time job that paid £40 a week and the club did not have a single goalkeeper at the time. Alex straight away gained a reputation as a disciplinarian, with striker Bobby McCulley later saying he had "never been afraid of anyone before but Alex was a frightening bastard from the start". His players admired his tactical decisions, however, and the club's results improved considerably.

The following October, Alex was invited to manage St. Mirren. While they were below East Stirlingshire in the league, they were a bigger club and although Alex felt a degree of loyalty towards East Stirlingshire, he decided to join St. Mirren after taking advice from Jock Stein.

Sir Alex was manager of St. Mirren from 1974 until 1978, producing a remarkable transformation in a team that were in the lower half of the old Second Division watched by crowds of just over 1,000, to First Division champions in 1977, discovering talents such as Billy Stark, Tony Fitzpatrick, Lex Richardson, Frank McGarvey, Bobby Reid and Peter Weir while playing superb attacking football. The average age of the team was 19 and the captain, Fitzpatrick, was 20.

St. Mirren have been the only club ever to sack Sir Alex. He claimed wrongful dismissal against the club at an tribunal but lost and was given no leave to appeal. According to a Billy Adams *Sunday Herald* article on 30 May 1999, the official version is that Sir Alex was sacked for various breaches of contract including unauthorised payments to players. He was counter-accused of intimidating behaviour towards his office secretary because he wanted players to get some expenses tax free. He didn't speak to her for 6 weeks, confiscated her keys and communicated only through a 17-year-old assistant. The tribunal concluded that Sir Alex was "particularly petty" and "immature". It was claimed during the tribunal by St. Mirren chairman, Willie Todd, that Ferguson had "no managerial ability".

On 31 May 2008, *The Guardian* published an interview with Todd (by now aged 87), who had sacked him all those years earlier. He explained that the fundamental reason for the dismissal was a breach of contract relating to Sir Alex having agreed to join Aberdeen. Ferguson told journalist Jim Rodger of the *Daily Mirror* that he had asked at least one member of the squad to go to Aberdeen with him. He also told the St. Mirren staff he was leaving. Todd expressed regret over what happened but blamed Aberdeen for not approaching his club to discuss compensation.

THE MANCHESTER UNITED PREMIER YEARS

Sir Alex joined Aberdeen in June 1978, replacing Billy McNeill who had only lasted one season before he was offered the chance to manage Celtic. Although Aberdeen were one of Scotland's major clubs, they had not won the league since 1955. The team had been playing well, however, and had not lost a league match since the previous December, having finished second in the league the previous season. He had now been a manager for 4 years, but was still not much older than some of the players and had trouble winning the respect of some of the older pros such as Joe Harper. The season did not go especially well, with Aberdeen reaching the semi-final of the Scottish F.A. Cup and the final of the league cup, but losing both matches and finishing 4th in the league.

In December 1979, they lost the league cup final again, this time to Dundee United after a replay. Sir Alex took the blame for the defeat, saying he should have made changes to the team for the replay.

Aberdeen had started the season poorly but their form improved dramatically in the new year and they won the Scottish league that season with a 5–0 win on the final day. It was the first time in 15 years that the league had not been won by either Rangers or Celtic. Ferguson now felt that he had the respect of his players, later saying "that was the achievement which united us. I finally had the players believing in me".

He was still a strict disciplinarian, though, and his players nicknamed him *Furious Fergie*. He fined one of his players, John Hewitt, for overtaking him on a public road, and kicked a tea urn at the players at half time after a poor first half. He was dissatisfied with the atmosphere at Aberdeen matches, and deliberately created a 'siege mentality' by accusing the Scottish media of being biased towards the Glasgow clubs, in order to motivate the team. The team continued their success with a Scottish Cup win in 1982. Ferguson was offered the managers' job at Wolves but turned it down as he felt that Wolves were in trouble and "[his] ambitions at Aberdeen were not even half fulfilled".

Ferguson led Aberdeen to even greater success the following season (1982–83). They had qualified for the European Cup

MANAGER

Winners' Cup as a result of winning the Scottish Cup the previous season, and impressively knocked out Bayern Munich, who had beaten Tottenham Hotspur 4–1 in the previous round. According to Willie Miller, this gave them the confidence to believe that they could go on to win the competition, which they did, with a 2–1 victory over Real Madrid in the final on 11 May 1983. Aberdeen became only the 3rd Scottish team to win a European trophy and Ferguson now felt that "he'd done something worthwhile with his life". Aberdeen had also performed well in the league that season, and retained the Scottish Cup with a 1–0 victory over Rangers, but Ferguson was not happy with his team's play in that match and upset the players by describing them as a "disgraceful performance" in a televised interview after the match· a statement that he later retracted.

After a sub-standard start to the 1983–84 season, Aberdeen's form improved and the team won the Scottish league and retained the Scottish Cup. Ferguson was awarded the OBE in the 1984 honours list, and was offered the managers' jobs at Rangers, Arsenal and Tottenham Hotspur during the season. Aberdeen retained their league title in the 1984–85 season, but had a disappointing season in 1985–86, finishing fourth in the league, although they did win both domestic cups. Ferguson had been appointed to the club's board of directors early in 1986, but that April he told Dick Donald, their chairman, that he intended to leave that summer.

Ferguson had been part of coaching staff for the Scottish national side during qualifying for the 1986 World Cup, but manager Jock Stein had collapsed and died on 10 September 1985 – at the end of the game in which Scotland qualified from their group for a play-off against Australia. Ferguson promptly agreed to take charge of the Scottish national side against the Australians and subsequently at the World Cup. To allow him to fulfil his international duties he appointed Archie Knox as his co-manager at Aberdeen.

Around this time, Tottenham Hotspur offered Ferguson the chance to take over from Peter Shreeves as manager, but he rejected this offer and the job went to Luton Town's David Pleat instead. There was also an offer for Ferguson to replace Don Howe as Arsenal manager, but he rejected this offer as well, and fellow Scot George Graham took the post instead.

That summer, there had been speculation that he would take over from Ron Atkinson at Manchester United, who had slumped to fourth in the English top flight after a 10-match winning start had made title glory seem inevitable. Although Ferguson remained at the club over the summer, he did eventually join Manchester United when Atkinson was sacked in November 1986.

Ferguson was appointed manager at Old Trafford on 6 November 1986. He was initially worried that many of the players, such as Norman Whiteside, Paul McGrath and Bryan Robson were drinking too much and was "depressed" by their level of fitness, but he managed to increase the players' discipline and United climbed up the table to finish the season in 11th place, having been 2first (second from bottom) when he took over.

His first game in charge was a 2-0 defeat at underdogs Oxford United on 8 November, followed seven days later by a goalless draw at newly promoted Norwich City, and then his first win (1-0 at home to QPR) on 22 November. Results steadily improved as the season went on, and by the time they recorded what would be their only away win of the league campaign at title challengers and deadly rivals Liverpool on Boxing Day, it was clear that United were on the road to recovery. 1987 began on a high note with a 4-1 victory over Newcastle United and United gradually pulled together in the second half of the season, with relatively occasional defeats on the way, and finished 11th in the final table.

Ferguson endured a personal tragedy three weeks after his appointment, when his mother Elizabeth died of lung cancer aged 64. Ferguson appointed Archie Knox, his assistant at Aberdeen, as his assistant at Manchester United.

On his arrival at Old Trafford, he told the media '*My greatest challenge is not what's happening at the moment, my greatest challenge was knocking Liverpool right off their f*****g perch. And you can print that*', in reference to his desire for United to overhaul Liverpool, who were the dominant club in the English league at the time.

In the 1987–88 season, Ferguson made several major signings, including Steve Bruce, Viv Anderson, Brian McClair and Jim Leighton.

The new players made a great contribution to a United team who finished in second place, nine points behind Liverpool. However, Liverpool's points lead had been in double digits for most of the season and while United had lost only five league games all season, they drew 12 games and there was clearly still some way to go before United could be a match for their deadly north western rivals.

United were expected to do well when Mark Hughes returned to the club two years after leaving for Barcelona, but the 1988–89 season was a disappointment for them, finishing eleventh in the league and losing 1–0 at home to Nottingham Forest in the FA Cup Sixth Round. They had begun the season slowly, going on a nine-match winless run throughout October and November (with one defeat and eight draws) before a run of generally good results took them to third place and the fringes of the title challenge by mid February. However, another run of disappointing results in the final quarter of the season saw them fall down to mid table.

During the season, United played in friendly matches against the Bermudan national team and Somerset County Cricket Club as part of the Bermudan team's tour of England. In the match against Somerset, both Ferguson himself and his assistant, Archie Knox, took to the field, with Knox even getting on the scoresheet. The match remains Ferguson's only appearance for the Manchester United first team.

For the 1989–90 season, Ferguson further boosted his squad by paying large sums of money for midfielders Neil Webb, Mike Phelan and Paul Ince, as well as defender Gary Pallister and winger Danny Wallace. The season began well with a 4–1 win over defending champions Arsenal on the opening day, but United's league form quickly turned sour. In September, United suffered a humiliating 5–1 away defeat against fierce rivals Manchester City. Following this and an early season run of six defeats and two draws in eight games, a banner declaring "Three years of excuses and it's still crap. Ta ra Fergie." was displayed at Old Trafford, and many journalists and supporters called for Ferguson to be sacked. - Ferguson later described December 1989 as "the darkest period [he had] ever suffered in the game", as United ended the decade just outside the relegation zone.

However, Ferguson later revealed that the board of directors had assured him that they were not considering dismissing him. Although naturally disappointed with the lack of success in the league, they understood the reasons for the sub-standard results (namely the absence of several key players due to injury) and were pleased with the way that Ferguson had reorganised the club's coaching and scouting system.

Following a run of seven games without a win, Manchester United were drawn away to Nottingham Forest in the third round of the FA Cup. Forest were performing well that season and were in the process of winning the League Cup for the second season running, and it was expected that United would lose the match and Ferguson would consequently be sacked, but United won the game 1–0 thanks to a Mark Robins goal and eventually reached the final. This cup win is often cited as the match that saved Ferguson's Old Trafford career.

United went on to win the FA Cup, beating Crystal Palace 1–0 in the final replay after a 3–3 draw in the first match, giving Ferguson his first major trophy as Manchester United manager. United's defensive frailties in the first match were unilaterally blamed on goalkeeper Jim Leighton, forcing Ferguson to drop his former Aberdeen player and bring in Les Sealey.

Although United's league form improved greatly in 1990–91, they were still inconsistent and finished sixth. There were some excellent performances that season, including a 6-2 demolition of Arsenal at Highbury, but results like an early 2-1 loss at newly promoted Sunderland, a 4–0 September hammering by Liverpool at Anfield, and a 2-0 home defeat by Everton in early March (the game where 17-year-old hot prospect Ryan Giggs made his senior debut) showed that United still had some way to go.

Even after the FA Cup Final victory in the previous season, some still had doubts about Ferguson's ability to succeed where all the other managers since Busby had failed — to win the league title. They were runners-up in the League Cup, losing 1–0 to Sheffield Wednesday. They also reached the final of the European Cup Winners' Cup, beating that season's Spanish champions Barcelona 2–1. After the match, Ferguson vowed that United would win the league the following season, and at long last he seemed to have won over the last of his sceptics after nearly five years in the job.

During the 1991 close season, Ferguson's assistant Archie Knox departed to Glasgow Rangers to become assistant to Walter Smith and Ferguson promoted youth team coach Brian Kidd to the role of assistant manager in Knox's place. He also made two major signings - goalkeeper Peter Schmeichel and defender Paul Parker - to bolster his side. There was much anticipation about the breakthrough of the young Ryan Giggs, who had played twice and scored once in the 1990-91 campaign, and the earlier emergence of another impressive young winger in the shape of Lee Sharpe, who despite their youth had made Ferguson feel able to resist plunging into the transfer market and buying a new player to take over from the disappointing Danny Wallace on the left wing. He had also added the Ukrainian Andrei Kanchelskis to the right wing, giving him a more attacking alternative to older right footed midfielders Mike Phelan and Bryan Robson.

The 1991–92 season did not live up to Ferguson's expectations and, in Ferguson's words, "many in the media felt that [his] mistakes had contributed to the misery" United won the League Cup and Super Cup for the first time, but lost out on the league title to rivals Leeds United after leading the table for much of the season. A shortage of goals and being held to draws by teams they had been expected to beat in the second half of the campaign had proved to be the undoing of a United side who had performed so well in the first half of the season.

Ferguson felt that his failure to secure the signing of Mick Harford from Luton Town had cost United the league, and that he needed "an extra dimension" to the team if they were to win the league the following season

During the 1992 close season, Ferguson went on the hunt

for a new striker. He first attempted to sign Alan Shearer from Southampton, but lost out to Blackburn Rovers. He also made at least one approach for the Sheffield Wednesday striker David Hirst, but manager Trevor Francis rejected all offers and the player stayed put. In the end, he paid £1 million for 23-year-old Cambridge United striker Dion Dublin – his only major signing of the summer.

After a slow start to the 1992–93 season (they were 10th of 22 at the beginning of November) it looked as though United would miss out on the league title (now the Premier League) yet again. However, after the purchase of French striker Eric Cantona from Leeds United for £1.2 million, the future of Manchester United, and Ferguson's position as manager, began to look bright. Cantona formed a strong partnership with Mark Hughes and fired the club to the top of the table, ending United's 26-year wait for a League Championship, and also making them the first ever Premier League Champions. United had finished champions with a 10-point margin over runners-up Aston Villa, whose 1–0 defeat at Oldham on 2 May 1993 had given United the title. Alex Ferguson was voted Manager of the Year by the League Managers' Association.

1993–94 brought more success. Ferguson added Nottingham Forest's 22-year-old midfielder Roy Keane to the ranks for a British record fee of £3.75million as a long term replacement for Bryan Robson, who was nearing the end of his career.

United led the 1993–94 Premier League table virtually from start to finish. Cantona was top scorer with 25 goals in all competitions despite being sent off twice in the space of five days in March 1994. United also reached the League Cup final but lost 3–1 to Aston Villa, managed by Ferguson's predecessor, Ron Atkinson. In the FA Cup final, Manchester United achieved an impressive 4–0 scoreline against Chelsea, winning Ferguson his second League and Cup Double, following his Scottish Premier Division and Scottish Cup titles with Aberdeen in 1984–85, though the League Cup final defeat meant that he had not yet achieved a repeat of the treble that he had achieved with Aberdeen in 1983.

Ferguson made only one close-season signing, paying Blackburn

MANAGER

Rovers £1.2million for David May. There were newspaper reports that Ferguson was also going to sign highly rated 21-year-old striker Chris Sutton from Norwich City, but the player headed for Blackburn Rovers instead.

1994–95 was a harder season for Ferguson. Cantona assaulted a Crystal Palace supporter in a game at Selhurst Park, and it seemed likely he would leave English football. An eight month ban saw Cantona miss the final four months of the season. He also received a 14-day prison sentence for the offence but the sentence was quashed on appeal and replaced by a 120-hour community service order. On the brighter side, United paid a British record fee of £7million for Newcastle's prolific striker Andy Cole, with young winger Keith Gillespie heading to the north-east in exchange. The season also saw the breakthrough of young players Gary Neville, Nicky Butt and Paul Scholes, who provided excellent cover for the long periods that United were left without some of their more experienced stars.

However, the championship slipped out of Manchester United's grasp as they drew 1–1 with West Ham United on the final day of the season, when a win would have given them the a third successive league title. United also lost the FA Cup final in a 1–0 defeat to Everton.

Ferguson was heavily criticised in the summer of 1995 when three of United's star players were allowed to leave and replacements were not bought. First Paul Ince moved to Internazionale of Italy for £7.5 million, long serving striker Mark Hughes was suddenly sold to Chelsea in a £1.5 million deal and Andrei Kanchelskis was sold to Everton.

Ferguson made an approach for Tottenham Hotspur winger Darren Anderton, but the player signed a new contract with the North London club. He then made a bid to sign Dutchman Marc Overmars from Ajax Amsterdam (the European Cup winners), but the player suffered a serious knee injury and was ruled out for months. Media reports suggested that United were going to make an approach for Juventus and Italy forward Roberto Baggio, who was generally regarded as the best player in the world at this time, but the player remained in his homeland and signed for AC Milan instead.

It was widely known that Ferguson felt that United had a number of young players who were ready to play in the first team. The youngsters, who would be known as "Fergie's Fledglings", included Gary Neville, Phil Neville, David Beckham, Paul Scholes and Nicky Butt, who would all go on to be important members of the team. And so the 1995-96 season began without a major signing, at a time when the likes of Arsenal, Liverpool and Newcastle United were making the headlines with big money deals.

When United lost the first league match of the 1995–96 season 3–1 to Aston Villa, the media swooped upon Ferguson with undisguised glee. They wrote United off because Alex Ferguson's squad contained so many young and inexperienced players. Match of the Day pundit, Alan Hansen infamously proclaimed that "you can't win anything with kids".

However, the young players performed well and United won their next five matches, exacting their revenge over Everton for the FA Cup defeat with a 3-2 win at Goodison Park and achieving a 2-1 away win over defending champions Blackburn Rovers who were now looking rather like relegation battlers than title contenders.

Cantona's return from suspension was a boost, but they found themselves 10 points behind Newcastle United by Christmas 1995. A 2-0 home win over the Tynesiders on 27 December narrowed the gap to seven points and a subsequent win over struggling QPR narrowed it to four points, but a 4-1 defeat for United at Tottenham on New Year's Day 1996 and a 0-0 home draw with Aston Villa saw the Magpies re-establish their wide lead and it looked certain that the league title was Newcastle's.

However a series of good results starting in mid January 1996 saw the gap close, and when United travelled to Newcastle and won 1-0 on 4 March, the gap was down to a single point. United went top of the league soon after the win at Newcastle, who continued to drop points in crucial games.

Early April saw Newcastle manager Kevin Keegan's famous

outburst on live television ("I'd love it if we beat them! Love it!") is generally regarded as the moment that Ferguson gained the upper hand against his opponent. United's Premier League title success was confirmed on the final day of the season, when they defeated a Middlesbrough side managed by former United captain Bryan Robson in a game which ended in a 3-0 win despite strong displays by Boro confounding pre-match reports that Robson would give his old team an easy ride.

They played Liverpool in that year's FA Cup final, winning 1-0 with a late goal by Cantona. This made them the first team in English football to repeat the double of the league title and FA Cup and more impressive was the fact that it had been achieved with a similar set of players to the ones who achieved the first double.

1996-97 saw Alex Ferguson guide Manchester United to their fourth Premier League title in five seasons. In late autumn, they suffered three league defeats in a row and conceded 13 goals in the process. They also lost their 40 year unbeaten home record in Europe to unfancied Turkish side Fenerbahçe. But they still reached the Champions League semi final, where they lost to Borussia Dortmund of Germany. At the end of the season, Cantona surprisingly retired from football.

Other success stories of the 1996-97 season were two Norweigan signings, striker Ole Gunnar Solskjaer (the club's top scorer that season) and defender Ronny Johnsen, who were bargain buys as they were little known outside the Premier League on their arrival the previous summer but went on to be key factors in United's fourth Premier League title.

Ferguson made two new signings to bolster United's challenge for the 1997-98 season, 31-year-old England striker Teddy Sheringham and defender Henning Berg. However the season ended trophyless as Arsenal won the Premier League under French manager Arsène Wenger, who started a long-lasting rivalry with Ferguson. For much of the season United had looked to be on the road to success. They led the table for much of the season before a series of disappointing results in the final quarter - combined with Arsenal taking advantage of games in hand - saw the league title head to North London. There was much promise in the European Cup as United recorded an impressive 3-2 win over Juventus in the group stages before being eliminated by AS Monaco in the quarter finals. Their FA Cup challenge began with an excellent 5-3 away win over holders Chelsea before a shock fifth round replay exit at a Barnsley side who ended the season relegated from the Premier League.

The summer of 1998 saw striker Dwight Yorke, Dutch defender Jaap Stam and the Swedish winger Jesper Blomqvist join Manchester United for a combined total of nearly £30million.

In December 1998, Ferguson's assistant Brian Kidd accepted an offer to manage Blackburn Rovers and he recruited Steve McClaren from Derby County as his successor. Ironically, Kidd's side were relegated in the penultimate game on the league season when United held them to a 0–0 draw.

1998–99 saw the club win an unprecedented treble of the Premier League title, FA Cup and Champions League. The season was characterised by highly dramatic matches. In the Champions League semi-final second leg, United conceded two early goals away to Juventus; however, inspired by Roy Keane, who would later miss the final through suspension, United came back to beat Juventus 3–2 and reach their first European Cup final since 1968. In the FA Cup semi-final, United faced close rivals Arsenal and appeared to be heading for defeat when Keane was sent off and Arsenal were awarded a last-minute penalty. Peter Schmeichel saved the penalty, and in extra time Ryan Giggs ran the length of the pitch to score perhaps the most memorable goal of his career to win the match. They then defeated Newcastle United 2–0 in the FA Cup Final at Wembley thanks to goals from Teddy Sheringham and Paul Scholes. The European triumph was the most incredible of all. With 90 minutes on the clock they were 1–0 down to Bayern Munich at the Nou Camp in Barcelona following a Mario Basler free kick, but in 3 minutes of injury time allowed by referee Pierluigi Collina, Teddy Sheringham, a substitute, equalised and extra time looked certain. But with just seconds left on the clock, Ole Gunnar Solskjær, also a late substitution, scored the winning goal and history was made.

On 12 June 1999, Alex Ferguson received a knighthood in recognition of his services to the game.

Manchester United ended the 1999–2000 season as champions with just three Premier League defeats, and a cushion of 18 points. The massive gap between United and the rest of the Premier League, although they had faced stiff competition from the likes of Arsenal and Leeds United until the final weeks of the season, caused some to wonder if the club's financial dominance was developing into a problem for the English game.

In April 2000, it was announced that United had agreed to sign Dutch striker Ruud van Nistelrooy from PSV Eindhoven for a British record fee of £18million. But the move was put on hold when van Nistelrooy failed a medical, and he then returned to his homeland in a bid to regain fitness, only to suffer a serious knee injury which ruled him out for almost a year.

28-year-old French goalkeeper Fabien Barthez was signed from Monaco for £7.8million—making him the most expensive goalkeeper to be signed by a British club and United won the title again, becoming only the fourth side in history to win the English league title three seasons in succession. They also matched Liverpool's record (set in 1991) of 10 successive top two finishes.

However, the press largely saw the 1999-2000 and 2000-01 campaigns as failures as United had failed to win the European Cup, falling at the quarter final stages to Real Madrid in 2000 and Bayern Munich in 2001.

During the 2001 close season Ruud van Nistelrooy joined, and soon after Manchester United again broke the British transfer record—this time paying Lazio £28.1million for Argentine attacking midfielder Juan Sebastián Verón, although he failed to live up to the high expectations his transfer fee suggested and he was sold to Chelsea for £15million only two years later.

Two games into the 2001–02 season, Dutch central defender Jaap Stam was sold to Lazio in a £16million deal. The reason for Stam's departure was believed to have been claims in his autobiography *Head to Head* that he had been illegally spoken to about a move to Manchester United by Alex Ferguson, before his previous club PSV Eindhoven had been informed. Ferguson replaced Stam with Internazionale's 36-year-old central defender Laurent Blanc.

Before the season began, Ferguson also lost his assistant Steve McClaren, who took over as manager of Middlesbrough, and gave the role to long-serving coach Jim Ryan until a more permanent successor could be found.

By 8 December 2001, after a terrible run of form which saw one win and six defeats on a period of seven league games, Manchester United were ninth in the Premier League — 11 points behind leaders Liverpool who had a game in hand. There were widespread fears that they might not even qualify for Europe, let alone win the league title.

Then came a dramatic turn around in form: between mid-December and late January, as eight successive wins saw Manchester United climb to the top of the Premier League and put their title challenge back on track. Despite this, United finished third in the League as rival Arsène Wenger clinched the title for Arsenal at Old Trafford with a 1–0 win in the penultimate game of the season after United dropped points in a couple of other crucial games during the run-in.

United were also unsuccessful in Europe, losing the Champions League semi-final on away goals to Bayer Leverkusen. Early exits from the League Cup and FA Cup meant that the season endless trophyless. As they were third in the league and had not reached a cup final, it was the first time since 1989 that they had finished a season without being winners or runners-up of a major competition.

The 2001–02 season was to have been Ferguson's last as Manchester United manager, and the looming date of his retirement was cited as a reason for the team's loss of form. Ferguson himself admitted that the decision to pre-announce his retirement had resulted in a negative effect on the players and on his ability to impose discipline. But in February 2002 he agreed to stay in charge for at least another three years.

MANAGER

The close season saw Manchester United break the British transfer record yet again when they paid Leeds United £30million for 24-year-old central defender Rio Ferdinand. That summer, Ferguson brought in Portuguese coach Carlos Queiroz as his assistant.

Manchester United won their eighth Premier League title yet just over two months before the end of the season they were eight points behind leaders Arsenal. But an improvement in form for United, and a decline for Arsenal, saw the Premier League trophy gradually slip out of the Londoners' grasp and push it back in the direction of Old Trafford. Ferguson described the 2002–03 title triumph as his most satisfying ever, due to the nature of a remarkable comeback. The excellent run-in had produced 10 wins and a draw (including 4-0 home win over Liverpool and a 6-2 away demolition of Newcastle United) from the final 11 games, and no defeats since Boxing Day. Not for the first time, Ferguson had proven to be a master of managerial mind-games, successfully rattling the composure of Arsenal and their otherwise unflappable manager Arsène Wenger.

Ferguson guided Manchester United to their eleventh FA Cup at the end of the 2003–04 season, but it was a disappointing season which had seen them finish third in the Premier League (which was won by an undefeated Arsenal side) and suffer Champions League elimination at the hands of eventual winners FC Porto. Rio Ferdinand missed the final four months of the season, as he served the beginning of an eight-month ban for missing a drugs test. New signings like Eric Djemba-Djemba and José Kléberson were disappointing, but there was at least one productive signing in teenage Portuguese winger Cristiano Ronaldo. Striker Luis Saha, added in January, also proved to be reasonably successful covering for the injured Ole Gunnar Solskjaer in attack.

At the beginning of the 2004–05 season, teenage striker Wayne Rooney (the world's most expensive teenager at more than £20million) and Argentine defender Gabriel Heinze joined United while Cristiano Ronaldo continued where he had left off the previous season by putting in more match-winning performances.

But the lack of a striker after van Nistelrooy spent most of the season injured saw the club finish third for the third time in four seasons. In the FA Cup they lost on penalties to Arsenal. A second round exit from the European Cup at the hands of AC Milan and a semi-final exit from the League Cup at the hands of eventual winners Chelsea (who also clinched the Premier League title) meant that 2004-05 was a rare instance of a trophyless season for United.

Ferguson's preparations for the season were disrupted by a high-profile dispute with major shareholder John Magnier, over the ownership of the racehorse Rock of Gibraltar. When Magnier and business partner J. P. McManus agreed to sell their shares to American business tycoon Malcolm Glazer, it cleared the way for Glazer to acquire full control of the club. This sparked violent protests from United fans, and disrupted Ferguson's plans to strengthen the team in the transfer market. In spite of this, United looked to solve their goalkeeping and midfield problems. For this, they signed the Dutch keeper Edwin van der Sar from Fulham and Korean star Park Ji-Sung from PSV.

The season was one of transition. On 18 November, Roy Keane officially left the club, his contract ended by mutual consent. United failed to qualify for the knock-out phase of the UEFA Champions' League. In the January transfer window Serbian defender Nemanja Vidic and French full-back Patrice Evra were signed, and the side finished second in the league, behind runaway leaders Chelsea. Winning the League Cup was a consolation prize for lack of success elsewhere. Ruud van Nistelrooy's future at Old Trafford seemed to be in doubt after not starting in the Carling Cup final, and he departed at the end of the season.

Michael Carrick was signed as a replacement for Roy Keane for £14 million, although the figure may eventually rise in the future to £18.6 million depending on appearances and results. United started the season well and for the first time ever won their first four Premier League games. They set the early pace in the Premier League and never relinquished top spot from the tenth match of the 38–game season. The January 2006 signings had a huge impact on United's performances; Patrice Evra and Nemanja Vidic came in to form a solid back line along with already existing players Rio Ferdinand and skipper Gary Neville. The signing of Michael Carrick, which was questioned and criticised by a large portion of the media, brought stability and further creativity in the United midfield, forming an effective partnership with Paul Scholes. Park Ji-Sung and Ryan Giggs both underlined their value to the first team squad by adding significant pace and incisiveness in attack with Wayne Rooney and Cristiano Ronaldo.

Ferguson celebrated the 20th anniversary of his appointment as manager of Manchester United on 6 November 2006. Tributes also came from Ferguson's players, both past and present, as well as his old foe, Arsène Wenger, his old captain, Roy Keane, and current players. The party was spoiled the following day when United endured a single-goal defeat at the hands of Southend in the fourth round of the Carling Cup. However, on 1 December it was announced that Manchester United had signed 35 year old Henrik Larsson on loan,a player that Alex Ferguson had admired for many years, and attempted to capture previously. On 23 December 2006, Cristiano Ronaldo scored the club's 2000th goal under the helm of Ferguson in a match against Aston Villa.

Manchester United subsequently won their ninth Premier League title but were denied a unique fourth double by Chelsea's Didier Drogba scoring a late goal in the FA Cup Final at Wembley.

In the Champions League, the club reached the semi-finals, recording a 7–1 home win over Roma in the quarter-final second leg, but lost at the San Siro to Milan 3–0 in the second leg of the semi-final after being 3–2 up from the first leg. Still, it was a strong sign that United were on their way back to dominance after a couple of years of being overshadowed by Arsenal and more particularly Chelsea.

For the 2007–08 season, Ferguson made notable signings to reinforce United's first team. Long-term target Owen Hargreaves joined from Bayern Munich, bringing an end to a year of negotiations. Ferguson further bolstered the midfield with the additions of young Portuguese winger Nani and Brazilian playmaker Anderson. The last summer signing was of West Ham United and Argentina striker Carlos Tévez after a complex and protracted transfer saga.

United had their worst start to a season under Ferguson, drawing their first two league games before suffering a 1–0 defeat to local rivals Manchester City. However, United recovered and began a tight race with Arsenal for the title. After a good run of form, Ferguson claimed that throughout his time at Manchester United, this was the best squad he had managed to assemble thus far.

On 16 February 2008, United beat Arsenal 4–0 in an FA Cup Fifth Round match at Old Trafford, but were knocked out by eventual winners Portsmouth (a mid table side in the league) in the quarter final on 8 March, losing 1–0 at home. United having had a penalty claim turned down, Ferguson alleged after the game that Keith Hackett, general manager of the Professional Game Match Officials Board, was "not doing his job properly". Ferguson was subsequently charged by the FA with improper conduct, which he decided to contest. This was the second charge Ferguson faced in the season, following his complaints against the referee after United lost 1–0 at Bolton Wanderers – a charge he decided not to contest.

On 11 May 2008, Ferguson led Manchester United to a tenth Premier League title, exactly 25 years to the day after he led Aberdeen to European glory against Real Madrid in the European Cup Winners' Cup. Nearest rivals Chelsea – level on points going into the final round of matches, but with an inferior goal difference – could only draw 1–1 at home to Bolton, finishing two points adrift of the champions. United's title win was sealed with a 2-0 win over Wigan Athletic, managed by former United captain Steve Bruce, who before the game blew the whistle on suggestions that he would give his old club an easy ride - just as Bryan Robson had done 12 years earlier.

On 21 May 2008, Ferguson won his second European Cup with Manchester United as they beat Chelsea 6–5 on penalties in the Luzhniki Stadium in Moscow, following a 1–1 draw after extra time in the first ever all-English UEFA Champions League Final. A penalty miss from Cristiano Ronaldo meant that John Terry's spot-kick would have given the trophy to Chelsea if successfully converted, but Terry blew his chance of glory and in the end it was Edwin van der Sar's blocking of a Nicolas Anelka penalty which gave the trophy to Manchester United for the second time under Ferguson and for the third time overall.

After winning the 2007–08 UEFA Champions League Ferguson had stated that his intention to leave Manchester United within the next three years, meaning that he would be gone by the summer of 2011.Manchester United Chief Executive David Gill moved quickly to calm the speculation about Alex Ferguson's pending retirement.

Although the team had a slow start to the 2008–09 season, United won the Premier League with a game to spare, making Ferguson the first manager in the history of English football to win the Premier League three times consecutively, on two separate occasions. Ferguson had now won 11 league titles at Manchester United, and the 2008–09 season title success put them level with Liverpool as league champions on a record 18 occasions in total. They also won the Football League Cup on penalties after a goalless Wembley draw with Tottenham Hotspur. They contested the 2009 Champions League final against FC Barcelona on 27 May 2009 and lost 2–0.

After the presentation ceremony, Ferguson conceded that he would stay on at United for as long as his health permitted him and that he would be glad to win the league title once more. This would make United's total league wins one more than rivals Liverpool, becoming the outright leader in total wins.

In 2009-10, Ferguson added another Football League Cup to his honours list as United defeated Aston Villa 2-1 in the Wembley final on 28 February 2010. However, his dreams of a third European Cup were ended a few weeks later when United were edged out of the competition in the quarter-finals by Bayern Munich on away goals. And their hopes of a record 19th league title were ended on the last day of the season when Chelsea beat them to the Premier

League title, crushing Wigan Athletic 8-0 and rendering United's 4-0 win over Stoke City meaningless.. Around this time, several newspapers carried reports that Ferguson was due to retire at the end of the 2010-11 season, but he has since denied these rumours and insisted that he wants to go out on a high and will not retire during a time of struggle.

On 11 October 1999, a special testimonial match was played in honour of Alex Ferguson's contribution to the team. Manchester United played against a World XI, consisting of various profiledplayers from around the world the World XI wont the game 4-2.

One recurring theme of Ferguson's management of Manchester United has been his view that no player is bigger than the club. He has consistently taken a "my way or the highway" approach in his dealings with players and the pressure of this management tactic has often been the cause of many notable players' departures. Over the years players such as Gordon Strachan, Paul McGrath, Paul Ince, Jaap Stam, Dwight Yorke, David Beckham and more recently, Ruud van Nistelrooy and Gabriel Heinze have left the club after varying degrees of conflict with Ferguson. It is also suggested that one of the most inspirational players in the club's history, Roy Keane was a victim of Ferguson's wrath following damning criticism of his team mates on the club's in-house television channel, MUTV. This disciplinary line that he takes with such highly paid, high-profile players has been mentioned as a reason for the ongoing success of Manchester United.

HONOURS

Player

St. Johnstone
Scottish First Division (1): 1962–63

Falkirk
Scottish First Division (1): 1969–70

Managerial

Ferguson was made an Inaugural Inductee of the English Football Hall of Fame in 2002 in recognition of his impact on the English game as a manager. In 2003, Ferguson became an inaugural recipient of the FA Coaching Diploma, awarded to all coaches who had at least 10 years' experience of being a manager or head coach.

He is the Vice-President of the National Football Museum, based in Preston, and a member of the Executive Committee of the League Managers Association, and the only manager to win the top league honours and the Double north and south of the border (winning the Premier League with Manchester United, and the Scottish Premier Division with Aberdeen).

St. Mirren
Scottish First Division (1): 1976–77

Aberdeen
Scottish Premier Division (3): 1979–80, 1983–84, 1984–85
Scottish Cup (4): 1981–82, 1982–83, 1983–84, 1985–86
Scottish League Cup (1): 1985–86
UEFA Cup Winners' Cup (1): 1982–83
UEFA Super Cup (1): 1983

Manchester United

Premier League (11): 1992–93, 1993–94, 1995–96, 1996–97, 1998–99, 1999–2000, 2000–01, 2002–03, 2006–07, 2007–08, 2008–09

FA Cup (5): 1989–90, 1993–94, 1995–96, 1998–99, 2003–04

League Cup (4): 1991–92, 2005–06, 2008–09, 2009–10

FA Charity/Community Shield (8): 1990*, 1993, 1994, 1996, 1997, 2003, 2007, 2008 (* shared)

UEFA Champions League (2): 1998–99, 2007–08

UEFA Cup Winners' Cup (1): 1990–91

UEFA Super Cup (1): 1991

Intercontinental Cup (1): 1999

FIFA Club World Cup (1): 2008

Individual

Football Writers' Association Tribute Award: 1996

Mussabini Medal: 1999

UEFA Champions League Manager of the Year: 1998–99

BBC Sports Personality of the Year Coach Award: 1999

BBC Sports Personality of the Year Team Award: 1999

IFFHS Club Coach of the Year: 1999

LMA Manager of the Decade: 1990s

Laureus World Sports Award for Team of the Year: 2000

BBC Sports Personality of the Year Lifetime Achievement Award: 2001

English Football Hall of Fame: 2002

Onze d'Or Coach of the Year (2): 1999, 2007

Professional Footballers' Association Merit Award: 2007

UEFA Team of the Year (2): 2007, 2008

Premier League 10 Seasons Awards (1992/3 – 2001/2)

Manager of the Decade

Most Coaching Appearances (392 games)

Premier League Manager of the Year (9): 1993–94, 1995–96, 1996–97, 1998–99, 1999–2000, 2002–03, 2006–07, 2007–08, 2008–09

Premier League Manager of the Month (24): August 1993, October 1994, February 1996, March 1996, February 1997, October

1997, January 1999, April 1999, August 1999, March 2000, April 2000, February 2001, April 2003, December 2003, February 2005, March 2006, August 2006, October 2006, February 2007, January 2008, March 2008, January 2009, April 2009, September 2009
LMA Manager of the Year (2): 1998–99, 2007–08
World Soccer Magazine World Manager of the Year (4): 1993, 1999, 2007, 2008

Orders and special awards

Officer of the Order of the British Empire (OBE): 1983
Commander of the Order of the British Empire (CBE): 1995
Knight Bachelor: 1999

PLAYER PROFILES LIST IN ORDER

1) RYAN GIGGS
2) ERIC CANTONA
3) WAYNE ROONEY
4) CRISTIANO RONALDO
5) ROY KEANE
6) PETER SCHMEICHEL
7) MARK HUGHES
8) DAVID BECKHAM
9) PAUL SCHOLES
10) STEVE BRUCE
11) BRYAN ROBSON
12) GARY NEVILLE
13) RIO FERDINAND
14) DENIS IRWIN
15) GARY PALLISTER
16) BRIAN MCCLAIR
17) RUUD VAN NISTELROOY
18) ANDY COLE
19) OLE GUNNAR SOLKSKJAR
20) PAUL INCE
21) EDWIN VAN DER SAR
22) DWIGHT YORKE
23) TEDDY SHERINGHAM

RYAN GIGGS

Full name: Ryan Joseph Giggs
Date of birth: 29 November 1973
Place of birth: Canton, Cardiff, Wales
Height: 5 ft 11 in
Playing position: Midfielder
Current club: Manchester United

YOUTH CAREER
1985–1987   Manchester City
1987–1990   Manchester United

SENIOR CAREER

Years	Team	Apps	(Gls)
1990	Manchester United	588	(108)

NATIONAL TEAM

1990	Wales U21	1	(0)
1991–2007	Wales	64	(12)

Ryan made his first appearance during the 1990–91 season and has been a regular player since the 1991–92 season. He holds the club record for competitive appearances, and the club record for team trophies won by a player (23). Since 1992, he has collected 11 Premier League winner's medals, 4 FA Cup winner's medals, 3 League Cup winner's medals and 2 Champions League winner's medals, not a bad career?. He also has runner-up medals from the Champions League, 2 FA Cup finals and 2 Football League Cup finals, as well as being part of 4 United teams to have finished 2nd in the league. In recent years, Ryan has captained the team on numerous occasions, particularly in the 2007–08 season when regular captain Gary Neville was ruled out with different injuries. Ryan is the only player to play every season of the Premier league for one club and score in every season of the Premier League for any club.

Ryan turned professional on 29th November 1990 (his 17th birthday), by which time he was described by various sources as the finest prospect in English football since George Best. At this time, we had recently won the FA Cup – the first major trophy since the appointment of Ferguson as manager in November 1986. After 2 precarious seasons in the league where we had finished mid table, we were finally starting to threaten the dominance of Liverpool and Arsenal, though we only managed to finish 6th that season. Ferguson's quest for a successful left winger had not been easy since the departure of Jesper Olsen two years earlier. First he had signed Ralph Milne, but the player was not a success and lasted just a season in the first team before Sir Alex secured the Southampton winger Danny Wallace in September 1989. However, Danny had failed to repeat the performances that had made him one of the highest rated wingers in his days on the South Coast, and by the time Ryan turned professional Wallace was battling with 19-year-old Lee Sharpe for the role of first choice left winger.

Ryan made his League debut against Everton at Old Trafford on 2 March 1991, as a sub for the injured Denis Irwin in a 2–0 defeat. In his first full start, Ryan was credited with his first ever goal in a 1–0 win in the Manchester derby on 4 May 1991, though it appeared to be a Colin Hendry own goal. However, Ryan was not included in the squad of 16 that defeated Barcelona in the UEFA Cup Winners' Cup final 11 days later. Lee Sharpe, who had now won the race to displace Wallace as our regular left winger, took to the field as United's left winger, while Wallace was selected as a sub.

He became a first-team regular early in the 1991–92 season, yet remained active with the youth system and captained the team, made up of many of "Fergie's Fledglings", to an FA Youth Cup triumph in 1992.

Ryan broke into the first team even though he was still aged only 17, a mark of his skill and maturity, and paved the way as the first of many United youth players to rise into the first team under Sir Alex. As the youngest member of the United first team squad, Ryan looked to the older players such as Bryan Robson for advice.

That season, Ryan played in the team that finished 2nd to Leeds United in the final year of the old First Division before the advent of the Premier League. We had led the table for much of the season before a run of dismal results in April saw us overtaken by the West Yorkshire side.

Ryan collected his first piece of silverware on 12 April 1992 as We defeated Nottingham Forest in the League Cup Final, after he had set up Brian McClair to score the only goal of the game. At the end of the season, he was voted PFA Young Player of the Year – the award which had been credited to his colleague Lee Sharpe a year earlier.

By the start of the 1992–93 season, the first season of the newly formed Premier League, he was firmly established as United's first choice left winger, and became known as one of British football's most prodigious young players. He played a key role in our first top division title win for 26 years, though we didn't go top until after Christmas and fought off competition from big spending Aston Villa and Blackburn Rovers as well as surprise title contenders Norwich City.

His emergence and the arrival of Eric 'The King' Cantona heralded the dominance of United in the new league. Sir Alex was very protective of him, refusing to allow Ryan to be interviewed until he turned 20, eventually granting the first interview to the BBC's Des Lynam for *Match of the Day* in the 1993–94 season. This was the season when we won the double and Giggs was one of our key players alongside the likes of Eric Cantona, Paul Ince and Mark Hughes. Lee Sharpe, the player Giggs had ousted on the left wing a couple of years earlier, was now vying with Andrei Kanchelskis for the right wing position – with both players having key parts in the club's success.

We topped the table from the fourth game in late August and were not overtaken all season. Giggs also played for United in the

Football League Cup final, where we lost 3–1 to Aston Villa, ending our hopes of a unique domestic treble.

He was afforded many opportunities not normally offered to footballers at his young age, such as hosting his own television show, *Ryan Giggs' Soccer Skills*, which aired in 1994, and also had a book based on the series. Giggs was part of the Premier League's attempt to market itself globally, re-forging its image after the hooliganism-blighted years of the 1980s and he featured on countless football and lad mag covers, becoming a household name, and fuelling the era where footballers started to become celebrity idols on a par with pop stars in and around the mid to late 1990s. Despite his aversion to attention, Giggs also became a teenage pin-up and was once described as the "Premiership's First Poster Boy" and the "boy wonder", arguably the original footballer who catapulted the term into the public lexicon. He was hailed as the first football star to capture the public imagination in a way unseen since the days of George Best, the irony was that Best and Bobby Charlton used to describe Giggs as their favourite young player, turning up at The Cliff training ground just to watch him, where Best once quipped, "One day they might even say that I was another Ryan Giggs."

His immense popularity heralded a new era in football fandom and was also once described as the "boy who converted a million innocent teenage hearts into United fans". He burst onto the football scene in the 1990s when football was surging in popularity and becoming less working class, and when photogenic young players like Giggs and Liverpool's Jamie Redknapp were adored like popstars. It was not uncommon to have roads blocked and traffic jams when Giggs was at booksignings.

Giggs showed such unique talent that words like "genius" and "magician" were often used by admiring team mates like Paul Ince, while Gary Pallister remarked that United defenders "got twisted blood trying to mark him in training". His more experienced team-mates admired him even before he made his first-team debut, constantly asking the manager when Giggs would be selected for the first team. As Steve Bruce commented, "when Ryan ran, he ran like the wind. You couldn't hear him he was that light on his feet. He had that natural body swerve, that way with a ball only the great players have got. No disrespect to Beckham and Scholesy, but he's the only one who was always going to be a superstar."

Ryan proved to be a great goalscorer, many of his memorable goals being shortlisted for various Goal of the Season awards. Widely regarded as among his best were those against Queens Park Rangers in 1993, Tottenham in 1994, Everton in 1995, Coventry in 1996, and the most remarkable of all, his solo-goal against Arsenal in the replay of the 1999 FA Cup semi-final. During extra time, Giggs picked up possession after Patrick Vieira gave the ball away, then ran from the half-way line, dribbled past the whole Arsenal back line, including Tony Adams, Lee Dixon and Martin Keown before launching his left-footed strike just under David Seaman's bar and beyond his reach. He famously whipped off his shirt as he ran to celebrate with his teammates. It also has the distinction of being the last ever goal scored in an FA Cup semi-final replay as, from the following season, the FA Cup semi-finals are decided in a single game, with extra time and a penalty shootout if required.

1994–95 saw Ryan restricted through injury to 29 Premier League games and only one goal, but later in the season he recovered his form and fitness, though it was too late to help United to any major trophies. A failure to beat West Ham United on the final day of the season saw us lose the Premier League title to Blackburn Rovers. A week later, he came on as a sub in the FA Cup final against Everton, but United lost 1–0 in a game I remember clearly like it was yesterday. It was a frustrating season for both player and club, and Giggs was not the only key player to be ruled out for crucial games. Roy Keane, Lee Sharpe and Andrei Kanchelskis had notable absences due to injuries, while Eric Cantona missed the final 4 months of the league campaign (and the first six weeks of the next) after being banned from football for an incident during a game at Crystal Palace in late January.

The 1995 close season brought more controversy as United sold Paul Ince, Mark Hughes and Andrei Kanchelskis and began the following season without a major signing, though they had added Andy Cole to their ranks for a national record £7 million halfway through the previous season.

In 1995–96, Giggs returned to full form and played a vital part in securing a second double, his goal against Everton at Goodison Park on 9 September 1995 being shortlisted for the "goal of the season" award, though it was eventually beaten by votes for a goal by Manchester City's Georgi Kinkladze. In November that season, Giggs scored 2 goals in a Premier League match against Southampton, arguably his finest performance of the season, where we won 4–1 to keep up the pressure on a Newcastle United side who actually went 10 points clear on 23 December but were finally overhauled by United in mid March. Giggs was also in the side for Our FA Cup final win over Liverpool on 11 May 1996, though Eric Cantona scored the late winner – the only goal of the game.

By now, Giggs had several new key colleagues in breakthrough youngsters Gary Neville, Phil Neville, Nicky Butt, David Beckham and Paul Scholes. Beckham took over from Andrei Kanchelskis on the right wing and Butt succeeded Paul Ince in central midfield to complete a new look United midfield along with Giggs and Roy Keane. This midfield line-up was arguably even better than the one that had featured Kanchelskis and Ince.

The following season, Ryan had his first real chance to shine in Europe. Having played a key role when we won our third league title in 4 seasons, he helped us reach the UEFA Champions League semi-finals, the first United side in 28 years to achieve this. However, our hopes of European glory were ended by Borussia Dortmund, who edged us out by winning each leg of the semi-final 1–0.

In 1997–98, we were pipped to the Premier League title by Arsenal, following a dismal run of form in March and early April, leaving us without a trophy for only the 2nd time since 1989. The following season, Giggs missed a lot of games through injury, but when he was fit his form was consistently excellent and he played in both of our cup finals that season. Memorable moments were his extra-time goal in the FA Cup semi-final against arch-rivals Arsenal to give us a 2–1 win, and his 90th minute equaliser in the home leg of the UEFA Champions League semi-final against

PLAYER PROFILES

Juventus, a 1–1 draw which was followed later by a remarkable 3–2 win in Turin where United came from two goals behind, that was an incredible game, very nervous though to watch.

The highpoint in the 1998–99 season was when Giggs set up the equalising goal scored by Teddy Sheringham in the 1999 UEFA Champions League Final that set us on our way to the Treble. Striker Ole Gunnar Solskjaer scored the winning goal with the last kick of the game two minutes later. Giggs was also the Man of the Match as United beat Palmeiras to claim the Intercontinental Cup later that year.

Giggs became our longest serving player when Denis Irwin left in May 2002, and he became a pivotal part of the club, despite still being in his twenties. Giggs continued to excel in the 4 years that followed the Treble triumph of 1999. United were Premier League champions in three of the four seasons following the treble, as well as reaching the UEFA Champions League quarter-finals three times and the semi-finals once. He celebrated his 10-year anniversary at Old Trafford with a testimonial match against Celtic at the start of the 2001–02 campaign. However, this was one of the most disappointing seasons we had endured since Giggs made his debut for us, as a dismal run of form in early winter ultimately cost us the league title and we were surprisingly knocked out of the Champions League on away goals in the semi finals by German underdogs Bayer Leverkusen. A year later, in the autumn of 2002, he bagged his 100th career goal in a draw with Chelsea at Stamford Bridge.

He played in his 4th FA Cup triumph on 22 May 2004, making him one of only two players (the other being Roy Keane) to have won the trophy four times while playing for Manchester United. He has also finished with a runners-up medal three times (1995, 2005 and 2007). His participation in the victory over Liverpool in September 2004 made him the third player to play 600 games for United, alongside Sir Bobby Charlton and Bill Foulkes. He was inducted into the English Football Hall of Fame in 2005 in recognition of his contribution to the English game.

After that season, Giggs signed a two-year contract extension with United when chief executive David Gill relented on his normal policy of not signing players over 30 to contracts longer than one year. He has subsequently signed three further one-year contact extensions, to keep him at Old Trafford until at least June 2011, when he will be 37. Giggs has also benefited from being largely injury-free aside from a series of hamstring problems.

On 6 May 2007, with Chelsea only able to manage a 1–1 draw with London rivals Arsenal, we became the champions of England. In doing so, Giggs set a new record of nine league titles, beating the previous record of eight he shared with Alan Hansen and Phil Neal (who won all of their titles with Liverpool). Giggs played a starring role in United's 2007 Charity Shield victory after netting in the first half to bring the game to a 1–1 draw, which led to penalty triumph for the Red Devils after keeper Edwin van der Sar saved all of Chelsea's first three penalties.

In the 2007–08 season, Alex Ferguson adopted a rotation system between Giggs and newcomers Nani and Anderson. Nevertheless, Giggs remained the favoured choice for the anticipated clash with Chelsea at Old Trafford and put in a cross with the outside of his boot for Carlos Tévez to score his first United goal.

Giggs scored his 100th league goal for us against Derby County on 8 December 2007, which we won 4–1 More landmarks have been achieved: on 20 February 2008 he made his 100th appearance in the UEFA Champions League in a game against Lyon and on 11 May 2008 he came on as a sub for Park Ji-Sung to equal Sir Bobby Charlton's record of 758 appearances for United. Fittingly, Giggs scored the 2nd goal in that match, sealing his, and our 10th Premier League title. Ten days later, on 21 May 2008, Giggs broke Bobby Charlton's appearance record when coming on as an 87th minute substitute for Paul Scholes in the Champions League Final against Chelsea. We of course would go on to win the Final, defeating Chelsea 6–5 on penalties after a 1–1 draw after extra time. Giggs converted what became the winning penalty in sudden-death for United (before Chelsea's Nicolas Anelka missed the final penalty) and joined Steve McManaman and team-mate Owen Hargreaves in becoming the only British players to have played in and won more than one Champions League final. (This is not true for European Cups as several Nottingham Forest players achieved this in 1979 and 1980 and several Liverpool players in 1977, 1978, 1981 and 1984.) Giggs lifted the Champions League trophy with Rio Ferdinand as captain Gary Neville had been out for nearly the entire season with an injury.

At the start of Manchester United's 2008–09 campaign, Sir Alex Ferguson began playing Giggs in central midfield, behind the forwards, instead of his favoured wing position. Giggs has since adapted very well to his new position and supplied two assists in as many games, against Middlesbrough and Aalborg. Sir Alex Ferguson said in an interview, "(Giggs) is a very valuable player, he will be 35 this November but at 35, he can be United's key player. At 25, Ryan would shatter defenders with his run down the flank, but at 35, he will play deeper." Giggs has begun taking his coaching badges and Ferguson has hinted that he would like Giggs to serve as his coaching staff after retirement like Ole Gunnar Solskjær did.

On 8 February 2009, Giggs maintained his record of being the only player to score in every season of the Premier League since its inception in 1992 by netting the only goal in a 1–0 win over West Ham United. Following speculation earlier in the year, in February 2009, Giggs signed a one-year extension to his current contract – which was due to expire in June 2009. After a successful season, Giggs was short-listed along with four other Manchester United team mates for the PFA Player of the Year. On 26 April 2009, Giggs received the award, despite having started just twelve games throughout the 08/09 season (at the time of receiving the trophy). This was the first time in his illustrious career that Giggs had received the award. Prior to the awards ceremony, Alex Ferguson had given his backing for Giggs to win the award and stated that it would be fitting, given Giggs' long term contribution to the game. Giggs made his 800th appearance for Manchester United on 29 April 2009, in the 1–0 semi-final win over Arsenal in the UEFA Champions League. On 16 May 2009, We won the Premier League after a 0–0 draw against Arsenal, both our and

Giggs' 11th Premier League titles.

On 12 September 2009, Giggs scored United's first goal in a 3–1 Premier League win against Tottenham Hotspur, at White Hart Lane, maintaining his record of having scored in every Premier League season since its inception, the only player to have done so. This game also marked Giggs' 700th start for United. Giggs scored his 150th goal for United, only the ninth player to do so for the club, against Wolfsburg in his first Champions League game of the season. The goal, as well as his previous strike of the season against Spurs, was direct from a free-kick, albeit with a huge deflection. It also made it a record-equalling 14th Champions League season in which he had scored, drawing him level with Raúl who had achieved the feat 15 days earlier. He then set up Michael Carrick to score the winner to give United a 2–1 win against the Champions League newcomers. On 28 November 2009, the eve of his 36th birthday, Giggs scored his 100th Premier League goal – all for Manchester United – scoring the final goal in a 4–1 victory over Portsmouth at Fratton Park. The goal along with his previous two strikes of the season was another free kick, stating his claim for regular set-piece taker since the departure of Cristiano Ronaldo, he also became only the 17th player to reach the milestone in the Premier League.

On 30 November 2009, the day after his 36th birthday, it was reported that Giggs would be offered an additional one-year contract which would run until the end of the 2010–11 season and see him past the 20th anniversary of his first game and first goal for United.On the same day, Giggs was nominated for BBC Sports Personality of the Year 2009. On 5 December 2009, Giggs' appearance against West Ham United – a game that he ended playing at left-back – equalled countryman Gary Speed's outfield record of 535 Premier League games. On 12 December, Giggs surpassed Speed's feat by playing against Aston Villa. The following day, Giggs won the BBC Sports Personality of the Year award.On 18 December 2009, Giggs signed a one-year contract extension with United, keeping him at the club until June 2011, taking him past the 20th anniversary of his first professional contract and that of his first team debut – a rare occurrence of a player reaching the 20-year mark with the same club and with unbroken service.On 31 December 2009, Giggs was named the Manchester United Player of the Decade.

On 24 April 2010, Giggs scored the first ever league penalties of his career in his 900th game for club and country. He netted two penalties in a 3–1 home win over Tottenham Hotspur, which was crucial as it sent United to the top of the Premier League after several weeks in second place behind Chelsea.

ERIC CANTONA

Full name: Eric Daniel Pierre Cantona
Date of birth: 24 May 1966
Place of birth: Marseille, France
Height: 6 ft 2 in
Playing position: Forward (retired)

YOUTH CAREER
000?–1981 SO Les Caillols

SENIOR CAREER

Years	Team	Apps	(Gls)
1983–1988	Auxerre	82	(23)
1985–1986	Martigues (loan)	15	(4)
1988–1991	Marseille	40	(13)
1989	Bordeaux (loan)	11	(6)
1989–1990	Montpellier (loan)	33	(10)
1991	Nîmes	16	(2)
1992	Leeds United	28	(9)
1992–1997	Manchester United	144	(64)
Total		**369**	**(131)**

NATIONAL TEAM
1987–1995	France	45	(20)

TEAMS MANAGED
2005 – France national beach soccer team

Eric made his first appearance for us in a friendly match against Benfica in Lisbon to mark Eusébio's 50th birthday. He made his competitive debut as a second half substitute against Manchester City at Old Trafford on 12 December 1992. United won 2-1, though the King made little impact that day.

Our season had been disappointing up to Cantona's signing.

PLAYER PROFILES

We were falling behind the likes of big spending Aston Villa and Blackburn Rovers in the race for the first FA Premier League title, as well as surprise challengers including Norwich City and QPR. Goalscoring had been a problem since the halfway point of the previous season - when it had cost us the league title.

Brian McClair and Mark Hughes were off form, and summer signing Dion Dublin had broken his leg early in the season, ruling him out of action for 6 months. However, King Eric quickly settled into the team, not only scoring goals but also creating chances for the other players. His first goal came in a 1-1 draw against Chelsea at Stamford Bridge on 19 December 1992, and his second came on Boxing Day in a thrilling 3-3 draw against Sheffield Wednesday at Hillsborough where we claimed a point after being 3-0 down at half time.

It was against Tottenham Hotspur on 9 January 1993, that Cantona really showed his class, scoring one and having a hand in the other goals in a 4-1 victory. However, controversy was never far away, and on his return to Elland Road to play Leeds a few weeks later, he spat at a fan and was fined £1,000 by the FA.

In Eric's first two seasons at Old Trafford, we went on an amazing run, winning the inaugural Premier League in 1993 by 10 points after an excellent second half of the season - largely inspired by Cantona - saw us crowned champions of England for the first time since 1967. By winning that title, Cantona became the first - and so far the only - player ever to win back-to-back English top division titles with different clubs.

In the 1993/94 season we retained the Premier League and Cantona's two penalties helped us to a 4-0 win over Chelsea in the FA Cup Final. He also collected a runners-up medal in the Football League Cup, in which we reached the final only to lose 3-1 to Aston Villa. He was also voted PFA Player of the Year for that season. However, the season was not without its moments of controversy not least when Cantona was sent off at the end of the Champions League exit at the hands of Galatasaray following an argument with the referee, and when he was dismissed in successive Premier League games - the first against Swindon Town, the second against Arsenal. The two successive red cards saw Cantona banned for five matches -including the FA Cup semi-final clash with Oldham Athletic, which we drew 1-1 to force a replay for which Cantona was available and helped them win 4-1. 1993-94 was the first season of squad numbers in the Premier League. Cantona was issued with the number 7 shirt; a squad number which he kept for the rest of his career at United.

In the 1994/95 season, Cantona continued his impressive form as we looked to win a 3rd successive league title, but on 25 January 1995 he was involved in an incident which attracted headlines and controversy worldwide. In an away match against Crystal Palace, Cantona was sent off by the referee for a vengeful kick on Palace defender Richard Shaw after Shaw had pulled his shirt. As he was walking towards the tunnel, he launched a 'kung-fu' style kick into the crowd, directed at Crystal Palace fan Matthew Simmons, followed by a series of punches. The infamous photograph of the moment Cantona's foot connected with Simmons, was used with permission on the front cover of Ash's single "Kung Fu". The front cover alone generated publicity in the British rock press, which helped the band get a hit single when it charted at number 57 in the same year.

At a press conference called later, Cantona gave what is perhaps his most famous quotation. Perhaps referring to how journalists would constantly monitor his behaviour, Cantona said, in a slow and deliberate manner: "When the seagulls follow the trawler, it's because they think sardines will be thrown into the sea. Thank you very much." He then got up from his seat and left, leaving many of the assembled crowd bemused. He was sentenced to 120 hours of community service after an appeal court overturned a two-week prison sentence for assault.

In accordance with the Football Association's wishes, Manchester United suspended Cantona for the remaining 4 months of the 1994–95 season, which ruled him out of first team action as we were still in the hunt for a 2nd double. He was also fined £20,000.

The Football Association then increased the ban to 8 months

PLAYER PROFILES

(up to and including 30 September 1995) and fined him a further £10,000. The FA Chief Executive Graham Kelly described his attack as "a stain on our game" that brought shame on football. FIFA then confirmed the suspension as worldwide, meaning that Cantona couldn't escape the ban by transferring to a foreign club. Manchester United also fined Cantona two weeks wages and he was stripped of the French captaincy; his club eventually lost the Premier League title to Blackburn. In 2007 he said, "I have a lot of good moments, but the one I prefer is when I kicked the hooligan."

Almost since the day of the kung fu incident, there had been endless media speculation that Cantona would leave English football when his ban finished, but Alex Ferguson persuaded him to stay in Manchester, despite interest from the Italian club Inter Milan (who managed to lure his team mate Paul Ince to Italy that year) and Cantona was once again inspirational.

In the 1995/96 season we had sold several key players at the start of the season and replaced them with players from the club's youth team and their prospects of winning the league were not looking good after a 3-1 defeat to Aston Villa on the opening day of the season.

Much hype surrounded Cantona's return game, against Liverpool on 1 October 1995 - by which time United had bounced back from the opening day defeat and were second in the league. There were also fears from various individuals that he might never be able to cope in English football again, as the torment and provocation from players and particularly supporters of rival teams might prove too much for him.

In his comeback game, Cantona set up a goal for Nicky Butt 2 minutes into the game, and then scored a penalty after Ryan Giggs had been upended. Eight months without competitive football had inevitably taken its toll and Cantona struggled for form prior to Christmas, and the gap between us and leaders Newcastle United had increased to 10 points by 24 December.

Things then changed, however, when in mid January a goal by Cantona in our league clash with West Ham United at Upton

Park triggered a 10-match winning run in the league. Over the second half of the season, several more United games ended in 1-0 wins with Cantona scoring the only goal, though it was actually a draw (in which Cantona equalised) with Queen's Park Rangers on 9 March which saw United finally overtake Newcastle on goal difference. They stayed there for the rest of the season, and any lingering doubts of the title's destination were ended on the final day of the season when United beat Middlesbrough 3-0 at the Riverside Stadium to clinch our third title in four seasons.

Fittingly, it was a 1-0 scoreline, and the same scorer, in that year's FA Cup Final against Liverpool, with Cantona becoming the first player from outside the home nations to lift the FA Cup as captain (regular captain Steve Bruce missed the game due to doubts about his fitness). The strike of that match happened with 5 minutes remaining and was perhaps the most famous goal of Cantona's career. A corner from the right side troubled Liverpool keeper David James who fisted the ball. The ball was deflected to Cantona, who had backed away when the corner was sent, who volleyed the ball to score the winning goal. Cantona gave a post-match interview saying: "You know that's life. Up and down." Manchester United became the first team to win "the double" twice.

Cantona was confirmed as United's captain for the 1996-97 season following the departure of Steve Bruce to Birmingham City.

Cantona galvanised the United team to greater success with the likes of Ryan Giggs and youngsters David Beckham, Paul Scholes, Nicky Butt and Gary Neville emerging under his influence. As we retained the league in the 1996-97 season, Cantona had won 4 league titles in 5 years with United (6 in 7 years including those won with Marseille and Leeds United), the exception being the 1994-95 season which he had missed the 2nd half of through suspension.

At the end of an admittedly lacklustre season by his standards, which was fuelled by our elimination at the hands of Borussia Dortmund in the semi-finals of the UEFA Champions League, he announced that he was retiring from football at the age of 30 which came as a surprise, and was met with great dismay by fans. His final competitive game came against West Ham on 11 May 1997, and his final appearance before retiring was five days later on 16 May in a testimonial for David Busst (a player whose career had been ended by an injury suffered against United the previous year) against Coventry City at Highfield Road, in which Cantona scored twice in a 2-2 draw. Cantona scored a total of 64 league goals for Manchester United, 11 in domestic cup competitions, and 5 in The Champions League, bringing his tally to 80 goals in less than 5 years.

WAYNE ROONEY

Full name: Wayne Mark Rooney
Date of birth: 24 October 1985
Place of birth: Croxteth, Liverpool
Height: 5 ft 10 in
Playing position: Striker
Current club: Manchester United

YOUTH CAREER
1996–2002 Everton

SENIOR CAREER

Years	Team	Apps	(Gls)
2002–2004	Everton	67	(15)
2004–	Manchester United	189	(91)

NATIONAL TEAM

2003–	England	64	(25)

Wayne Wonder made his United debut on 28 September 2004 in a 6–2 Champions League group stage win over Fenerbahçe, scoring a hat-trick along with an assist. However, his first season at Old Trafford ended trophyless as we could only manage a third place finish in the league (having been champions or runners-up on all but 2 previous occasions since 1992) and failed to progress to the last 8 of the UEFA Champions League. United had more success in the cup competitions, but we were edged out of the League Cup in the semi finals by a Chelsea side who also won the League title that season, and a goalless draw with Arsenal in the FA Cup final was followed by a penalty shoot-out defeat. However, Wayne was United's top league scorer that season with 11 goals, and was credited with the PFA Young Player of the Year award.

In September 2005, Wayne was sent off in a UEFA Champions

League clash with Villarreal which finished 0–0 for sarcastically clapping the referee who had booked him for an unintentional foul on an opponent. His first trophy with United came in the 2006 League Cup, and he was also named man of the match after scoring twice in United's 4–0 win over Wigan Athletic in the final. In the Premier League, however, an erratic start to the season left title glory looking unlikely for United and their title hopes were ended in late April when they lost 3–0 at home to champions Chelsea and had to settle for second place. Rooney's goalscoring further improved in the 2005–06 season, as he managed 16 goals in 36 Premier League games.

Rooney was sent off in an Amsterdam Tournament match against Porto on 4 August 2006 after hitting Porto defender Pepe with an elbow. He was punished with a 3 match ban by the FA, following their receipt of a 23-page report from referee Ruud Bossen that explained his decision. Wayne wrote a letter of protest to the FA, citing the lack of punishment handed down to other players who were sent off in friendlies. He also threatened to withdraw the FA's permission to use his image rights if they did not revoke the ban, but the FA had no power to make such a decision.

During the first half of the 2006–07 season, Rooney ended a 10 game scoreless streak with a hat-trick against Bolton Wanderers, and he signed a 2 year contract extension the next month that tied him to United until 2012. By the end of April, a combination of 2 goals in an 8–3 aggregate quarter-final win over Roma and two more in a 3–2 semi-final first leg victory over AC Milan brought Rooney's total goal amount to 23 in all competitions and tied him with teammate Cristiano Ronaldo for the team goalscoring lead. By the end of that season, he had scored 14 league goals.

Rooney collected his first Premier League title winner's medal at the end of the 2006–07 season, but has yet to pick up an FA Cup winner's medal; he had to settle for a runners-up medal in the 2007 FA Cup Final.

On 12 August 2007, Rooney fractured his left metatarsal in United's opening-day goalless draw against Reading; he had suffered the same injury to his right foot in 2004. After being sidelined for 6 weeks, he returned for United's 1–0 Champions League group stage win over Roma on 2 October, scoring the match's only goal. However, barely a month into his return, Rooney injured his ankle during a training session on 9 November, and missed an additional two weeks. His first match back was against Fulham on 3 December, in which he played 70 minutes. Rooney missed a total of 10 games and finished the 2007–08 season with 18 goals (12 of them in the league), as United clinched both the Premier League and the Champions League, in which they defeated league rivals Chelsea in the competition's first-ever all-English final.

On 4 October 2008 in an away win over Blackburn Rovers, Rooney became the youngest player in league history to make 200 appearances. On 14 January after scoring what turned out to be the only goal 54 seconds into the 1–0 win over Wigan Athletic, Rooney limped off with a hamstring ailment in the eighth minute. His replacement, Carlos Tévez, was injured himself shortly after entering the game, but stayed on. Rooney was out for three weeks, missing one match apiece in the League Cup and FA Cup, along with four Premier League matches. On 25 April 2009, Rooney scored his final league goals of the season against Tottenham. United scored 5 goals in an emphatic second half display to come from 2–0 down winning the game 5–2. Rooney grabbed two goals, set up two and provided the assist that led to the penalty for United's first goal. Rooney ended the season with 20 goals in all competitions, behind Ronaldo as leading United scorer for the season. Once again, he managed 12 goals in the league.

Rooney's start to the 2009/10 campaign got off to great scoring ways, grabbing a goal in the 90th minute of the 2009 Community Shield, though United lost the game to Chelsea on penalties. He then scored the only goal of the opening game of the 2009–10 season against Birmingham City, taking his overall United tally to 99. He failed to score in the next game, a historic 1–0 defeat to the hands of newly-promoted Burnley at Turf Moor. On 22 August 2009, he became the 20th Manchester United player to have scored over 100 goals for the club, finding the net twice in a

5–0 away win at Wigan Athletic, a game which also saw Michael Owen notch his first goal for United.

On 29 August 2009, United played Arsenal at Old Trafford. Rooney scored the equaliser from the penalty spot after Andrei Arshavin had put the Gunners ahead. The game finished 2–1 to Manchester United after Abou Diaby scored an own goal. Five days later Rooney commented on his penalty against Arsenal: "Everyone who watches me play knows I am an honest player, I play the game as honestly as I can. If the referee gives a penalty there is nothing you can do." On 28 November 2009, Rooney scored his first hat-trick for three years in a 4–1 away victory against Portsmouth, with two of them being penalties. On 27 December 2009, he was awarded Man of the Match against Hull. He was involved in all the goals scored in the game, hitting the opener and then giving away the ball for Hull's equalizing penalty. He then forced Andy Dawson into conceding an own goal and then set up Dimitar Berbatov for United's third goal which gave them a 3–1 victory. On 30 December 2009, three days on from their victory over Hull, he grabbed another goal in United's 5–0 thrashing of Wigan in their final game of the decade. On 23 January 2010, Rooney scored all four goals in Manchester United's 4–0 win over Hull City; three of the goals came in the last 10 minutes of the match. This was the first time in his career that he bagged four in one match. On 27 January 2010, he continued his great scoring run by heading the winner in the second minute of stoppage time against derby rivals Manchester City. This gave United a 4–3 aggregate win, taking them into the final, it was his first League Cup goal since netting two in the 2006 final.

On 31 January 2010, Rooney scored his 100th Premier League goal in a 3–1 win over Arsenal for the first time in the league at the Emirates, notably his first Premier League goal also came against Arsenal. On 16 February 2010, Rooney hit his first European goals of the season, scoring two headers in the 3–2 away win against A.C. Milan in their first ever win against them at the San Siro. On 28 February 2010, he scored another header against Aston Villa (his fifth consecutive headed goal in a row) which resulted in Manchester United winning the Carling Cup final 2–1.In the second leg of United's European tie against AC Milan, Rooney scored a brace in a resounding 4–0 home victory, taking his tally of goals this season to 30. He then added 2 more to his tally just 5 days later at Old Trafford, in a 3–0 win over Fulham.

On 30 March 2010, during United's Champions League Quarter-final first leg defeat against Bayern Munich (at Munich's Allianz Arena), Rooney crumpled when he twisted his ankle in the last minute. There were fears that he had received serious ligament damage or even a broken ankle, but it was announced that the injury was only slight ligament damage, and that he would be out for 2 to 3 weeks, missing United's crunch match with Chelsea and the return leg against Munich next week. The team list for second leg of the Champions League Quarter-final yielded a massive surprise when Rooney was given a starting place in the United lineup.Despite a 3–0 lead by the 40th minute, Munich snatched 2 goals back (with United forced down to 10 men after Rafael Da Silva was sent-off). Rooney was substituted after re-damaging his ankle. Manchester United, although they won the second leg 3–2, exited from the Champions League on the away goals rule.

On 25 April 2010, Rooney was named the 2010 PFA Players' Player of the Year, It's a shame Wayne didn't have the best World Cup like we all expected but he is still one of the best players in the World in my eyes, and I'm sure a lot of other peoples aswell. He is still young and has a really long time left in the game.

CRISTIANO RONALDO

Full name: Cristiano Ronaldo dos Santos Aveiro
Date of birth: 5 February 1985
Place of birth: Funchal, Madeira, Portugal
Height: (6 ft 1 in)
Playing position: Winger/Forward
Current club: Real Madrid

YOUTH CAREER

1993–1995 Andorinha
1995–1997 Nacional
1997–2001 Sporting CP

SENIOR CAREER

Years	Team	Apps	(Gls)
2001–03	Sporting CP	25	(3)
2003–09	Manchester United	196	(84)
2009–	Real Madrid	29	(26)

NATIONAL TEAM

2001–02	Portugal U17	9	(6)
2003	Portugal U20	5	(1)
2002–03	Portugal U21	6	(3)
2004	Portugal U23	3	(1)
2003–	Portugal	76	(23)

Cristiano became our first-ever Portuguese player when he signed for £12.24 million after the 2002–03 season. He requested the number 28 (his number at Sporting Lisbon), as he did not want the pressure of living up to the expectation linked to the number 7 shirt, which had previously been worn by players such as George Best, Bryan Robson, Eric Cantona, and David Beckham. "After I joined, the manager asked me what number I'd like. I said 28. But Sir Alex said 'No, you're going to have No. 7,' and the famous shirt was an extra source of motivation. I was forced to live up to such an honour."

Cristiano made his United debut as a 60th-minute substitute in a 4–0 home victory over Bolton Wanderers. He scored his first goal for Manchester United with a free kick in a 3–0 win over Portsmouth on 1 November 2003. He scored Our 1000th Premier League goal on 29 October 2005 in a 4–1 loss to Middlesbrough. He scored 10 goals in all competitions, and fans voted him to his first FIFPro Special Young Player of the Year award in 2005.

In November and December 2006, Cristiano received consecutive Barclays Player of the Month honours, becoming only the 3rd player in Premier League history to do so after Dennis Bergkamp in 1997 and Robbie Fowler in 1996. He scored his 50th United goal against city rivals Manchester City on 5 May 2007 as we claimed our first Premier League title in 4 years, and he was voted into his 2nd consecutive FIFPro Special Young Player of the Year award at the end of the year.

Despite rumours circulating in March 2007 that Real Madrid were willing to pay an unprecedented £80 million (£54 million) for Ronaldo, he signed a 5-year, £120,000-a-week (£31 million total) extension with United on 13 April, making him the highest-paid player in team history.

He amassed a host of personal awards for the season. He won the PFA Players' Player of the Year and PFA Young Player of the Year awards, joining Andy Gray (in 1977) as the only players to receive this honour. In April, he completed the treble by winning the PFA Fans' Player of the Year. Ronaldo was also one of eight Manchester United players named in the 2006–07 PFA Premier League Team of the Year.

Ronaldo's 2007–08 season began with a red card for a headbutt on Portsmouth player Richard Hughes during United's second match of the season, for which he was punished with a 3-match ban. Ronaldo said he had "learned a lot" from the experience and would not let players "provoke" him in the future. After scoring the only goal in a Champions League away match against Sporting, Ronaldo also scored the injury-time winner in the return fixture as Manchester United topped their Champions League group.

He finished 2nd to Kaká for the 2007 Ballon d'Or, and was 3rd in the running for the FIFA World Player of the Year award, behind Kaká and Lionel Messi.

Ronaldo scored his first hat trick for us in a 6–0 win against Newcastle United at Old Trafford on 12 January 2008, bringing United up to the top of the Premier League table. He scored his twenty-third league goal of the season in a 2–0 win against Reading, equalling his entire total for the 2006–07 season. During a 1–1 Champions League first knockout round draw against Lyon on 20 February, an unidentified Lyon supporter continuously aimed a green laser at Ronaldo and United teammate Nani, prompting an investigation by UEFA. One month later, Lyon were fined £2,427 for the incident.

On 19 March 2008, Ronaldo captained United for the first time in his career in a home win over Bolton, scoring both goals in the 2–0 victory. The second of the goals was his 33rd of the campaign, which set a new club single-season scoring record by a midfielder and thus topped George Best's 40-year-old total of 32 goals in the 1967–68 season. Ronaldo scored another brace in a 4–0 win over Aston Villa on 29 March, which at the time gave him 35 goals in 37 domestic and European matches as both a starter and substitute. Ronaldo's scoring streak was rewarded with his becoming the first winger to win the 2007–08 European Golden Shoe, finishing 8 points ahead of Mallorca's Dani Güiza.

In the 2007–08 Champions League final on 21 May against league rivals Chelsea, Ronaldo scored the opening goal after 26 minutes, which was negated by a Chelsea equaliser in the 45th minute as the match ended 1–1 after extra time. His misfire in the penalty shoot-out put Chelsea in position to win the trophy, but John Terry shot wide right after slipping on the pitch surface, and Manchester United emerged victorious 6–5 on penalties. Ronaldo was named the UEFA Fans' Man of the Match, and wrapped up the campaign with a career-high 42 goals in all competitions, falling four short of Denis Law's team-record mark of 46 in the 1963–64 season.

On 5 June 2008, Sky Sports reported that Ronaldo had expressed an interest in moving to Real Madrid if they offered him the same amount of money the team had allegedly promised him earlier in the year. Manchester United filed a tampering complaint with FIFA on 9 June over Madrid's alleged pursuit of Ronaldo, but FIFA declined to take any action. Speculation that a transfer would happen continued until 6 August, when Ronaldo confirmed that he would stay at Manchester for at least another year.

Ronaldo underwent ankle surgery at the Academic Medical Center in Amsterdam on 7 July. He returned to action on 17 September in United's UEFA Champions League goalless group-stage draw with Villarreal as a substitute for Park Ji-Sung, and scored his first overall goal of the season in a 3–1 League Cup third round win over Middlesbrough on 24 September.

In a 5–0 win over Stoke City on 15 November 2008, Ronaldo scored his 100th and 101st goals in all competitions for Manchester United, both from free kicks. The goals also meant that Ronaldo had now scored against each of the other 19 teams in the Premier League at the time.

On 2 December, Ronaldo became Manchester United's first Ballon d'Or recipient since George Best in 1968. He finished with 446 points, 165 ahead of runner-up Lionel Messi. He was awarded the Silver Ball after finishing with two goals as United won the Club World Cup on 19 December.

On 8 January 2009, Ronaldo was uninjured in a single-car accident in which he wrote off his Ferrari 599 GTB Fiorano in a tunnel along the A538 near Manchester Airport. A breathalyzer test he gave to police officers at the scene was negative, and he attended training later that morning.

4 days later, he became the first Premier League player ever to be named the FIFA World Player of the Year, in addition to being the first Portuguese player to win the award since Luís Figo in 2001.

Ronaldo scored his first Champions League goal of the season, and first since the final against Chelsea, in a 2–0 victory over Internazionale that sent United into the quarter-finals. In the second leg against Porto, Ronaldo scored a 40-yard game-winning goal as United advanced to the semi-finals. He later called it the best goal he had ever scored. Ronaldo participated in his second consecutive Champions League final, but made little impact in United's 2–0 loss to Barcelona. He finished with 53 appearances in all competitions, which was 4 higher than the previous year, but scored 16 fewer goals (26) than his career-best total of 42 from the previous season.

On 11 June 2009, Manchester United accepted an unconditional offer of £80 million from Real Madrid for Ronaldo after it was revealed that he again had expressed his desire to leave the club. It was confirmed by a representative of the Glazer family that the sale was fully condoned by Ferguson.

When Ronaldo had eventually completed his transfer to Real, he expressed his gratitude towards Ferguson for helping him develop as a player, saying, "He's been my father in sport, one of the most important factors and most influential in my career."

ROY KEANE

Full name: Roy Maurice Keane
Date of birth: 10 August 1971
Place of birth: Cork, Ireland
Height: 5 ft 10 in
Playing position: Midfielder
Current club: Ipswich Town (manager)

YOUTH CAREER
1979–1989 Rockmount

SENIOR CAREER

Years	Team	Apps	(Gls)
1989–1990	Cobh Ramblers	12	(1)
1990–1993	Nottingham Forest	114	(22)
1993–2005	Manchester United	323	(33)
2005–2006	Celtic	10	(1)
Total		**459**	**(57)**

NATIONAL TEAM

1990–1991	Republic of Ireland U21	4	(0)
1991–2005	Republic of Ireland	66	(9)

TEAMS MANAGED
2006–2008 Sunderland
2009– Ipswich Town

There was no guarantee that Roy would go straight into the first team despite the £3.75m fee paid to Nottingham Forest in July 1993. Bryan Robson and Paul Ince had established a formidable partnership in the centre of midfield, having just inspired Manchester United to their first league title since 1967. Robson, however, was now 36 years old and in the final stages of his playing career, and a series of injuries kept him out of action at the start of the 1993–94 season. Keane took full advantage of his run in the team, scoring twice on his home debut against Sheffield United on 18 August 1993 and grabbing the winner in the Manchester derby three months later, when United overturned a 2–0 deficit at Maine Road to beat Manchester City 3–2. He had soon established himself as a permanent fixture in Alex Ferguson's side, and by the end of the season he had won his first trophy as a professional as United retained their Premier League title in May. Two weeks later, Keane broke his Wembley losing streak by helping United to a 4–0 victory over Chelsea in the FA Cup Final, sealing the club's first ever Double.

The following season was less successful, however, as United were beaten to the league title by Blackburn Rovers and beaten 1–0 in the FA Cup final by Everton. He received his first red card as a Manchester United player in an FA Cup semi-final against Crystal Palace after stamping on Gareth Southgate, and, as punishment, was suspended for three matches and fined £5,000. This incident was the first of eleven red cards Keane would accumulate in his United career, and one of the first signs of his fiery temper leading to indiscipline on the field.

The summer of 1995 saw a period of change at United, with Ince leaving for Inter Milan as well as striker Mark Hughes moving to Chelsea and Andrei Kanchelskis being sold to Everton. Younger players such as David Beckham, Nicky Butt and Paul Scholes were brought into the team, which left Keane as the most experienced player in midfield. Despite a slow start to the 1995–96 campaign, United pegged back title challengers Newcastle, who had built a commanding twelve-point championship lead by Christmas, to secure another Premier League title. Keane's second Double in three years was confirmed with a 1–0 win over bitter rivals Liverpool to win the FA Cup for a record ninth time.

The next season saw Keane in and out of the side due to a series of knee injuries and frequent suspensions. He picked up a costly yellow card in the first leg of the UEFA Champions League semi-final against Borussia Dortmund, which ruled him out of the return leg at Old Trafford. United lost both legs 1–0, but this was compensated for by winning another league title a few days later.

After Eric Cantona's unexpected retirement, Keane took over as club captain, although he missed most of the 1997-98 season because of a cruciate ligament injury caused by an attempt to tackle Leeds United player Alf-Inge Haåland in the ninth Premier League game of the season. As Keane lay prone on the ground, Haåland stood over Keane, accusing the injured United captain of having tried to hurt him and of feigning injury to escape punishment; an allegation which would lead to an infamous dispute between the two players four years later. Keane did not return to competitive football that campaign. He watched from the sidelines as United squandered an eleven-point lead over Arsenal to miss out on the Premier League title. Many pundits cited Keane's absence as a crucial factor in the team's surrender of the league trophy. He initially expressed doubts as to whether he would play again due to the severity of his injury, but he recovered in time to begin pre-season training for the new campaign.

Any fears that Keane's injury may have reduced his effectiveness as a player were dispelled in the 1998-99 season, when he returned to captain the side to an unprecedented treble of the FA Premier League, FA Cup, and UEFA Champions League. One of his finest performances in this campaign was an inspirational display against Juventus in the second leg of the Champions League semi-final, when he helped haul his team back from two goals down to win 3–2, a game regarded around Europe as one of the best performances on a football field in the modern era of European football. He scored from a header to start United's comeback and continually drove the team forwards at every opportunity. His performance in Turin has been described as his finest hour as a footballer. Earlier in the match, however, Keane had received a yellow card that ruled him out of the final after a trip on Zinedine Zidane.

"It was the most emphatic display of selflessness I have seen on a football field. Pounding over every blade of grass, competing if he would rather die of exhaustion than lose, he inspired all around him. I felt it was an honour to be associated with such a player." Sir Alex Ferguson on Keane's performance against Juventus in 1999.

PLAYER PROFILES

In the final, United defeated Bayern Munich 2-1 at Nou Camp, but Keane had mixed emotions about the victory due to his suspension. Recalling his thoughts before the game, Keane said: "Although I was putting a brave face on it, this was just about the worst experience I'd had in football." Later that year, Keane scored the only goal in the finals of the Intercontinental Cup, as United defeated Palmeiras.

Contract negotiations dominated the landscape during the summer after the treble, with Keane turning down United's initial £2 million-a-year offer amid rumours of a move to Italy. His higher demands were eventually met midway through the 1999-00 season, committing him to United until 2004. Keane was angered when club officials explained an increase in season ticket prices was a result of his improved contract and asked for an apology from the club. Days after the contract was signed, Keane celebrated by scoring the winning goal against Valencia in the Champions League, although United's interest in the competition was ended by Real Madrid in the quarter-finals, partly due to an unfortunate Keane own-goal in the second leg. He was voted PFA Players' Player of the Year and Football Writers' Association Footballer of the Year at the end of the season after leading United to their sixth Premier League title in eight years.

Keane caused controversy in December 2000, when he criticised sections of United supporters after the Champions League victory over Dynamo Kiev at Old Trafford. He complained about the lack of vocal support given by some fans when Kiev were dominating the game, stating: "Away from home our fans are fantastic, I'd call them the hardcore fans. But at home they have a few drinks and probably the prawn sandwiches, and they don't realise what's going on out on the pitch. I don't think some of the people who come to Old Trafford can spell 'football', never mind understand it." Keane's rant started a debate in England about the changing atmosphere in football grounds, and the term 'prawn sandwich brigade' is now part of the English football vocabulary.

He made headlines again in the 2001 Manchester Derby, a game in which Alf-Inge Haåland played. Five minutes from the final whistle, he was sent off for a blatant knee-high foul on the Norwegian in what was seen by many as an act of revenge. He initially received a three game suspension and a £5,000 fine from the FA, but further punishment was to follow after the release of Keane's autobiography in August 2002, in which he stated that he intended "to hurt" Haåland. Keane's account of the incident was as follows:

"I'd waited long enough. I fucking hit him hard. The ball was there (I think). Take that you cunt. And don't ever stand over me sneering about fake injuries."

An admission that the tackle was in fact a premeditated assault, left the FA with no choice but to charge Keane with bringing the game into disrepute. He was banned for a further 5 matches and fined £150,000 in the ensuing investigation. Despite widespread condemnation, he later maintained in his autobiography that he had no regrets about the incident: "My attitude was, fuck him. What goes around comes around. He got his just rewards. He fucked me over and my attitude is an eye for an eye."

United finished the 2001-02 season trophyless for the first time in 4 years. Domestically, they were eliminated from the FA Cup by Middlesbrough in the fourth round and finished third in the Premier League, their lowest final position in the league since 1991. Progress was made in Europe, however, as United reached the semi-finals of the UEFA Champions League, their furthest advance since their successful campaign of 1999. They were eventually knocked out on away goals after a 3–3 aggregate draw with Bayer Leverkusen, despite Keane putting United 3–2 up, and after the defeat, Keane blamed United's loss of form on some of his team-mates' fixation with wealth, claiming that they had "forgot about the game, lost the hunger that got you the Rolex, the cars, the mansion."

Earlier in the season, Keane had publicly advocated the breakup of the Treble-winning team as he believed the team-mates who had played in United's victorious 1999 Champions League final no longer had the motivation to work as hard.

In August 2002 he was fined £150,000 by Ferguson and

suspended for three matches for elbowing Sunderland's Jason McAteer, and this was compounded by an added five-match suspension for the controversial comments about Haåland. Keane used the break to undergo an operation on his hip, which had caused him to take painkillers for a year beforehand. Despite early fears that the injury was career-threatening, and suggestions of a future hip-replacement from his surgeon, he was back in the United team by December.

"I'd come to one firm conclusion, which was to stay on the pitch for 90 minutes in every game. In other words, to curb the reckless, intemperate streak in my nature that led to sendings-off and injuries." Keane on his 'new' style of play.

During his period of rest after the operation, Keane reflected on the cause of his frequent injuries and suspensions. He decided that the cause of these problems was his reckless challenges and angry outbursts which had increasingly blighted his career. As a result, he became more restrained on the field, and tended to avoid the disputes and confrontations with other players. Some observers felt that the "new" Roy Keane had become less influential in midfield as a consequence of the change in his style of play, possibly brought about by decreased mobility after his hip operation. However, after his return, Keane displayed the tenacity of old, leading the team to another league title in May 2003.

Throughout the 2000s, Keane maintained a healthy rivalry with Arsenal captain Patrick Vieira. The most notable incident between the two took place at Highbury in 2005 at the height: of an extreme period of bad blood between United and Arsenal. Vieira was seen confronting United defender Gary Neville in the tunnel before the game over his fouling of José Antonio Reyes in the previous encounter between the two sides prompting Keane to verbally confront the Arsenal captain. The incident was broadcast live on Sky Sports, with Keane clearly heard telling match referee Graham Poll to "Tell him [Vieira] to shut his fucking mouth!" After the game, which United won 4-2, Keane controversially criticised Vieira's decision to play internationally for France instead of his birthplace of Senegal. However, Vieira later suggested that having walked out on his National team in the World Cup finals Keane was not in a good position to comment on such matters. Referee Poll later revealed that he should have sent off both players before the match had begun, though was under pressure not to do so.

Overall, Keane would lead United to 9 major honours, making him the most successful captain in the club's history. Keane scored his 50th goal for Manchester United on 5 February 2005 in a league game against Birmingham City. His appearance in the 2005 FA Cup final, which United lost to Arsenal in a penalty shootout, was his seventh such game, an all-time record in English football at the time. Keane also jointly holds the record for the most red cards received in English football, being dismissed a total of 13 times in his career. He was inducted into the English Football Hall of Fame in 2004 in recognition of his undoubted impact on the English game, and became the only Irish player to be selected into the FIFA 100, a list of the greatest living footballers picked by Pelé.

PETER SCHMEICHEL

Full name: Peter Bolesław Schmeichel
Date of birth: 18 November 1963
Place of birth: Gladsaxe, Denmark
Height: 6 ft 4 in
Playing position: Goalkeeper

YOUTH CAREER
1972–1975 Høje-Gladsaxe
1975–1981 Gladsaxe-Hero

SENIOR CAREER

Years	Team	Apps	(Gls)
1981–1984	Gladsaxe-Hero	46	(0)
1984–1987	Hvidovre	78	(6)
1987–1991	Brøndby	119	(2)
1991–1999	Manchester United	292	(0)
1999–2001	Sporting CP	50	(0)
2001–2002	Aston Villa	29	(1)
2002–2003	Manchester City	29	(0)
Total		643	(9)

NATIONAL TEAM
1987–2001	Denmark	129	(1)

Following Peter's displays on the international scene, Manchester United bought him in 1991 for £530,000, a price which was described in 2000 by Manchester United manager Alex Ferguson as the "bargain of the century" Schmeichel played the bulk of his career for United, 8 years in total. With United, He won 5 FA Premier League titles, 3 FA Cups, 1 League Cup, and the UEFA Champions League.

Manchester United finished 2nd in Schmeichel's first season (also winning the Football League Cup for the first time in the club's history), but it was on the international stage that Schmeichel enjoyed his biggest success that year. In the Danish national team under new national manager Richard Møller Nielsen, Schmeichel was Denmark's starting goalkeeper at the Euro 92 tournament which they won. He saved a penalty kick from Marco van Basten in the semi-final, and most notably held a cross with one hand in the final. He made a string of important saves during the tournament, and was elected "The World's Best Goalkeeper 1992".

In the 1992–93 season, 22 clean sheets from Schmeichel helped United win the Premier League championship for the first time in 26 years. Schmeichel was once again named "The World's Best Goalkeeper" in 1993. In January 1994, Schmeichel fell out with Ferguson, as United had squandered a 3–0 lead to draw 3–3 with Liverpool. The two had a row where Schmeichel "said the most horrible things", and he was subsequently sacked by Ferguson. A few days later, Schmeichel made an improvised apology to the other players. Unknown to him, Ferguson was eavesdropping on this, and he let Schmeichel stay at Manchester United. Schmeichel and United repeated the Premier League championship win at the end of the season.

Despite being a goalkeeper, he could also single-handedly provide a deadly attacking threat. He would run into the box on corner kicks if his team was behind. The sight of him going up for the corner was a great distraction to opposing defenders. He scored a goal in this fashion in a 1995 UEFA Cup match against Rotor Volgograd. He scored in the last minutes of the game, though United was eliminated from the tournament on the away goals rule.

In April 1996, during a game against Coventry City, defender David Busst colided with United defender Denis Irwin and suffered a compound fracture of the leg. The break was so bad that the bone pierced through the skin and his blood had to be cleared off the pitch. Schmeichel, who witnessed the incident, reportedly vomited at the sight and had to receive counselling afterwards.

Schmeichel competed with Denmark at the Euro 96 hosted by England. The defending European Champions went out in the preliminary group stage, despite delivering results equivalent to the Euro 92 tournament.

Following a February 1997 match against Arsenal, Schmeichel was accused of racism by Arsenal striker Ian Wright. During the game, Schmeichel and Wright had a number of controversies, and at the end of the game, the two players confronted each other on their way off the pitch. After the game, news emerged of a police inquiry into a November 1996 match between the two clubs, where it was alleged that Schmeichel had made a racist remark. After months of politicizing by the FA and the PFA, who wanted a "converted" Schmeichel as their posterboy of the "Kick Racism out of Football" campaign, no evidence was found and the case was dropped.

Under new national manager Bo Johansson, Schmeichel was a part of the Danish squad at the 1998 FIFA World Cup. He was one of the leading members of the Danish campaign, which ended in a 3–2 quarter-final defeat to Brazil.

Schmeichel ended his Manchester United career on the highest note, when Schmeichel and United won the Treble, the FA Premier League title, FA Cup and UEFA Champions League, in the same season. In that year's FA Cup semi-final against Arsenal, Schmeichel saved a penalty kick by Dennis Bergkamp in the last minutes of the game, to send the game into extra time. In the absence of the suspended Roy Keane, he captained United in the UEFA Champions League final in May 1999. German opponents Bayern Munich had a 1–0 lead until the dying minutes of the game, when United received a corner kick. Schmeichel ran into the attack attempting to cause confusion, and Teddy Sheringham scored the equalising goal. A few seconds later, Ole Gunnar Solskjær scored the 2–1 winner for United to ensure that Schmeichel's United career ended on the highest possible note. In an unforgettable celebratory moment, Schmeichel was shown cartwheeling gleefully in his area after Solskjær's winning goal.

MARK HUGHES

Full name: Leslie Mark Hughes
Date of birth: 1 November 1963
Place of birth: Ruabon, Wrexham, Wales
Height: 5 ft 10 in
Playing position: Forward

YOUTH CAREER
1978–1980 Manchester United

SENIOR CAREER

Years	Team	Apps	(Gls)
1980–1986	Manchester United	89	(37)
1986–1988	Barcelona	28	(4)
1987–1988	Bayern Munich (loan)	18	(6)
1988–1995	Manchester United	256	(82)
1995–1998	Chelsea	95	(25)
1998–2000	Southampton	52	(2)
2000	Everton	18	(1)
2000–2002	Blackburn Rovers	50	(6)
Total		606	(163)

NATIONAL TEAM
1984–1999	Wales	72	(16)

TEAMS MANAGED
1999–2004 Wales
2004–2008 Blackburn Rovers
2008–2009 Manchester City

MANCHESTER UNITED (1980–1986)

M ark joined Manchester United after leaving school in the summer of 1980, having been spotted by the team's North Wales talent scout Hugh Roberts. However he did not make his first team debut for 3 years — in a 1–1 draw away to Oxford United in the FA Cup, in the 1983–84 season. Like many other United legends, "Sparky" quickly became a favourite by scoring on his debut.

When Mark made his United debut, the club's striker partnership consisted of 27-year-old Irishman Frank Stapleton and 18-year-old Ulsterman Norman Whiteside, and breaking up that partnership would not be an easy challenge for Hughes. But Hughes quickly broke into the first team, partnering Frank Stapleton in attack while Norman Whiteside was switched to midfield to partner Ray Wilkins and stand in for the injury prone Remi Moses. The departure of Wilkins to AC Milan at the end of the season saw manager Ron Atkinson decide to use Whiteside as a first choice midfielder, enabling Hughes to keep his place in the first team, and he was rewarded handsomely as he scored 25 goals in 55 games in all competitions as United achieved an FA Cup final victory over Everton. They also finished fourth in the league.

He managed a further 20 goals in the 1985–86 season, where they led until February having won their first 10 league games of the season, before a dismal second half of the season saw them slip into fourth place in the final table. That season saw him score 17 goals in the Football League First Division – it would remain the highest goals tally in a season throughout his career.

BACK TO MANCHESTER UNITED (1988–1995)

In May 1988, Hughes returned to Manchester United, now managed by Sir Alex Ferguson, for a then club record of £1.8 million. As he had done in his first spell at Old Trafford, Hughes proved to be a dynamic goalscorer and was a key player for the club over the next 7 years.

He was voted PFA Player of the Year in 1988–89, his first season back in England, though United disappointed in the league and finished 11th after an erratic season which had seen them go 10 league games without a win in the autumn but then go on a strong run after the turn of the new year to lift them to third place, only for a late season collapse to drag them down to mid table. He was the very first Manchester United player to be credited with that award despite the accolade being in its 16th season.

A year later, he scored twice as United drew 3–3 with Crystal Palace in the FA Cup final, before a Lee Martin goal in the replay gave United their first major trophy in five years. He was United's top goalscorer that season, scoring 15 goals in all competitions (13 of them in the league).

The following season, Hughes scored both goals against old club Barcelona as United lifted the UEFA Cup Winners' Cup. Once again, he was their top scorer, this time with 21 goals in all competitions. He was the joint top scorer in the league alongside Steve Bruce on 13 goals. They also reached the Football League Cup final that year, but United suffered a shock 1–0 defeat to a Sheffield Wednesday side managed by Ron Atkinson, who had been Hughes's manager in his first spell at Old Trafford. He was also voted PFA Player of the Year again this season.

In 1991–92, Hughes suffered the disappointment of missing out on a league title medal as United were pipped to the title by Leeds United, but had some compensation in the form of a League Cup winner's medal. A year after that, he finally collected an English league title medal as United won the first-ever Premier League title. Hughes collected yet more silverware in 1994 as United won the league title as well as the FA Cup, with Hughes scoring in the final. He also scored Manchester United's consolation goal in their 3–1 defeat in the 1994 League Cup Final at the hands of Aston Villa at Wembley in that season. In doing this, he became only the second player (after Norman Whiteside in 1983) to score in the finals of both the domestic cups in the same season. This has since been achieved a third time by Didier Drogba in 2007.

Hughes came close to winning both the Premier League and FA Cup again in 1995, but a failure to beat West Ham on the final day of the season and the inability to score an equaliser against Everton in the FA Cup final a year later condemned United to their first trophyless season in six years.

In April 1994, he scored a spectacular equaliser in the final minute of extra time in the FA Cup semi-final against Oldham Athletic, a goal which has been described by many as one of the finest ever scored by any Manchester United player.

1994–95 was Hughes's last season at United as he agreed to join Chelsea in a surprise £1.5 million deal. There had been speculation about his future at United since January that year, as the arrival of Andy Cole had put his future in the first team under doubt, though he was given a lifeline in the first team after Eric Cantona received an 8-month ban for assaulting a spectator against Crystal Palace. There was also talk that Cantona would be on his way out of Old Trafford, as Internazionale were interested in signing him, but when Cantona signed a new three-year contract Hughes knew that Cantona was likely to be straight back in the side after his suspension finished on 30 September 1995, and knew that his best chance of first-team football would be away from Old Trafford.

Between Cole's arrival and the Cantona incident, Hughes had suffered a knee injury as he courageously scored United's goal in a 1–1 draw at Newcastle United in the Premier League. It was feared that he would be out until the following season as knee ligament damage was suspected, but the injury turned out to be less serious than originally feared and he was back in action by the end of the following month. His injury also put paid to talk of a £2.5million move to Everton that was being mooted in the aftermath of Cole's arrival.

By the time of his departure from Manchester United, he was the last player at the club to have been there before the appointment of Alex Ferguson as manager in November 1986.

DAVID BECKHAM

Full name:David Robert Joseph Beckham
Date of birth:2 May 1975
Place of birth:Leytonstone, London
Height:6 ft 0 in
Playing position:Midfielder
Current club:Los Angeles Galaxy

YOUTH CAREER
Brimsdown Rovers
1987–1991 Tottenham Hotspur
1991–1993 Manchester United

SENIOR CAREER

Years	Team	Apps	(Gls)
1993–2003	Manchester United	265	(62)
1995	Preston North End (loan)	5	(2)
2003–2007	Real Madrid	116	(13)
2007–	Los Angeles Galaxy	41	(7)
2009	Milan (loan)	18	(2)
2010	Milan (loan)	11	(0)

NATIONAL TEAM

1992–1993	England U-18	3	(0)
1994–1996	England U-21	9	(0)
1996–	England	115	(17)

D avid was part of a group of young players at the club who guided the club to win the FA Youth Cup in May 1992, with Beckham scoring in the second leg of the final against Crystal Palace. He made his first appearance for United's first-team that year, as a substitute in a League Cup match against Brighton and Hove Albion, and signed his first professional contract shortly afterwards. United reached the final of the Youth

Cup again the following year, with Beckham playing in their defeat by Leeds United, and he won another medal in 1994 when the club's reserve team won their league, although he didn't play in any first team games that season.

On 7 December 1994, Beckham made his Champions League debut, scoring a goal in a 4–0 victory at home to Galatasaray in the final game of the group stage. However, this victory was of little use as they finished third out of four in their group behind Barcelona on goal difference.

He then went to Preston North End on loan for part of the 1994–95 season to get some first team experience. He impressed, scoring two goals in five appearances, notably scoring directly from a corner kick. Beckham returned to Manchester and finally made his Premier League debut for Manchester United on 2 April 1995, in a goal-less draw against Leeds United.

United manager Sir Alex Ferguson had a great deal of confidence in the club's young players. Beckham was part of a group of young talents Ferguson brought in to United in the 1990s "Fergie's Fledglings", which included Nicky Butt and Gary and Phil Neville. When experienced players Paul Ince, Mark Hughes, and Andrei Kanchelskis left the club after the end of the 1994–95 season, his decision to let youth team players replace them instead of buying star players from other clubs (United had been linked with moves for players including Darren Anderton, Marc Overmars, and Roberto Baggio, but no major signings were made that summer), drew a great deal of criticism. The criticism increased when United started the season with a 3 1 defeat at Aston Villa, with Beckham scoring United's only goal of the game; however, United won their next 5 matches and the young players performed well.

Beckham swiftly established himself as United's right–sided midfielder (rather than a right-winger in the style of his predecessor Andrei Kanchelskis) and helped them to win the Premier League title and FA Cup double that season, scoring the winner in the semi-final against Chelsea and also provided the corner that Eric Cantona scored from in the FA Cup Final. Beckham's first title medal had, for a while, looked like it wouldn't be coming that season, as United were still 10 points adrift of leaders Newcastle United at the turn of the new year, but Beckham and his team-mates had overhauled the Tynesiders at the top of the league by mid March and they remained top until the end of the season.

Despite playing regularly (and to a consistently high standard) for Manchester United, Beckham did not break into the England squad before Euro 96.

At the beginning of the 1996–97 season David Beckham was given the number 10 shirt that had most recently been worn by Mark Hughes. On 17 August 1996 (the first day of the Premier League season), Beckham became something of a household name when he scored a spectacular goal in a match against Wimbledon. With United leading 2–0, Beckham noticed that Wimbledon's goalkeeper Neil Sullivan was standing a long way out of his goal, and hit a shot from the halfway line that floated over the goalkeeper and into the net.When Beckham scored his famous goal, he did so in shoes custom-made for Charlie Miller ("Charlie" embroidered on boots), which had been given to Beckham by mistake. In a UK poll conducted by Channel 4 in 2002, the British public voted the goal #18 in the list of the 100 Greatest Sporting Moments. During the 1996–97 season, he became an automatic first-choice player at United helping them to retain the Premier League championship, and being voted PFA Young Player of the Year by his peers.

On 18 May 1997, Eric Cantona retired as a player and left the coveted number 7 shirt free, and with Teddy Sheringham arriving from Tottenham Hotspur as Cantona's successor, Beckham left his number 10 shirt for Sheringham and picked up the number 7 jersey. Some fans had felt the number 7 shirt should be retired after Cantona had himself retired, but the shirt number remains in use to this day (most recently by another England star Michael Owen).

United started the 1997–98 season well but erratic performances in the second half of the season saw United finish second behind Arsenal.

At that year's world cup he scored against Columbia to ensure England's progression to the last 16 but was then dismissed for a petulant kick out at Simeone when England were leading 2-1. After England's exit he was blamed by manager Glenn Hoddle in particular and the majority of England fans in general. It seemed Beckham had taken the wrap for the nation's failings.

The following 1998–99 season, he was part of the United team that won the Treble of the Premier League, FA Cup and Champions League, a unique feat in English football. There had been speculation that the criticism that he had received after being sent off in the World Cup would lead to him leaving England, but he decided to stay at Manchester United.

To ensure they would win the Premier League title, United needed to win their final league match of the season, at home to Tottenham Hotspur (with reports suggesting that the opposition would allow themselves to be easily beaten to prevent their deadly local rivals Arsenal from retaining the title), but Tottenham took an early lead in the match. Beckham scored the equaliser and United went on to win the match and the league.

Beckham played centre-midfield in United's FA Cup final win over Newcastle United and for the 1999 UEFA Champions League Final against Bayern Munich, since United's first string centre-midfielders were suspended for the match. United were losing the match 1–0 at the end of normal time, but won the trophy by scoring two goals in injury time. Both of the goals came from corners taken by Beckham. Those crucial assists, coupled with great performances over the rest of the season, led to him finishing runner up to Rivaldo for 1999's European Footballer of the Year and FIFA World Player of the Year awards.

Despite Beckham's achievements in the 1998–99 season, he was still unpopular among some opposition fans and journalists, and he was criticised after being sent off for a deliberate foul in Manchester United's World Club Championship match against Necaxa. It was suggested in the press that his wife was a bad influence on him, and that it might be in United's interests to sell him, but his manager publicly backed him and he stayed at the club. During the 1999–2000 season, there was a talk of a transfer to Juventus in Italy, but this never happened.

THE MANCHESTER UNITED PREMIER YEARS

By the early 2000s, the relationship between Ferguson and Beckham had begun to deteriorate, possibly as a result of his fame and commitments away from football. In 2000, Beckham was given permission to miss training to look after his son Brooklyn, who had gastroenteritis, but Ferguson was furious when Victoria Beckham was photographed at a London Fashion Week event on the same night, claiming that Beckham would have been able to train if Victoria had looked after Brooklyn that day. He responded by fining Beckham the maximum amount that was permitted (two weeks' wages – then £50,000) and dropping him for a crucial match against United's rivals Leeds United. He later criticised Beckham for this in his autobiography, claiming he had not been *"fair to his teammates"* Beckham had a good season for his club, though, and helped United to win the Premier League by a record margin.

"He was never a problem until he got married. He used to go into work with the academy coaches at night time, he was a fantastic young lad. Getting married into that entertainment scene was a difficult thing – from that moment, his life was never going to be the same. He is such a big celebrity, football is only a small part.'" – Alex Ferguson speaking about Beckham's marriage in 2007.

Beckham helped United retain the Premier League title in 1999–2000 by an 18-point margin – after being pushed by Arsenal and Leeds United for much of the season, United won their final 11 league games of the season, with Beckham scoring five goals during this fantastic run of form. He managed six league goals that season, and scored eight goals in all competitions. He was a key player in United's third successive league title in 2000–01 – only the fourth time that any club had achieved three league titles in a row. He scored nine goals that season, all in the Premier League.

On 10 April 2002, Beckham was injured during a Champions League match against Deportivo La Coruña, breaking the second metatarsal bone in his left foot. There was speculation in the British media that the injury might have been caused deliberately, as the player who had injured Beckham was Argentine Aldo Duscher, and England and Argentina were due to meet in that year's World Cup. The injury prevented Beckham from playing for United for the rest of the season and they missed out on the Premier League title to Arsenal (also being knocked out of the European Cup by Bayer Leverkusen on away goals in the semi-finals), but he signed a three-year contract in May, following months of negotiations with the club, mostly concerning extra payments for his image rights. The income from his new contract, and his many endorsement deals, made him the highest-paid player in the world at the time.

2001–02 was arguably Beckham's best season as a United player, though. He scored 11 goals in 28 league games, and a total of 16 goals in 42 games in all competitions, the best tally of his career.

Following an injury early in the 2002–03 season, Beckham was unable to regain his place on the Manchester United team, with Ole Gunnar Solskjær having replaced him on the right side of midfield. His relationship with his manager deteriorated further on 15 February 2003 when, in the changing room following an FA Cup defeat to Arsenal, a furious Alex Ferguson threw or kicked a boot that struck Beckham over the eye, causing a cut that required stitches. The incident led to a great deal of transfer speculation involving Beckham, with bookmakers offering odds on whether he or Ferguson would be first to leave the club. Although the team had started the season badly, their results improved greatly from December onwards and they won the league, with Beckham managing a total of 11 goals in 52 games in all competitions.

He was still a first-choice player for England, however, and he was awarded an OBE for services to football on 13 June 2003.

Beckham had made 265 Premier league appearances for United and scored 61 goals. He also made 81 Champions league appearances, scoring 15 goals. Beckham won six Premier League titles, two FA Cups, one European Cup, one Intercontinental Cup, and one FA Youth Cup in the space of 12 years. By this stage, he was their joint second longest serving player behind Ryan Giggs (having joined them at the same time as Nicky Butt, Gary Neville and Paul Scholes).

PAUL SCHOLES

Full name: Paul Scholes
Date of birth: 16 November 1974
Place of birth:Salford
Height:5 ft 7 in
Playing position:Midfielder
Current club: Manchester United

YOUTH CAREER
1991–1994   Manchester United

SENIOR CAREER

Years	Team	Apps	(Gls)
1994–	Manchester United	444	(101)

NATIONAL TEAM

1997–2004	England	66	(14)

Paul was not a member of Manchester United's 1992 FA Youth Cup-winning squad that included future senior teammates David Beckham, Nicky Butt, Gary Neville and Ryan Giggs, but he was part of the youth team that reached the final in the following season, alongside Phil Neville. Scholes turned professional on 23 July 1993 and was issued with the number 24 shirt, but did not make his breakthrough into the senior squad until the 1994–95 season, when he made seventeen league appearances and scored five goals. His debut came on 21 September 1994, where he scored twice in a 2–1 victory over Port Vale in the Football League Cup. Scholes came on as a substitute in the 1995 FA Cup final against Everton, which United lost 1–0.

In 1995–96, after Mark Hughes moved to Chelsea, Scholes had even more first-team opportunities. He stood in for the suspended Eric Cantona as Andrew Cole's strike partner for the first two months of the campaign. Scholes (now wearing the number 22 shirt) scored fourteen goals in all competitions as United became the first English team to win the double twice. He picked up another Premier League winners medal in 1996–97 (changing his shirt number once again, this time to number 18, which he has held ever since), but was restricted to three goals in sixteen league games.

Scholes moved to the midfielder and forward attack positions in the 1997–98 after Roy Keane suffered a knee injury in late September and did not play again that season. United finished the season without a major trophy, only the second time in the 1990s that this happened.

In 1998–99, Scholes was a key player in Manchester United's Premier League title, FA Cup, and UEFA Champions League Treble success. He scored one of Manchester United's two goals against Newcastle in the FA Cup final. He also scored an away goal against Internazionale in the Champions League quarter-final, but was ruled out of the final victory over Bayern Munich through suspension.

Scholes netted a career-high twenty goals in all competitions in the 2002–03 season, a number that dipped to fourteen the next year, despite a career-best four FA Cup goals in comparison to his total of five in his first nine seasons. He helped Manchester United reach the 2005 FA Cup Final but saw his penalty saved by Jens Lehmann as they lost to Arsenal in a penalty shootout. He was ruled out for the second half of the 2005–06 campaign with blurred vision. The cause of this was initially uncertain, sparking fears that it could end his career. He overcame this problem through the beginning of the year and he appeared in Manchester United's final game of the season against Charlton Athletic. Reportedly, Scholes' vision has not completely recovered.

On 22 October 2006, in the 2–0 Premier League victory over Liverpool in which Scholes also scored, twelve years after marking his Red Devils debut with a League Cup brace against Port Vale, Scholes became the ninth United player to play in five hundred matches, joining Sir Bobby Charlton, Bill Foulkes, Denis Irwin, and current teammates Giggs and Gary Neville.

Scholes was dismissed during Manchester United's 1–0 away victory over Liverpool F.C. on 3 March 2007, for swinging an arm at Xabi Alonso. It marked his first league expulsion since April 2005. A month later, he was sent off in the first leg of Manchester United's Champions League quarter final at A.S. Roma.

On 23 August, he was shortlisted for a spot in the National Football Museum Hall of Fame, which ultimately went to Dennis Bergkamp.

Scholes suffered knee ligament damage during a training session the night before Manchester United's Champions League Group F matchup with Dynamo Kiev on 23 October 2007, and was out of action until the end of January 2008. He returned as a substitute in Manchester United's 3–1 win over Tottenham Hotspur in the fourth round of the FA Cup. On 23 April 2008, Scholes made his 100th Champions League appearance in a semi-final 0–0 draw at FC Barcelona, and scored the only goal in a 1–0 victory in the second leg that sent United into the final. During the final he suffered an injury and a yellow card after a clash with Claude Makélélé, he returned until he was substituted by Giggs in the 87th minute and did not take part in the penalty shoot-out that was won 6–5 by United after a 1–1 extra-time draw.

Scholes was inducted into the English Football Hall of Fame in September 2008. In a December 2008 interview with the *Daily Mirror*, he said he planned to retire from football completely in two years. "I think I've got two years left at the most, I'm looking forward to finishing and everything that goes with it."

On 24 January 2009, Scholes scored his first goal of the season against Tottenham Hotspur in the FA Cup. His shot from outside the box in the 34th minute deflected in off Tom Huddlestone to bring the game to 1–1, while United would go on to win 2–1. On 18 February, Scholes scored his first Premier League goal in over a year in a 3–0 win over Fulham, a swerving volley that hit Mark Schwarzer and rebounded in. On 22 April, he made his 600th appearance for Manchester United in a 2–0 win over Portsmouth.

On 15 September 2009, Scholes scored his first Champions League goal since netting the winner against Barcelona in the semi-final a year and a half ago. He netted the solitary goal in the 77th minute away to Besiktas, giving Manchester United a winning start to their 2009–10 European campaign. On 3 November 2009, Scholes hit his second goal of the campaign, again coming in the Champions League. This time he scored the second United goal in the 3–3 draw with CSKA Moscow, which was another headed goal. On 5 December 2009, Scholes scored his first league goal of the season and his 99th Premier League goal overall, hitting the first in a 4–0 away win at West Ham.

On 27 January 2010, Scholes hit his first goal of the new year and his first in the League Cup for seven years in a 3–1 win in the Manchester derby. He hit the opener in United's semi-final second leg against Manchester City, eventually winning the game 4–3 on aggregate. On 16 February 2010, Scholes hit his third Champions League goal of the season against Milan in a 3–2 win; it was also United's first ever away goal against Milan. This gave United their first ever away win over Milan and also made Scholes the first ever player to score against both Internazionale and Milan at the San Siro in the Champions League.

On March 6, 2010, Scholes became the 19th player in Premier League history to score 100 goals and also the third United player after Ryan Giggs and Wayne Rooney to do so this season, netting the only goal in a 1–0 win over Wolves at Molineux.On 16 April 2010, Scholes signed a new one-year contract with United, keeping him at the club until the end of the 2010–11 season. On 17 April 2010, Scholes scored a last minute winner against rivals Man City, giving United a 1–0 win and the perfect way to celebrate signing a new contract just the day before. This also gave him his second derby goal in the last two games against their great city rivals

STEVE BRUCE

Full name: Stephen Roger Bruce
Date of birth:31 December 1960
Place of birth: Corbridge, Northumberland
Height:6 ft 0 in
Playing position: Centre back
Current club: Sunderland (manager)

YOUTH CAREER
1977–1978 Gillingham

SENIOR CAREER

Years	Team	Apps	(Gls)
1978–1984	Gillingham	205	(29)
1984–1987	Norwich City	141	(14)
1987–1996	Manchester United	309	(36)
1996–1998	Birmingham City	72	(2)
1998–1999	Sheffield United	10	(0)
Total		737	(81)

NATIONAL TEAM

1979–1980	England Youth	8	(0)
1987	England B	1	(0)

TEAMS MANAGED
1998–1999	Sheffield United
1999–2000	Huddersfield Town
2001	Wigan Athletic
2001	Crystal Palace
2001–2007	Birmingham City
2007–2009	Wigan Athletic
2009–	Sunderland

PLAYER PROFILES

Steve made his Manchester United debut in a 2–1 win over Portsmouth on 19 December 1987, and played in 21 of United's remaining 22 league fixtures, helping the club to a top two place in the First Division for the first time since 1980. The team could only finish in mid-table the following season, however, prompting manager Alex Ferguson to bring in a number of new players, including Gary Pallister, who joined the club in August 1989 from Middlesbrough. His partnership with Bruce in the centre of defence was described in 2006 by the then-United captain, Gary Neville, as the best in the club's history. Bruce and Pallister were part of the team which won the 1990 FA Cup final against Crystal Palace in a replay.

Following the lifting of the five-year ban on English clubs from European competitions, which had been imposed after the Heysel Stadium Disaster, United became England's first entrants into the UEFA Cup Winners' Cup in the 1990–91 season. Bruce played regularly, and scored three goals, in the team's progress to the final against FC Barcelona.

He came close to scoring the first goal, only for Mark Hughes to deflect the ball over the line and claim the goal, and United went on to win the game 2–1. This was a particularly high-scoring season for Bruce, who found the net 13 times in the First Division and 19 times in total in all competitions. He also played again at Wembley, in the Football League Cup final, in which United were defeated by Sheffield Wednesday of the Second Division.

Bruce missed several weeks of the 1991–92 season when he underwent an operation on a longstanding hernia problem, in which Leeds United, after a season-long tussle, beat the "Red Devils" to the championship by four points. Bruce was, however, able to help United win their first-ever League Cup in April 1992, captaining the team in the final in place of the injured Bryan Robson. Injuries continued to take their toll upon Robson during the 1992–93 season, leading to Bruce captaining the team in the majority of United's matches during the first season of the new Premier League. Bruce scored two late goals in a win over Sheffield Wednesday which proved decisive in United winning the inaugural Premier League title, the first time the club had won the championship of English football since 1967, and he and Robson received the trophy jointly after the home victory over Blackburn Rovers on 3 May.

At the height:of his success with United, Bruce was contacted by Jack Charlton, manager of the Republic of Ireland national team, who had discovered that, due to his mother's place of birth, Bruce was eligible to play for Ireland. Bruce states in his autobiography that further investigation revealed that, while his earlier appearance for England B in a friendly match was not an issue, his appearances for the England Youth team in a UEFA-sanctioned tournament prohibited him from playing for the senior team of another country. He has subsequently claimed, however, that he chose not to play for Ireland as it would have caused problems for his club at a time when the Premier League restricted the number of foreign players that a club could include in its team.

United dominated English football in the 1993–94 season, winning a second consecutive Premier League title and then defeating Chelsea in the FA Cup final to become only the fourth team, and Bruce the first English captain, to win The Double in the twentieth century, The 1994–95 season was a disappointing one for Bruce and United, however, as the club failed in its bid to win a third consecutive Premier League title and lost to Everton in the FA Cup final.

During the following season Bruce was offered the job of manager by three different clubs, but Ferguson refused to allow him to pursue the opportunities as he felt the player still had a role to play in the United team. Bruce made a further 30 Premier League appearances, as United managed to overcome a twelve-point deficit to Newcastle United to win the championship once again. A week later, however, he was left out of United's squad for the FA Cup final, due to a slight injury. At the end of the match Eric Cantona, who had captained the team and scored the only goal in a 1–0 win over Liverpool, attempted to persuade Bruce to be the one to receive the trophy, but Bruce declined. Ferguson denied that Bruce's omission was a sign that his time at the club was nearing an end, but Bruce, then 35 years old, believed that he would be unlikely to be selected for the team during the year remaining on his contract. He opted instead to join First Division club Birmingham City on a free transfer, having signed a contract valued at nearly £2 million over two years, which made him one of the highest-paid players in the country.

BRYAN ROBSON

Full name:Bryan Robson
Date of birth:11 January 1957
Place of birth:Chester-le-Street
Height:5 ft 11 in
Playing position:Midfielder
Current club:Thailand (Head coach)
Manchester United (Global ambassador)

YOUTH CAREER
1972–1974 West Bromwich Albion

SENIOR CAREER

Years	Team	Apps	(Gls)
1974–1981	West Bromwich Albion	198	(40)
1981–1994	Manchester United	345	(74)
1994–1996	Middlesbrough	25	(1)

NATIONAL TEAM

1979–1980	England U21	7	(2)
1979–1990	England B	3	(1)
1980–1991	England	90	(26)

TEAMS MANAGED
1994–1996	Middlesbrough (player-manager)
1996–2000	Middlesbrough
2000–2001	Middlesbrough (joint with Terry Venables)
2003–2004	Bradford City
2004–2006	West Bromwich Albion
2007–2008	Sheffield United
2009–	Thailand

PLAYER PROFILES

"Money wasn't my main motivation. I simply wanted to be a winner."

Bryan Robson explains his reasons for joining United

Bryan moved to United for a British record transfer fee of £1.5 million on 1 October 1981 and signed the contract on the Old Trafford pitch two days later. The record was not broken until Liverpool paid £1.9 million for Newcastle striker Peter Beardsley in the summer of 1987. Robson made his United debut on 7 October 1981 in a 1–0 defeat away at Tottenham Hotspur in the League Cup. His league debut for his new club came three days later, in a goalless draw against Manchester City at Maine Road. This was his first appearance in the Manchester United number 7 shirt, which he went on to make his own. Robson scored his first goal for United on 7 November 1981 in a 5–1 win over Sunderland at Roker Park. He ended his first season at United with 32 games and five goals. Meanwhile, his England career was flourishing as the World Cup neared; he scored in a 4–0 thrashing of Northern Ireland at Wembley and added a brace in the last warm-up game in Helsinki against Finland before scoring in record time (27 seconds) against France in their first game in Spain. Unfortunately, although unbeaten in the tournament, England were knocked out in the second group stage.

Robson tore his ankle ligaments during the 1983 League Cup semi-final victory over Arsenal, meaning that he missed the final, which United lost to Liverpool. He regained his fitness in time for the FA Cup semi-final, again against Arsenal, and scored in a 2–1 win. The final against Brighton ended in a 2–2 draw. Robson scored twice in the replay, but declined the chance to become the first player in 30 years to score an FA Cup final hat-trick, instead allowing regular penalty taker Arnold Muhren to convert a spot-kick to seal a 4–0 victory and enable Robson to lift his first trophy as United captain. The following season he helped the club enjoy a great run in the Cup Winners Cup. Robson scored twice in the 3–0 quarter-final second leg victory over FC Barcelona at Old Trafford, overturning a 2–0 first leg deficit to progress 3–2 on aggregate. He missed both legs of the semi-final defeat by Juventus due to a hamstring injury, but whilst in Turin for the second leg was given permission by United to speak to Juve regarding a proposed transfer. The move never took place as neither Juventus nor any other club were prepared to meet United's £3 million asking price. Robson's injury also meant that he missed several crucial late season games as United's title challenge slipped away and they finished fourth, with Liverpool becoming champions for the 15th time. Robson instead extended his contract with United in 1984, signing a seven-year deal worth around £1 million which would keep him there until at least 1991. In 1985 he captained the club to another FA Cup triumph, this time over Everton where a Norman Whiteside goal denied their opponents the chance of a unique treble, as they had already won the league title and the European Cup Winners' Cup.

Robson and United began the following season in fine form with ten successive victories which suggested the championship could be on its way back to Old Trafford for the first time since 1967. But their form slipped after Christmas and they finished the season trophyless in fourth place behind champions Liverpool, runners-up Everton and third-placed West Ham. Injuries, notably a dislocated shoulder suffering in February 1986, restricted Robson to just 21 out of 42 league appearances for United in 1985-86, though he did manage seven goals.

Robson remained in favour with his employers after Ron Atkinson was sacked as United manager in November 1986 and replaced by Alex Ferguson. But it was not until 1990 that Robson was to lift another trophy. He scored United's first goal in the FA Cup Final against Crystal Palace in the first match which ended in a 3–3 draw. United won the replay 1–0 and Robson thus became the first United captain to lift the cup three times. Robson had faced his familiar fight against injury once again in that 1989-90 campaign, restricted to 20 appearances out of 38 in the league, as United finished 13th - their lowest finish since relegation in 1974. Robson's testimonial match took place on 20 November 1990 and saw United lose 3–1 to Celtic at Old Trafford. During 1990–91, he was restricted to 17 league appearances due to an injury suffered at the World Cup and didn't make a first team appearance until December 1990. During his absence, United had been captained by fellow midfielder Neil Webb, but Robson regained the captain's armband on his return.

He was fit for the European Cup Winners' Cup final in which United beat Barcelona 2–1 in Rotterdam with both goals coming from Mark Hughes.

Robson was still a regular choice for United during the 1991–92 season despite competition from likes of Paul Ince, Neil Webb and Andrei Kanchelskis. During that season he made his 90th and final appearance for the England team, who by this stage were being managed by Graham Taylor. But the 1991–92 season ended in disappointment for Robson as United were overhauled in the First Division championship race by Leeds. He missed their League Cup final victory over Nottingham Forest through injury and his first-team chances were starting to look increasingly numbered as he faced competition from other players within the United squad and the press reported that Alex Ferguson was hoping to sign a new, younger midfielder, although no such addition took place in 1992. Robson still captained the club in most of his first-team appearances, but Steve Bruce was captaining the side when Robson was absent.

Robson made just 14 league appearances during the 1992–93 season, which was the first season of the new Premier League. The club's regular central midfielders for this season were Paul Ince (who had been at United since 1989) and Brian McClair (who was shifted from the attacking positions following the late November arrival of Eric Cantona), while his other favoured position on the right side of midfield was either occupied by Mike Phelan or the younger, wider-lying Andrei Kanchelskis and Lee Sharpe.

He scored on the final day of the season against Wimbledon – it was his only senior goal of that campaign. By that game United were Premiership champions and Robson finally won the league championship medal that he had been trying to gain since his days at West Bromwich Albion some 15 years earlier. It was not just injuries that were restricting the 36-year-old Robson's first-team chances. Eric Cantona had been signed during the 1992–93 campaign and played up front with Mark Hughes, while Hughes's former strike-partner Brian McClair had been converted into a midfielder. This counted against Robson and the biggest blow came in the summer of 1993 when United signed Nottingham Forest's Roy Keane.

With the introduction of squad numbers for the 1993-94 Premier League, Robson was issued with the number 12 shirt, while the number 7 shirt that he had worn in virtually every game of his career went to Eric Cantona instead.

But Robson was still able to make enough appearances for another Premiership champions medal in 1993–94, and scored one of their four goals in the FA Cup semi-final replay victory over Oldham at Maine Road. Unfortunately, he was dropped from the squad for the FA Cup final, a decision which manager Alex Ferguson later admitted was one of the hardest of his career. His very last appearance in a United shirt came on the last day of the season, 8 May 1994, when United drew 0-0 at home with Coventry City. He had played 461 times for them in all competitions, scoring 99 goals, and was widely regarded as one of their finest players ever.

GARY NEVILLE

Full name: Gary Alexander Neville
Date of birth: 18 February 1975
Place of birth: Bury
Height: 5 ft 11 in
Playing position: Right back
Current club: Manchester United

YOUTH CAREER
1991–1992 Manchester United

SENIOR CAREER

Years	Team	Apps	(Gls)
1992–	Manchester United	397	(5)

NATIONAL TEAM

1995–2007	England	85	(0)

The older of the Neville brothers joined Manchester United as an apprentice upon leaving school in 1991, and captained the youth side to FA Youth Cup glory in his first season. He made his senior debut for United in September 1992 against Torpedo Moscow in the UEFA Cup. Gary emerged as part of Alex Ferguson's youth-oriented side of the 1990s (nicknamed Fergie's Fledglings, an updated take on the 1950s equivalent Busby Babes) that included his brother Phil, Ryan Giggs, David Beckham, Nicky Butt and Paul Scholes. In the 1994–95 season, he became first-choice right back when Paul Parker was ruled out by injury, and has remained so ever since, although in his first season as a regular player he often found himself on the sidelines as Denis Irwin was switched to right back with Lee Sharpe (normally a winger) filling the left back role.

He formed a partnership with Beckham on the right wing, regularly contributing assists.

In the summer of 2004, Neville signed a four-year contract extension with United. Following Roy Keane's departure in November 2005, Neville was appointed the new captain,

In January 2006, his actions were the subject of some controversy after his celebration in front of the visiting Liverpool fans at Old Trafford, when he was seen to run from the half-way line towards the opposing fans to celebrate the 90th minute injury-time winning headed goal by United defender Rio Ferdinand. His actions were criticized by Liverpool and fellow England defender Jamie Carragher, sections of the media and police who blamed him for disturbances between fans after the game. He was subsequently charged with improper conduct by The Football Association. Neville contested this, asking if it was preferable for players to act like "robots" and show no emotions. He was fined £5,000 and warned about his future conduct.

Thus far, Gary Neville has won eight Premier League titles, three FA Cups, two European Cups, an Intercontinental Cup, a FIFA Club World Cup, and one League Cup, the last of which was his first trophy as captain.

Neville recovered from an injury suffered against Bolton in March 2007 and in his first match back, a reserve game against Everton in January 2008, he scored a rare goal in the 2first minute of the game which helped Manchester United to a 2–2 draw.

On 9 April 2008, Neville made his long-awaited comeback against Roma in the UEFA Champions League quarter-final second leg at Old Trafford as an 81st minute substitute for Anderson. Neville was welcomed back to the pitch with a standing ovation, and was promptly given the captain's armband. It was Neville's 99th Champions League appearance. However, he was not selected for the European Cup final squad on 21 May, though he did join in with the post-match celebrations after United won on penalties following a 1–1 draw with Chelsea. Instead, Rio Ferdinand and Giggs lifted the trophy together having shared the captaincy during Neville's absence.

Neville started his first game in seventeen months when he captained Manchester United for the 2008 FA Community Shield against Portsmouth on 10 August 2008. He then made another start against Zenit St. Petersburg in the UEFA Super Cup, before making his first start at home since his injury against Villarreal in the opening group game of the UEFA Champions League 2008–09. On 21 September 2008, Neville started his first league game in almost 18 months when he played against Chelsea. Gary Neville extended his stay at Old Trafford until June 2010.

On 27 October 2009, Neville was sent off for a tackle on Adam Hammill in United's 2–0 away win against Barnsley in the League Cup Fourth Round. He has played in an unfamiliar role at centre back due to a long-term injury to Rio Ferdinand and various minor injuries to Nemanja Vidic and Jonny Evans.

Neville added another medal to his honours list on 28 February 2010 when he came on as a substitute in the League Cup final win over Aston Villa. He did feature in enough league games to qualify for what would have been his ninth title medal, but United were beaten to the Premier League title by Chelsea who finished ahead of them by a single point.

His first squad number at Manchester United was number 27, which was issued to him when squad numbers were launched in the Premier League for the 1993–94 season. For the 1995–96 season, however, he was issued with the number 20 shirt which had been vacant since the departure of Dion Dublin the previous autumn. A year later however, the departure of Paul Parker enabled Neville to take up the number 2 shirt which he has held ever since.

RIO FERDINAND

Full name: Rio Gavin Ferdinand
Date of birth: 7 November 1978
Place of birth: Peckham, London
Height: 6 ft 2.5 in
Playing position: Centre back
Current club: Manchester United

YOUTH CAREER
Eltham Town
1988–1990   Millwall
1990–1993   Queens Park Rangers
1993–1995   West Ham United

SENIOR CAREER

Years	Team	Apps	(Gls)
1995–2000	West Ham United	127	(2)
1996	Bournemouth (loan)	10	(0)
2000–2002	Leeds United	54	(2)
2002–	Manchester United	221	(6)

NATIONAL TEAM

1997–2000	England U21	5	(0)
1997–	England	78	(3)

O n 22 July 2002, Ferdinand joined fellow Premier League side Manchester United on a five-year deal to become the most expensive British footballer in history, the world's most expensive defender again (a title he had lost in 2001 to Lilian Thuram). The fee included a basic element in the high £20 millions, and some conditional elements, which allowed Leeds to tell their fans that they were selling him for over £30 million. Leeds United later took a single payment in place of all the contingent elements when they were desperate for cash during their financial crisis. The final book value of Ferdinand's contract in Manchester United's accounts was £33 million. This included agents' fees, with Leeds receiving just under £30 million. Ferdinand suffered from a lack of form at the start of his Manchester United career, particularly illustrated by his performance against Real Madrid in the Champions League and in a 1–0 defeat by his former club Leeds United at Elland Road.

In 2003, he failed to attend a drug test, claiming he had forgotten because he was preoccupied with moving houses and instead went shopping. The FA Disciplinary Committee chaired by Barry Bright imposed an eight month ban from January 2004 at club and international level and a £50,000 fine, meaning he would miss the rest of the league season and some of the next along with all of Euro 2004. Manchester United appealed against the verdict and sought to draw parallels to the case of Manchester City player Christian Negouai, who was fined £2,000 for missing a test. However, FIFA president Sepp Blatter stated that such comparisons are inappropriate due to differences between the two cases. Negouai had been stuck in traffic and was willing to take the test, while Ferdinand was charged with "failure or refusal" to attend the test. Both the FA and FIFA sought to have the ban increased to 12 months (half the possible maximum). In the end, the original verdict was upheld.

Ferdinand went on to win the Premier League title with Manchester United in his first season. He has also collected a winner's medal in the 2006 League Cup, with runners-up medals in the 2003 League Cup and the 2005 FA Cup.

On 14 December 2005, in a game against Wigan Athletic, Ferdinand scored his first goal for United, en route to a 4–0 victory. This was his first goal after more than three years at Old Trafford. He followed this up with a powerfully headed goal against West Bromwich Albion. He then scored a last minute winner against Liverpool at Old Trafford, possibly his most important Manchester United goal to date. In the corresponding fixture in the following season on 22 October 2006, Rio scored again in a 2–0 victory.

Following impressive and consistent performances in the league,

Rio Ferdinand was named in the 2006–07 PFA Premiership Team of the Season alongside seven of his Manchester United team-mates.

Ferdinand started the 2007–08 season well, he was part of a United defence that managed to keep six clean sheets in a row in the Premier League, before conceding an early goal to Aston Villa at Villa Park on 20 October 2007. It was also during this game where Ferdinand scored his first goal of the season, which was United's third goal of that game, with a left foot strike which took a very strong deflection off one of Villa's defenders. Just three days later, Ferdinand scored his first European goal for United by opening the scoring against Dynamo Kyiv, with a superb header. United dominated the game and won 4–2. On 12 January 2008 Ferdinand bagged a rare Premier League goal in a 6–0 hammering of Newcastle United at Old Trafford.

In their FA Cup quarter-final match against Portsmouth on 8 March 2008 when Manchester United dominated, Ferdinand made a rare appearance as a goalkeeper, after Edwin van der Sar left the pitch with a groin injury and the replacement keeper, Tomasz Kuszczak, was sent off after conceding a penalty. Despite diving the right way, he was unable to save Sulley Muntari's spot kick, and Manchester United were eliminated from the FA Cup.

On 6 April 2008, against Middlesbrough, Ferdinand limped out of the match due to a foot injury. He was rated doubtful whether he would face Roma in the UEFA Champions League quarter-final second leg on 9 April 2008. He would play the full 90 minutes, though he received three stitches at half-time.

After United's 2–1 loss to Chelsea in the Premier League in April 2008 Ferdinand, angry at the defeat, swore at Chelsea stewards and tried to kick a wall in the tunnel, but instead kicked a female steward, Tracy Wray. Ferdinand claimed to have merely brushed her with his foot Ferdinand said he apologised and sent the steward some flowers. However Wray disagreed and in the *The Sun* she showed the large bruise on her leg caused by Ferdinand 'brushing her with his foot'. Her husband also claimed that Ferdinand did not apologise or send flowers.

It was announced on 16 April 2008 that, along with Michael Carrick and Wes Brown, Ferdinand had agreed to sign a new five-year contract, worth around £130,000 a week, which would keep him with United until 2013. The contract was finally signed on 15 May 2008.

On 21 May 2008, Ferdinand captained Manchester United to a Champions League Final victory versus Chelsea. He accepted the trophy together with Ryan Giggs, as Giggs was the on field captain for most of the matches during that season during Gary Neville's absence due to injury.

In an interview with BBC Radio 5 Live he criticised FIFA's approach to tackling racism in football, stating that not enough was being done to punish those guilty of homophobic or racist abuse at matches. Regarding taunts aimed at Emile Heskey in England's 4–1 victory against Croatia in Zagreb, Ferdinand remarked:

"Croatia were fined a few thousand quid. What's that going to do? That is not going to stop people shouting racist or homophobic abuse...If things like this keep happening you have to take points off them. Then the punters will realise the team is going to be punished."

On 28 January 2010 Ferdinand was banned for four games after being found guilty of violent conduct for elbowing an opponent in a game against Hull City

DENIS IRWIN

Full name: Denis Joseph Irwin
Date of birth: 31 October 1965
Place of birth: Cork, Ireland
Height: 5 ft 8 in
Playing position: Full back

SENIOR CAREER

Years	Team	Apps	(Gls)
1983–1986	Leeds United	72	(1)
1986–1990	Oldham Athletic	167	(4)
1990–2002	Manchester United	368	(22)
2002–2004	Wolves.	75	(3)
Total		**682**	**(29)**

NATIONAL TEAM

1986–1987	Republic of Ireland U21	3	(0)
1990	Republic of Ireland B	1	(0)
1990–1999	Republic of Ireland	56	(4)

Irwin began his career with Leeds United in 1983, making 72 appearances in the Second Division, before moving on to Oldham Athletic on a free transfer in 1986. He helped Oldham reach the semi-finals of the FA Cup and the final of the Football League Cup in 1990 before he was transferred to Manchester United for a fee of £625,000.

In 12 years at Old Trafford, he made 296 Premier League appearances and won seven Premier League title medals, as well as three FA Cup winners medals (1994, 1996 and 1999), a League Cup winner's medal and Champions League and Cup Winners' Cup honours. He was comfortable in either of the full back positions and an expert at free kicks and penalties, and even in his mid thirties he was United's first choice left-back in preference to the much younger Phil Neville.

PLAYER PROFILES

Irwin made his last appearance for Manchester United at Old Trafford against Charlton Athletic on the final day of the 2001–02 Premier League season (12 May 2002), which ended in a 0–0 draw. For his final game as a Manchester United player, Alex Ferguson awarded him the captain's armband.

Irwin joined Wolverhampton Wanderers on a free transfer in July 2002, coincidentally at the same time as his former Manchester United teammate Paul Ince made the move to the West Midlands club, having previously been at Middlesbrough. Irwin scored twice in his first season at Wolves, against Burnley and Grimsby.

After Wolves won promotion to the Premier League in 2003, Irwin was applauded by the Manchester United supporters when he walked onto the pitch at Old Trafford. Wolves were relegated at the end of the 2003–04 season, and the 38-year-old Irwin then announced his retirement.

GARY PALLISTER

Full name: Gary Andrew Pallister
Date of birth: 30 June 1965
Place of birth: Ramsgate, Kent
Height: 6 ft 5 in
Playing position: Centre back

SENIOR CAREER

Years	Team	Apps	(Gls)
1984–1989	Middlesbrough	156	0(5)
1985	Darlington (loan)	7	0(0)
1989–1998	Manchester United	31	(12)
1998–2001	Middlesbrough	55	(1)

NATIONAL TEAM

1988–1996	England	22	(0)
1989–1992	England B	9	(0)

His footballing career started at non-league Billingham Town, but at the age of 19, he joined his boyhood heroes Middlesbrough as a defender, making 156 League appearances over nearly five seasons, with a seven-game loan spell at Darlington in 1985, before he moved to Manchester United on 29 August 1989 for £2.3 million. It was the national record for a defender at the time, as well as being the highest fee between British clubs and the second highest fee to be paid by a British club - second only to Ian Rush's return to Liverpool from Juventus a year earlier.

Already one of the most respected defenders in the English game, he had the rare achievement of representing the English national side before appearing in the top flight, in early 1988 when still playing in the Second Division for Middlesbrough. Later that year he helped Boro win their second successive promotion and reach the First Division just two years after they almost went out of business, but was unable to keep them there and they were relegated on the final day of the 1988-89 season. As one of the highest regarded defenders in England, his days at Ayresome Park were looking numbered as soon as Boro were relegated but he did begin the 1989-90 season still at the club in the Second Division before his move to United was completed.

Although it was his excellent defensive displays that helped Manchester United to the league title along with Steve Bruce at the heart of the defence, forming one of the best central defensive partnerships in the club's history, in the 1992–93 season, he scored a memorable goal in the final home game of the season against Blackburn Rovers. Into stoppage time, with his team winning 2–1, he stepped up to drive a free-kick into the bottom corner from the edge of the penalty area. It was his first goal of the season and just about summed up an incredible season for Manchester United. It also meant that every outfield regular had scored at least once that season. He partnered Bruce in central defence for virtually every game until he left United to join Birmingham City on a free transfer at the end of the 1995-96 season. The following campaign saw Pallister partnered with either Bruce's former understudy David May or with new signing Ronny Johnsen, and ended with United winning their fourth league title in five seasons.

The final season Pallister played for Manchester United was the 1997–98 season in which Manchester United came second in the league table, losing by one point to Arsenal.

During his time at Manchester United, Pallister won the FA Cup in 1990, 1994 and 1996, Cup Winners' Cup in 1991, Football League Cup in 1992, Premier League title in 1993, 1994, 1996 and 1997. He was also part of the team that came second in the league in 1992, 1995 and 1998, as well as the team that finished runners-up in the League Cup in 1991 and 1994 and the FA Cup in 1995. By the time of his departure from Old Trafford after nine years, he was the only player to have collected winner's medals in all of the club's successes under Alex Ferguson's management, and second only to Brian McClair (who left United at the same time) he was the club's longest serving player.

Transferred back to Middlesbrough for £2.5million (actually more than he had cost United nine years earlier) in July 1998 (his departure from Old Trafford at least partly prompted by United's acquisition of Jaap Stam), he scored once against Southampton in 55 League appearances, as well as appearing in two FA Cup matches and four League Cup matches.

His final playing season, in which Middlesbrough finished 14th in the table, was 2000–01. He was brought back to Teesside by manager Bryan Robson, who had played alongside Pallister at Old Trafford until 1994.

He retired from playing due to a succession of injuries on 4 July 2001, at the age of 36, just three weeks after the appointment of Steve McClaren as manager following the departure of Bryan Robson.

He has since become a regular TV football pundit, appearing on the BBC and ITV.

BRIAN MCCLAIR

Full name Brian John McClair
Date of birth   8 December 1963
Place of birth   Bellshill, Scotland
Height: 5 ft 10 in
Playing position: Forward   Midfielder
Current club Manchester United
(Director of Youth Academy)

SENIOR CAREER

Years	Club	App	(Gls)
1980–1981	Aston Villa	0	(0)
1981–1983	Motherwell	40	(15)
1983–1987	Celtic	145	(99)
1987–1998	Manchester United	355	(88)
1998	Motherwell	11	(0)
Total		**551**	**(202)**

NATIONAL TEAM

1986–1993	Scotland	30	(2)

TEAMS MANAGED

1998–1999	Blackburn Rovers (assistant)	
2006–	Manchester United (Director of Youth Academy)	

He joined United for £850,000 in July 1987 — despite Celtic initially wanting £2million for him, a fee which would have made him the most expensive player at the time to have signed for any British club.

In 11 years at Old Trafford, he made a total of 468 appearances and scored 126 goals in all competitions. In later years, as his first team opportunities were reduced, McClair became somewhat of a cult hero at United due to his Choccy's Diary being published in the official Manchester United magazine.

In his first season for Manchester United he scored 24 league goals, becoming the first United player to surpass 20 league goals in one season since George Best in the 1967–68 season. His first goal for United came in the third game of the season, a 2-0 home win over Watford. He scored in the next game, a 3-1 away win over Charlton Athletic. He scored a brace in the 4-2 away over Sheffield Wednesday on 10 October 1987, and a further one in the late December win over defending champions Everton. He put a further double over Sheffield Wednesday in the March return game at Old Trafford, and scored a hat-trick against Derby County in early April. In the final two games of the season (against Portsmouth and Wimbledon) he managed two further braces. Only Liverpool's John Aldridge managed more First Division goals that season. He managed a total of 31 goals in all competitions, but a late penalty miss in the fifth round of the FA Cup at Arsenal meant that United lost the tie 2-1 and he was denied the chance of silverware as well as building on his already highly impressive goals tally.

1988-89 was a trying season for United after the excellent progress of 1987-88. After a season playing alongside Peter Davenport, McClair now found himself paired with returning hero Mark Hughes (back at United after two unhappy years abroad) and much was expected of the newly formed partnership. By the end of November, McClair had scored just twice in the league and Hughes had found the net eight times, and United were mid table after a run of eight draws and one defeat. Results improved over the next couple of months as United crept to the fringes of the title challenge, but fell away in the final quarter of the season as United finished 11th. McClair and Hughes both managed 16 goals in all competitions, with Hughes being leading scorer in the league with 14 goals opposed to McClair's 10.

He was on the winning side at United triumphed 1–0 over Crystal Palace in the 1990 FA Cup Final replay at Wembley Stadium on 17 May 1990, five days after drawing 3–3 in the first match. In the league, however, it had been a disappointing time for McClair as he scored just five goals and United finished 13th — their lowest finish since they were relegated from the top flight 16 years earlier. He was now facing competition from highly promising young striker Mark Robins, who had scored 10 goals in 23 first team games that season.

He did however score the winning goal for United in the 1991 UEFA Super Cup against Red Star Belgrade, which followed his part in their European Cup Winners' Cup triumph over Barcelona. McClair had now won the fight to keep his place in the first team as he rediscovered his goalscoring touch and Mark Robins was now struggling to get into the team.

In October 1990, McClair was involved in controversy when in reaction to a late challenge he repeatedly kicked Arsenal's Nigel Winterburn in the back as he lay prone on the ground, sparking a 21 man brawl. It was later claimed that Winterburn had taunted McClair after his penalty miss in the Cup game at Highbury four years before. Manchester United had a point deducted for this, and Arsenal (who went on to be league champions that season) had two points docked.

In 1992, McClair scored the only goal in the 1992 League Cup Final against Nottingham Forest at Wembley, though he missed out on a league title winner's medal as United's shortage of goals in the second half of the season cost them the championship, which was clinched by Leeds United. Alex Ferguson then made unsuccessful bids for strikers David Hirst and Alan Shearer, sparking speculation that either Brian McClair or Mark Hughes would be forced out of the first team by the new signings, but in the end the new striker signed was Dion Dublin, who was bought as backup for McClair and Hughes.

Having been the main striker for United during his first season, and then partnering Mark Hughes when the Welshman returned from Barcelona, McClair was switched to a central midfield role when Eric Cantona joined United in November 1992, the casualty of this position being the veteran Bryan Robson, who from this point onwards was mostly used as a substitute.

When Roy Keane was signed the following summer, McClair's first team opportunities became increasingly limited. He did, however, manage another Cup Final appearance and another goal at Wembley, coming off the bench to score United's fourth goal as they beat Chelsea 4-0 in the 1994 FA Cup Final. He was rarely left out of the squad, often coming on as a substitute to play in midfield or attack.

When squad numbers were introduced in the Premier League for the 1993-94 season (its second edition) McClair was issued with the number 9 shirt that had traditionally been his during the days of 1-11 shirt numbering. However, this number went to Andy Cole at the start of the 1996-97 season, after which McClair wore the number 13 shirt.

Despite his infrequent first team appearances, McClair elected to stay on at United as a squad player, providing reliable cover in midfield and attack and making over 40 appearances (in the first eleven or as a substitute) in 1994–95. He was still trucking along in 1996–97, and on the first day of that season, McClair was credited with an assist for David Beckham's spectacular goal from the halfway line against Wimbledon. McClair had a hand in another memorable goal that season, assisting Eric Cantona in his famous chipped goal against Sunderland at Old Trafford. On 15 April 1997, a crowd of over 44,000 attended McClair's testimonial game against former club Celtic at Old Trafford.

He scored a total of 127 goals for United, the last two coming against Coventry City in a 4-0 away league win on 22 November 1995, although he made some 60 first team appearances over the next two and a half years (mostly as a substitute).

RUUD VAN NISTELROOY

Full name: Rutgerus Johannes Martinus van Nistelrooj
Date of birth: 1 July 1976
Place of birth: Oss, North Brabant, Netherlands
Height: 6ft 2 in
Playing position: Striker
Current club: Hamburg

SENIOR CAREER

Years	Team	Apps	(Gls)
1994–1997	Den Bosch	69	(17)
1997–1998	Heerenveen	31	(13)
1998–2001	PSV Eindhoven	67	(62)
2001–2006	Manchester United	150	(95)
2006–2010	Real Madrid	68	(46)
2010–	Hamburg	11	(5)

NATIONAL TEAM

1998–2008	Netherlands	64	(33)

Van Nistelrooy finally signed a five-year contract a year after after having failed one in 2000. He downplayed United's £19 million investment to reporters, saying "The price is not heavy for me – it lifts me up because it means United have big confidence in me." During his first season, Van Nistelrooy scored 23 goals in 32 league games. He broke the record he shared with Mark Stein, Alan Shearer and Thierry Henry, by scoring in eight consecutive league games. He also scored 10 Champions League goals, and was named the PFA Players' Player of the Year. The following season, he finished as the top Premier League scorer with 25 in 34 games, including three hat-tricks, and he ended the season on another eight-game scoring streak. He started the

2003–04 season by scoring twice in his first two league matches, which boosted his goals in consecutive games record to 10 matches in a row. He scored his 100th goal for the club in a 4–3 victory over Everton on 7 February 2004. He scored two goals, one a penalty, in United's victory over Millwall in the 2004 FA Cup Final.

Van Nistelrooy missed most of the 2004–05 season due to injury, but nonetheless scored a Champions League-best eight goals. One of them was his thirtieth career European goal, which he scored in a 2–2 Champions League group stage draw with Lyon on 16 September 2004, overtaking Denis Law's previous club record of 28 goals. Law later said to reporters, "I'm delighted for Ruud. It could not happen to a nicer guy." Manchester United were eliminated by eventual finalists Milan in the knockout stage after going scoreless in both legs.

At the start of the 2005–06 season, Van Nistelrooy scored in United's first four Premier League games. He finished as the second-highest league scorer with 21 goals, behind Arsenal's Thierry Henry. By the end of his fifth season with United, Van Nistelrooy had amassed 150 goals in fewer than 200 starts.

Van Nistelrooy was benched for the League Cup final against Wigan Athletic, fuelling speculation of a rift between him and coach Alex Ferguson, which Van Nistelrooy denied. He was nonetheless left on the bench for six consecutive league matches, and though he then returned to the starting line-up and scored match-winners against West Ham United and Bolton Wanderers, fresh doubt spread over Van Nistelrooy's future when he was benched for United's season finale win over Charlton Athletic. Ferguson claimed that Van Nistelrooy was angry at the decision and left the stadium three hours before kick-off.

On 9 May 2006, Setanta Sports reported that Van Nistelrooy's exclusion from the squad was due to a training session fight between him and team-mate Cristiano Ronaldo. Van Nistelrooy allegedly criticised Ronaldo's tendency to hold onto the ball instead of passing to his team-mates, which sparked the fight, after which Van Nistelrooy remarked, "Go crying to your daddy." The article claimed that this was not a reference to Ronaldo's father (who had died earlier in the season), but to United's Portuguese assistant coach, Carlos Queiroz.

Van Nistelrooy signed with Spanish side Real Madrid on 28 July 2006, departing Manchester United after five seasons with a total of 150 goals in 220 appearances, as well as the club's all-time European scoring record with 38 goals.

ANDY COLE

Full name: Andrew Alexander Cole
Date of birth: 15 October 1971
Place of birth: Nottingham, England
Height: 5 ft 10 in
Playing position: Striker
Current club: None

YOUTH CAREER
1988–1989   Arsenal

SENIOR CAREER

Years	Team	Apps	(Gls)
1989–1992	Arsenal	1	(0)
1991	Fulham (loan)	13	(3)
1992–1993	Bristol City	41	(20)
1993–1995	Newcastle United	70	(55)
1995–2001	Manchester United	195	(93)
2001–2004	Blackburn Rovers	83	(27)
2004–2005	Fulham	31	(12)
2005–2006	Manchester City	22	(9)
2006–2007	Portsmouth	18	(3)
2007	Birmingham City (loan)	5	(1)
2007–2008	Sunderland	7	(0)
2008	Burnley (loan)	13	(6)
2008	Nottingham Forest	10	(0)
Total		**509**	**(229)**

NATIONAL TEAM

1991	England U20	3	(0)
1992–1993	England U21	8	(4)
1994	England B	1	(1)
1995–2002	England	15	(1)

PLAYER PROFILES

On 10 January 1995, Andy Cole was sold by former club Newcastle to rivals Manchester United in a shock deal worth £7 million – £6 million cash plus £1 million-rated Keith Gillespie going in the opposite direction, setting a new record for most expensive British transfer at the time. This record was broken five months later by Arsenal's £7.5 million acquisition of Dennis Bergkamp from Internazionale.

Despite joining halfway through the 1994–95 season, Cole still managed to score 12 goals in just first 18 Premier League games for United. This included his first, the winner in a 1–0 victory over Aston Villa on 4 February at Old Trafford and five in the 9–0 rout of Ipswich Town, a Premier League record. However, he missed two simple chances against West Ham United on the final day of the season as they could only manage a 1–1 draw and the league title went to Blackburn Rovers instead. He was cup-tied for the FA Cup final a week later. Without him, United lost to Everton 1–0. United were also without the banned Eric Cantona and the injured Andrei Kanchelskis, the club's next two highest scorers that season after Cole.

His first full season in 1995–96 with Manchester United proved to be difficult, as Cole struggled to find his trademark form in a side now built around the much heralded return of Eric Cantona. Though Cole scored in four successive games during the winter, including an important opening goal in United's 2–0 defeat of title rivals Newcastle United on 27 December, Cole was badgered by fans and critics alike across much of the season for only scoring 14 times and missing many chances. However, Cole picked up his form in the business end of the season and scored critical goals including the winner in the FA Cup semi-final against Chelsea to send United to Wembley again. He then collected his first Premier League title winners medal and scored the second goal in United's 3–0 defeat of Middlesbrough on the final day of the season to help United win the Premier League title for the third time in four years. He also played in their FA Cup final victory to become part of England's first ever side to win the double twice.

Before the 1996–97 season began, Cole had to deal with being offered to Blackburn Rovers as part-exchange in a £12 million deal that would have brought Alan Shearer to Old Trafford but the offer was turned down and Shearer opted for Newcastle instead. Despite Alex Ferguson's clear indication to Cole that he was looking for another striker, after the Shearer deal fell through, Cole fought to stay at the club and was handed the number 9 shirt (having previously worn 17). The arrival of Ole Gunnar Solskjær – and being the victim of two broken legs suffered after a tackle by Neil Ruddock in a reserve game against Liverpool – restricted Cole's first-team chances further, but he managed to still play in 20 Premier League games (10 as a substitute) for the season, ending the season strongly with several crucial goals in both the league and UEFA Champions League (where he scored a goal voted the season's best European goal against Porto) to complete his comeback from injury. He then scored the title sealing goal away at Anfield – the scene of his broken legs just half a season earlier – against Roy Evans' "Spice Boys" Liverpool team and thereby aided United in winning their fourth title in five years, with Cole qualifying for another Premier League title medal.

For the 1997–98 season, the retirement of Eric Cantona saw Cole emerge as first choice striker once again, and he discovered his best form ever for the club, becoming the joint top goalscorer in the Premier League during the course of the season with 18 goals, including a slew of spectacular goals – one of which, a chip against Everton, had the fans' vote as the Manchester United goal of the season. Cole also developed a strong partnership with Teddy Sheringham (despite considerable personal friction between the two), but United finished trophyless for only the second time in 9 seasons as they lost to Arsenal in the end. Cole achieved several personal landmarks in this campaign, scoring his first European hat-trick for the club in an away match at Feyenoord, as well as ending the season as runner-up in the PFA Players' Player of the Year award to Arsenal's Dennis Bergkamp. Despite this accreditation, and being the leading goalscorer in all competitions that season with 25, Cole was omitted from England's 1998 World Cup squad by then-manager Glenn Hoddle. Cole remained upbeat when interviewed and when asked about his new found return to success, Cole claimed that he had found freedom in his life after the injuries of the previous season, saying he had great joy with his newborn son, and lived for him and his family in his faith as a Born again Christian. He also claimed the friendship of Ryan Giggs, his room-mate on away games, was a major motivating factor through the tough times when fans doubted him at United.

Cole faced competition from new signing Dwight Yorke, Teddy Sheringham and Ole Gunnar Solskjær during the 1998–99 season but ended up developing an immensely successful partnership with Yorke both on and off the pitch that season, the year in which his striking partnership with Yorke contributed 53 goals between them and was rated as one of the most feared attacking partnerships not just in the Premier League, but in all of Europe as well, with the pair scoring against sides like Barcelona away at the Nou Camp, and repeating the form all season with incredible one touch passes and assists that at times seemed to demonstrate a telepathic understanding between the pair.

Cole played a key role in the side's unique treble of the Premier League title, FA Cup and UEFA Champions League and scored the winning goal in United's final Premier League game of the season against Tottenham Hotspur, a result which meant United finished one point ahead of rivals Arsenal to win the Premier League title. He also scored United's third and winning goal in their Champions League semi-final second leg against Juventus, sealing their place in the final for the first time in over 30 years. Also in this season, Cole scored his 100th Premier League goal in a top of the table clash against Arsenal at Old Trafford on 17 February; the match ended 1–1.

Cole was United's top scorer again in 1999–2000 with 19 goals in 28 Premier League games. He collected his fourth Premier League title medal in five seasons, and scored over 20 goals in all competitions for the third successive season. Cole scored many goals for United including the only goal of the game in their top of the table clash against their closest rivals Leeds United. He also joined an elite group during this season by scoring his 100th goal for the club in a 2–2 draw against Wimbledon. Injury just prior to Euro 2000 led to Cole missing out on another major competition for his country.

Another title followed in 2000–01 when, despite suffering from an injury that restricted his appearances, Cole scored 13 goals in all competitions, including four in the European Cup allowing him at the time to become Manchester United's record goal scorer in European competition of all time.

Cole made one last appearance for Manchester United in the UEFA Celebration Match six years later, on 13 March 2007, coming on at half time for a friendly game between Manchester United and European XI in celebration of the 50th anniversary of the European Community and 50 years of Manchester United in the European Cup

OLE GUNNAR SOLSKJAER

Full name: Ole Gunnar Solskjær
Date of birth:26 February 1973
Place of birth: Kristiansund, Norway
Height: 5 ft 10 in
Playing position: Forward/Winger

YOUTH CAREER
1989–1990 Clausenengen

SENIOR CAREER

Years	Team	Apps	(Gls)
1990–1994	Clausenengen	109	(115)
1994–1996	Molde	42	(31)
1996–2007	Manchester United	235	(91)
Total		**386**	**(238)**

NATIONAL TEAM

1995–2007	Norway	67	(23)

TEAMS MANAGED
2008–   Manchester United Reserves

Ole had scored 31 goals in 42 matches for Molde in the Norwegian Premier League, and he did not disappoint at the start of his Manchester United career, scoring six minutes into his debut as a substitute against Blackburn Rovers in the Premiership in the 1996-97 season.

He had joined United in July 1996 for a fee of £1.5million, being something of a surprise acquisition as he was almost unknown outside his homeland and at the time United were still in the hunt for Blackburn Rovers and England striker Alan Shearer, who then joined Newcastle United for a world record £15million. As the only striker to arrive at Old Trafford that year, it was widely expected that his first season would be spent as a backup to Eric Cantona and Andy Cole with only occasional first team opportunities. But within weeks of his arrival it was clear that he would be a key part of the first team sooner than had been anticipated, and would also prove himself to be one of the biggest Premier League bargains of the season.

He was issued with the number 20 shirt (previously worn by Dion Dublin and then by Gary Neville) upon his arrival; it was a squad number he would retain for the rest of his Manchester United career.

Solskjær scored 18 Premiership goals for United in his first season, helping United win the title in the last weeks of the season. The British media nicknamed him the "Baby-Faced Assassin" because of his youthful looks and his deadly finishing. He will perhaps be best remembered as a "super-sub", having earned wide acclaim for a remarkable habit of coming into matches late on as a substitute and scoring goals. Alex Ferguson remarked that Solskjær has a knack of sitting on the bench and studying the game without taking his eye off the action. One of his most impressive feats was coming off the bench to score four goals in the last 12 minutes of United's 8-1 thrashing of Nottingham Forest. He scored another four goals in a match a season later against Everton in a 5-1 victory for Manchester United.

Solskjær stayed at Old Trafford even though other clubs showed interest in the player in 1998. He even refused an offer from Tottenham Hotspur, after Manchester United had accepted a bid for him. The Norwegian went on to score the winning goal in the 1999 UEFA Champions League Final, helping the team secure the Treble and cementing his own place in the United folklore. Another defining moment in his career, was in the end of the league match against Newcastle in 1998. The match was tied at 1-1, and Manchester United needed at least a draw to keep up with Arsenal in the race for the league title. At the end of the game Newcastles Robert Lee had a great goalscoring opportunity, when Solskjær ran across the entire field to commit a professional foul, thus denying Newcastle the winning goal. Solskjær did this knowing he would be sent off, and suspended in the coming matches. Supporters regarded this as a perfect example of how Solskjær put the club before personal interests.

These feats made him a favourite among the United supporters, inspiring songs such as "Who Put the Ball in the Germans' Net?" and "You Are My Solskjær". Even when he had been absent on the pitch for a long time due to injury, United fans would still fill matches with chants sung in Solskjær's honour.

After a few years of playing in the role of super-sub, Solskjær got a chance as a starter in the 2001-02 season, paired up with Dutch striker Ruud van Nistelrooy. He took the opportunity with characteristic incisiveness, forcing Andrew Cole and Dwight Yorke onto the bench.

By 2002-03, after both Andrew Cole and Dwight Yorke had left Old Trafford, Solskjær had only Diego Forlán and van Nistelrooy to compete with for a place in the starting line-up. Still, Ferguson's persistence in playing van Nistelrooy up front with Paul Scholes, or as a lone striker meant that opportunities were limited.

Solskjær was subsequently given his time again when David Beckham picked up an injury and Ferguson played the Norwegian on the right wing. While proving himself to be an able crosser of the ball, Solskjær also popped up with goals, scoring a total of 16 in the season. He was selected to play on the right in important matches, such as in the league game against Arsenal and the Champions League quarter-final against Real Madrid, while Beckham was left on the bench. He also captained the team in a number of matches. Solskjær played for Norway in the 1998 FIFA World Cup and Euro 2000.

At the start of 2003-04, Solskjær found himself as United's first-choice right winger. However, a knee injury suffered against Panathinaikos on 16 September 2003 put Solskjær out of action until February 2004. Solskjær returned from the injury for the season run-in and was man of the match in the FA Cup Semi Final victory over Arsenal. He also played in the 2004 FA Cup final, which the club won. Solskjær was forced to undergo intensive knee surgery in August 2004 and had to miss the 2004-05 season entirely. While he eventually recovered his fitness, it was difficult for the 32-year-old to carve his niche again among the heavyweight attack of Manchester United. The Old Trafford faithful, however, displayed almost fanatical loyalty in their desire to see Solskjær in action again.

To show their continuing support, fans added a banner to the collection that lines the Stretford End reading "20 LEGEND" (Solskjær wore number 20 for United). Solskjær further solidified his status amongst United fans when he became a patron of the supporters action group, Manchester United Supporters Trust (MUST), previously Shareholders United.

Solskjær made his long-awaited return to action on 5 December 2005, playing for United's reserves against Liverpool. Spectators numbering 2,738 showed up to witness the comeback of the popular Norwegian - an above-average turn-out for a reserve team match. He made his first-team return as a substitute in the match against Birmingham City on 28 December. He then finally made his first start more than a year later in the FA Cup match against Burton Albion, before playing a full game as a captain in the re-play. His return to full fitness slowly continued with regular appearances in the reserves, until on 8 March 2006 when, during a game against Middlesbrough, he was accidentally caught by Ugo Ehiogu, breaking his cheekbone. While facing the possibility of missing the rest of the season, he nevertheless appeared as a substitute against Sunderland on Good Friday.

Solskjær had a very successful pre season tour in the summer of 2006 gaining Ferguson's praise who also said he would re-consider his plan to buy a new striker. He returned to Premiership action in 23 August 2006 when he scored in an away match against Charlton Athletic, his first Premiership goal since April 2003. Ferguson commented after the match that "it was a great moment for Ole, United fans everywhere, the players and the staff" and that "Ole has been through a torrid time with injuries for the last two years, but he's persevered and never lost faith and has got his repayment tonight. Everyone is over the moon for him." He continued his come-back by scoring the winning goal in the Champions League clash with Celtic on 13 September, fulfilling his post-injury ambition to score another goal at Old Trafford. Solskjær's first Premiership goal at Old Trafford since the return came on October 1 when he netted both goals in the 2-0 win against Newcastle United. His goalscoring form continued with when he started the away match against Wigan Athletic and struck a sublime finish to round off a 3-1 victory and again against Crewe Alexandra on 25 October 2006, scoring the first in a 2-1 victory. After a further injury sustained in Copenhagen, Solskjær again returned on form scoring the third goal in the 3-1 win over Wigan on Boxing Day. Solskjær continued his form by scoring United's opening goal in their 3-2 win over Reading on the 30 December. Additionally, he came on as a substitute to score an injury-time winner in the 2-1 victory over Aston Villa in the 3rd Round of the FA Cup on 7 January 2007.

After a match against Reading, Solskjær had further surgery on his knee. However, it was not as serious as his previous operations, and he was put out of action for only a month. He was predicted to be available for the 31 March game against Blackburn Rovers. United boss Alex Ferguson said: "It was good timing with the international break coming up. It gave us the opportunity to get the thing done." Solskjær did make his comeback from injury against Blackburn Rovers as a late substitute, and even scored in the 89th minute to seal Manchester United's 4-1 win.

On 5 June 2007, it was announced that Solskjær had undergone minor surgery after he reported discomfort in his knee while training with Norway. The surgery was a success, but Solskjær failed to fully recover and announced his retirement from professional football on 27 August 2007. Finally, on 4 September at the home game against Sunderland, his retirement was officially announced over the Old Trafford tannoy, with Solskjær walking onto the pitch to a standing ovation. As of his retirement, Solskjær holds the record for the most goals scored for Manchester United as a substitute, scoring 28 goals off the bench.

On 2 August 2008, a testimonial was played in honour of Solskjær at Old Trafford against Espanyol. Over 68,000 fans were present as United eventually got the winner from substitute Fraizer Campbell. Solskjær appeared in the 68th minute, replacing Carlos Tévez. He hit the target three times and was credited for his role in influencing the young Campbell's play. At the end of the game, he addressed the fans with a speech, thanking the staff, players, fans and his family.

PAUL INCE

Full name: Paul Emerson Carlyle Ince
Date of birth: 21 October 1967
Place of birth: Ilford, London, England
Height: 5 ft 10 in
Playing position: Midfielder

YOUTH CAREER
1982–1984 West Ham United

SENIOR CAREER

Years	Team	Apps	(Gls)
1984–1989	West Ham United	72	(7)
1989–1995	Manchester United	206	(25)
1995–1997	Internazionale	54	(10)
1997–1999	Liverpool	65	(14)
1999–2002	Middlesbrough	93	(7)
2002–2006	Wolves	115	(10)
2006	Swindon Town	3	(0)
2007	Macclesfield Town	1	(0)
Total		**609**	**(72)**

NATIONAL TEAM

1989	England U21	2	(0)
1992	England B	1	(0)
1992–2000	England	53	(2)

TEAMS MANAGED
2006–2007 Macclesfield Town
2007–2008 Milton Keynes Dons
2008 Blackburn Rovers
2009–2010 Milton Keynes Dons

Paul completed his highly controversial transfer to Manchester United for £1 million from West Ham in September 1989. Ince had been photographed in a Manchester United kit long before the transfer was complete, which appeared in the *Daily Express*. Ince received hateful abuse from West Ham United fans for many years afterwards. The initial move was postponed after he failed a medical, but was quickly completed on 14 September 1989 after he later received the all-clear. In a recent article in *Four Four Two* magazine, when answering questions about his career from readers, he got his chance to explain the story.

"I spoke to Alex Ferguson and the deal was close to being done. I then went on holiday, and my agent at the time, Ambrose Mendy, said it wasn't worth me coming back to do a picture in a United shirt when the deal was completed, so I should do one before I left, and it would be released when the deal was announced. Lawrence Luster of the *Daily Star* took the picture and put in the library. Soon after, their sister paper, the *Daily Express*, were looking for a picture of me playing for West Ham, and found the one of me in the United shirt in the pile. They published it and all hell broke loose.

"I came back from holiday to discover West Ham fans were going mad. It wasn't really my fault. I was only a kid, I did what my agent told me to do, then took all the crap for it."

Ince eventually made his Manchester United debut in a 5–1 win over Millwall, though his next game for United came in a 5–1 hammering at the hands of Manchester City and became a strong presence in the midfield alongside long serving captain Bryan Robson and (when he wasn't out of the team injured) fellow new midfielder Neil Webb.

United won the FA Cup in his first season, defeating Crystal Palace 1–0 in a replay at Wembley after initially drawing 3–3. In both of these games, Ince was selected at right-back in favour of Viv Anderson, with his favoured central midfield position being occupied by Mike Phelan.

Over the next four seasons, Robson's United career gradually wound down until he finally left to manage Middlesbrough in

1994. During this time, Ince found himself playing alongside several other different central midfielders, including Mike Phelan, Neil Webb and Darren Ferguson. The arrival of striker Eric Cantona in November 1992 saw Brian McClair become Ince's regular central midfield partner until the arrival of Roy Keane the following season.

Meanwhile, Ince became United's key midfielder, with snapping tackles, raking passes and some tremendously hit shots, though he was not too prolific a goalscorer. One of his best games came in January 1994, when he scored twice in a 2–2 away draw with former club West Ham in the Premier League.

He won his second winners' medal when United defeated Barcelona in the final of the European Cup Winners Cup in Rotterdam in 1991 and received his third another year later when United beat Nottingham Forest in the 1992 League Cup final.

The next year, Manchester United were competing in the inaugural Premiership season with Ince and his best friend at the time, Ryan Giggs at the fore and part of a now legendary team that included Mark Hughes, Eric Cantona, Peter Schmeichel, Andrei Kanchelskis, Steve Bruce and Denis Irwin. Seeking a first League title for 26 years, United won it and Ince completed his domestic medal set just three years after joining the club.

Manchester United continued to dominate the domestic game in 1993–94 and Ince was the midfield general in the side which won the "double" of Premiership and FA Cup in 1994. A year later and Ince suffered more of the all too familiar chants of JUDAS when he and Manchester United went to West Ham on the last day of the season, needing a win to retain their Premiership crown. Sadly for them, they could only draw the game and Blackburn Rovers took the title. It went from bad to worse as Ince featured then in the United team which also lost the FA Cup final to Everton. During that season, his central midfield partner Roy Keane had missed 17 of United's 42 league games due to injury, meaning that Ince often found himself partnered with Brian McClair and – particularly towards the end of the season – the 20-year-old Nicky Butt.

In the summer of 1995, Ferguson sold him to Internazionale

of Milan for £7.5 million – at the time one of the costliest transfer fees involving an English player. Ferguson had long sustained a tempestuous relationship with Ince, labelling him a "bottler" and a "fucking big-time Charlie", which many fans saw as the prime reason for Ince being sold, rather than on footballing or economic grounds. Ince's sale caused massive unrest among United supporters, and the discontent deepened when United turned to the much younger Nicky Butt as his successor rather than buying a more experienced player. A similar uproar followed the subsequent sale of Ince's team mates Mark Hughes and Andrei Kanchelskis, although the younger players who filled their places in the team contributed greatly to United's "double double" success in the 1995–96 season as well as the triumphs of subsequent seasons.

While at United, Ince had collected two Premier League title medals as well as two FA Cup winner's medals and one winner's medal each in the European Cup Winners' Cup and Football League Cup. He had also collected runners-up medal's in the League Cup twice and the FA Cup once.

EDWIN VAN DER SAR

Full name: Edwin van der Sar
Date of birth: 29 October 1970
Place of birth: Voorhout, Netherlands
Height: 6 ft 5.5 in
Playing position: Goalkeeper
Current club: Manchester United

YOUTH CAREER
Foreholte vv Noordwijk

SENIOR CAREER

Years	Team	Apps	(Gls)
1988–1999	Ajax	226	(1)
1999–2001	Juventus	66	(0)
2001–2005	Fulham	127	(0)
2005–	Manchester United	153	(0)

NATIONAL TEAM
1995–2008	Netherlands	130	(0)

V an der Sar moved to Manchester United on 10 June 2005 for a reported fee of £2 million, although the exact transfer fee was undisclosed. Manchester United manager Sir Alex Ferguson considered him the best goalkeeper to have played for the club since Peter Schmeichel.

On 5 May 2007, his penalty save helped assure a 1–0 triumph over Manchester City in the Manchester derby. The following day, Chelsea's failure to beat Arsenal at the Emirates ensured Manchester United's ninth Premier League trophy and Van der Sar's first. He was also named to the 2006–07 PFA Team of the Year. Three months later, he was a catalyst in Manchester United's 16th FA Community Shield victory, as he saved three consecutive penalties in a shootout after Manchester United and Chelsea played to a 1–1 draw at the end of regular time.

The 2007–08 season was Van der Sar's best season since his arrival; he had several great performances despite a niggling groin injury. He would help United secure their second successive Premier League title on the final day and win the Champions League by saving the final penalty of the shoot-out from Nicolas Anelka.

Van der Sar signed a one-year extension to his current contract with Manchester United on 12 December 2008, keeping him at the club until at least the end of the 2009–10 season.

On 27 January 2009, Van der Sar helped Manchester United set a new club and Premier League record for consecutive clean sheets – the club's 5–0 win over West Bromwich Albion meant that they had gone 11 games and 1,032 minutes without conceding a goal, beating the previous record of 10 matches and 1,025 minutes set by Petr Cech in the 2004–05 season. He then broke the overall English league record in the club's following game four days later, beating the previous record of 1,103 minutes, set by Steve Death of Reading in 1979.

Another clean sheet, against West Ham on 8 February 2009, extended the record to 1,212 minutes, beating the British top-flight record of 1,155 minutes previously set by Aberdeen's Bobby Clark in 1971. Finally, on 18 February 2009, Van der Sar further extended the record to 1,302 minutes, and in doing so, he broke José María Buljubasich's single-season world record of 1,289 minutes, set in the Chilean Clausura in 2005. His clean sheet record ended on 4 March, when he made an error allowing Peter Løvenkrands of Newcastle United to score after 9 minutes. In total, Van der Sar had gone 1,311 minutes without conceding in the league.These clean sheets were a major factor in United clinching their 11th Premiership title as United won a lot of games 1–0 to clinch the title ahead of Liverpool. With a total of 21 clean sheets he also won the Barclays Golden Glove for 2008–09. However, he missed out on winning his third Champions League winners medal as United succumbed to a 2–0 defeat at the hands of Barcelona on 27 May 2009. Nevertheless, he won Best European Goalkeeper award from UEFA for the second time, 14 years after he first won it at Ajax. He was one of the five United players shortlisted for the PFA Players' Player of the Year award but it went to United teammate Ryan Giggs instead, however he was included into the PFA Team of the Year.

Van der Sar sustained a finger injury during the Audi Cup pre-season tournament, forcing him to miss the first 12 matches of Manchester United's 2009–10 season. On 6 October 2009, Van Der Sar returned to action for United, playing 90 minutes in the reserves against Everton. On 17 October 2009, he returned to action in the first team, playing in United's 2–1 victory over Bolton Wanderers. On 21 November 2009, Van Der Sar would suffer injury again and be kept out of action for 12 games, with the combination of his wife suffering a brain haemorrhage just before Christmas. On 16 January 2010, Van Der Sar returned to action in a 3–0 win over Burnley.

Van der Sar signed a one-year extension to his current contract with Manchester United on 26 February 2010, keeping him at the club until at least the end of the 2010–11 season

DWIGHT YORKE

Full name: Dwight Eversley Yorke
Date of birth: 3 November 1971
Place of birth: Canaan, Trinidad and Tobago
Height: 5 ft 9 in
Playing position: Forward/Midfielder

YOUTH CAREER
1988–1989 Signal Hill Comprehensive School

SENIOR CAREER

Years	Team	Apps	(Gls)
1989–1998	Aston Villa	232	(73)
1998–2002	Manchester United	95	(47)
2002–2004	Blackburn Rovers	60	(12)
2004–2005	Birmingham City	13	(2)
2005–2006	Sydney FC	21	(7)
2006–2009	Sunderland	58	(6)
Total		**479**	**(147)**

NATIONAL TEAM
1989–2009 Trinidad and Tobago   72   (19)

In his first season Yorke was a key player in guiding his club to a unique treble of the Premiership title, FA Cup and UEFA Champions League, and forming a legendary partnership with Andy Cole. Yorke finished the season as the top league goalscorer with 18 goals and contributed goals against Bayern München, Barcelona, Internazionale and Juventus in the Champions League. Yorke was also a regular member of United's 1999-2000 title winning team, contributing 22 goals in all competitions. Despite a less successful third season personally, Yorke did hit a hat-trick in the top of the table clash with Arsenal as United went on to win a third successive title.

Yorke's limited appearances in the 2001-02 season led to rumours that he'd fallen with United boss, Sir Alex Ferguson, following his much publicised relationship with British model Jordan. After a January move to Middlesbrough fell through. Yorke was sold to Blackburn Rovers for £2 million during the close-season.

TEDDY SHERINGHAM

Full name: Edward Paul Sheringham
Date of birth: 2 April 1966
Place of birth: Highams Park, London
Height: 6 ft 0 in
Playing position: Striker

YOUTH CAREER
Leytonstone and Ilford

SENIOR CAREER

Years	Team	Apps	(Gls)
1983–1991	Millwall	220	(93)
1985	Aldershot (loan)	5	(0)
1985	Djurgårdens IF (loan)	21	(13)
1991–1992	Nottingham Forest	47	(14)
1992–1997	Tottenham Hotspur	166	(76)
1997–2001	Manchester United	104	(31)
2001–2003	Tottenham Hotspur	70	(22)
2003–2004	Portsmouth	32	(9)
2004–2007	West Ham United	76	(28)
2007–2008	Colchester United	19	(3)
Total		**760**	**(289)**

NATIONAL TEAM

1988	England U21	1	(0)
1993–2002	England	51	(11)

In June 1997, Sheringham agreed to join Manchester United in a £3.5million deal. He was signed to replace the iconic Eric Cantona whose retirement had left the Old Trafford faithful demanding a big name to fill the gap. His first competitive game for the club was against his former employers, Tottenham, at White Hart Lane. Throughout the game, Sheringham suffered jeers and boos from his former fans, who had been angered by the fact that Sheringham had accused Tottenham of lacking ambition when he made his transfer. In the 60th minute with the score at 0–0, Sheringham missed a penalty, although ended up on the winning side as two late goals gave United the win.

Sheringham's first season at Old Trafford was difficult, although he scored 14 goals in all competitions he failed to meet expectations as the 1997–98 season ended without a trophy. Towards the end of the 1997–98 season, during a game at Bolton, an incident occurred that furthered the animosity with fellow striker Andy Cole. When Bolton scored, Sheringham blamed Cole, his strike partner and Cole then refused to talk to him. The breakdown in their relationship was never resolved, and reputedly they never spoke again. This had started three years previously when Sheringham had snubbed Cole as the latter made his international debut.

Speculation that Sheringham would leave United increased just after the 1998–99 season got underway, when Dwight Yorke moved to Old Trafford from Aston Villa. Sheringham's first-team chances were relatively limited but he still managed to get enough Premiership games to qualify for a title winner's medal at the end of the season — at the age of 33 he had finally won a major trophy. A week later he scored one of United's two goals in the FA Cup final to yield his second honour. Four days after the FA Cup triumph, Sheringham scored a dramatic stoppage-time equaliser against Bayern Munich in the Champions League final. With seconds of stoppage-time remaining, Ole Gunnar Solskjær scored from Sheringham's headed flick on, and United won a treble of the Premiership, FA Cup and European Cup with Sheringham – having not won a major honour in his 15 year career on leaving Spurs – now having won every top-level trophy in the club game.

Sheringham did not get as many first-team chances as he might have hoped for during 1999-00, but he still played enough times to merit another Premiership title medal. In 2000–01, Sheringham played some of the best football of his career as he was United's top goalscorer, displacing Dwight Yorke as the preferred first-team player, as well as being voted Player of the Year by both the PFA and FWA. His fine form ensured that he was still involved with the national side despite being in his 35th year, being named in the squad for the 2002 World Cup. He still maintains a legendary status with the Old Trafford faithful, appearing as a special half-time guest at Ole Gunnar Solskjaer's testimonial match.

SQUAD LISTS 1992-2010

1992/93

David Beckham
Clayton Blackmore
Steve Bruce
Nicky Butt
Eric Cantona
Dion Dublin
Darren Ferguson
Ryan Giggs
Keith Gillespie
Mark Hughes
Paul Ince
Denis Irwin
Andrei Kanchelskis
Lee Martin
Brian McClair
Gary Neville
Gary Pallister
Paul Parker
Mike Phelan
Bryan Robson
Peter Schmeichel
Lee Sharpe
Danny Wallace
Gary Walsh
Neil Webb

1993/94

Steve Bruce
Nicky Butt
Eric Cantona
Dion Dublin
Darren Ferguson
Ryan Giggs
Mark Hughes
Paul Ince
Denis Irwin
Andrei Kanchelskis
Roy Keane
Lee Martin
Brian McClair
Colin McKee
Gary Neville
Gary Pallister
Paul Parker
Mike Phelan
Bryan Robson
Peter Schmeichel
Les Sealey
Lee Sharpe
Ben Thornley
Gary Walsh

1994/95

David Beckham
Steve Bruce
Nicky Butt
Eric Cantona
Chris Casper
Andy Cole
Simon Davies
Ryan Giggs
Keith Gillespie
Mark Hughes
Paul Ince
Denis Irwin
Andrei Kanchelskis
Roy Keane
David May
Brian McClair
Phil Neville
Gary Neville
John O'Kane
Gary Pallister
Paul Parker
Kevin Pilkington
Peter Schmeichel
Paul Scholes
Lee Sharpe
Graeme Tomlinson
Gary Walsh

1995/96

David Beckham
Steve Bruce
Nicky Butt
Eric Cantona
Andy Cole
Terry Cooke
Simon Davies
Ryan Giggs
Denis Irwin
Roy Keane
David May
Brian McClair
Pat McGibbon
Gary Neville
Phil Neville
John O'Kane
Gary Pallister
Paul Parker
Kevin Pilkington
William Prunier
Peter Schmeichel
Paul Scholes
Lee Sharpe
Ben Thornley

SQUAD LISTS 1992-2010

1996/97

Michael Appleton
David Beckham
Nicky Butt
Eric Cantona
Chris Casper
Michael Clegg
Andy Cole
Terry Cooke
Jordi Cruyff
Simon Davies
Ryan Giggs
Denis Irwin
Ronny Johnsen
Roy Keane
David May
Brian McClair
Phil Neville
Gary Neville
John O'Kane
Gary Pallister
Karel Poborsky
Peter Schmeichel
Paul Scholes
Ole Gunnar Solskjaer
Ben Thornley
Raimond van der Gouw

1997/98

David Beckham
Henning Berg
Wes Brown
Nicky Butt
Michael Clegg
Andy Cole
Jordi Cruyff
John Curtis
Ryan Giggs
Danny Higginbotham
Denis Irwin
Ronny Johnsen
Roy Keane
David May
Brian McClair
Philip Mulryne
Gary Neville
Phil Neville
Erik Nevland
Gary Pallister
Kevin Pilkington
Karel Poborsky
Peter Schmeichel
Paul Scholes
Teddy Sheringham
Ole Gunnar Solskjaer
Ben Thornley
Michael Twiss
Raimond van der Gouw
Ronnie Wallwork

1998/99

David Beckham
Henning Berg
Jesper Blomqvist
Wes Brown
Nicky Butt
Michael Clegg
Andy Cole
Jordi Cruyff
John Curtis
Ryan Giggs
Jonathan Greening
Denis Irwin
Ronny Johnsen
Roy Keane
David May
Philip Mulryne
Gary Neville
Phil Neville
Erik Nevland
Alex Notman
Peter Schmeichel
Paul Scholes
Teddy Sheringham
Ole Gunnar Solskjaer
Jaap Stam
Raimond van der Gouw
Ronnie Wallwork
Mark Wilson
Dwight Yorke

1999/2000

David Beckham
Henning Berg
Mark Bosnich
Nicky Butt
Luke Chadwick
Michael Clegg
Andy Cole
Jordi Cruyff
Nick Culkin
John Curtis
Quinton Fortune
Ryan Giggs
Jonathan Greening
David Healy
Danny Higginbotham
Denis Irwin
Ronny Johnsen
Roy Keane
David May
Phil Neville
Gary Neville
John O'Shea
Paul Rachubka
Paul Scholes
Teddy Sheringham
Mikael Silvestre
Ole Gunnar Solskjaer
Jaap Stam
Massimo Taibi
Michael Twiss
Raimond van der Gouw
Ronnie Wallwork
Richie Wellens
Mark Wilson
Dwight Yorke

SQUAD LISTS 1992-2010

2000/2001

Gary Neville
Mikael Silvestre
Ole Gunnar Solskjaer
David Beckham
Paul Scholes
Ryan Giggs
Fabien Barthez
Roy Keane
Teddy Sheringham
Wes Brown
Nicky Butt
Phil Neville
Dwight Yorke
Andy Cole
Denis Irwin
Jaap Stam
Luke Chadwick
Ronny Johnsen
Ronnie Wallwork
Raimond van der Gouw
Quinton Fortune
Jonathan Greening
Michael Stewart
Michael Clegg
Andy Goram
John O'Shea
David May
Paul Rachubka
David Healy
Henning Berg
Bojan Djordjic
Danny Webber

2001/2002

Fabien Barthez
David Beckham
Laurent Blanc
Wes Brown
Nicky Butt
Roy Carroll
Luke Chadwick
Michael Clegg
Andy Cole
Jimmy Davis
Bojan Djordjic
Diego Forlan
Quinton Fortune
Ryan Giggs
Denis Irwin
Ronny Johnsen
Roy Keane
David May
Daniel Nardiello
Phil Neville
Gary Neville
John O'Shea
Lee Roche
Paul Scholes
Mikael Silvestre
Ole Gunnar Solskjaer
Jaap Stam
Michael Stewart
Raimond van der Gouw
Ruud van Nistelrooy
Juan Sebastian Veron
Ronnie Wallwork
Danny Webber
Dwight Yorke

2002/2003

Fabien Barthez
David Beckham
Laurent Blanc
Wes Brown
Nicky Butt
Roy Carroll
Luke Chadwick
Rio Ferdinand
Darren Fletcher
Diego Forlan
Quinton Fortune
Ryan Giggs
Roy Keane
Mark Lynch
David May
Daniel Nardiello
Gary Neville
Phil Neville
John O'Shea
Danny Pugh
Felipe Ricardo
Kieran Richardson
Lee Roche
Paul Scholes
Mikael Silvestre
Ole Gunnar Solskjaer
Michael Stewart
Mads Timm
Ruud van Nistelrooy
Juan Sebastian Veron
Danny Webber

2003/2004

Phil Bardsley
David Bellion
Wes Brown
Nicky Butt
Roy Carroll
Eric Djemba-Djemba
Chris Eagles
Rio Ferdinand
Darren Fletcher
Diego Forlan
Quinton Fortune
Ryan Giggs
Tim Howard
Eddie Johnson
Roy Keane
Jose Kleberson
Daniel Nardiello
Phil Neville
Gary Neville
John O'Shea
Danny Pugh
Kieran Richardson
Cristiano Ronaldo
Louis Saha
Paul Scholes
Mikael Silvestre
Ole Gunnar Solskjaer
Paul Tierney
Ruud van Nistelrooy

SQUAD LISTS 1992-2010

2004/2005

David Bellion
Wes Brown
Roy Carroll
Eric Djemba-Djemba
Chris Eagles
Sylvan Ebanks-Blake
Rio Ferdinand
Darren Fletcher
Diego Forlan
Quinton Fortune
Ryan Giggs
Gabriel Heinze
Tim Howard
David Jones
Roy Keane
Jose Kleberson
Liam Miller
Gary Neville
Phil Neville
John O'Shea
Gerard Pique
Kieran Richardson
Cristiano Ronaldo
Wayne Rooney
Giuseppe Rossi
Louis Saha
Paul Scholes
Mikael Silvestre
Alan Smith
Jonathan Spector
Ruud van Nistelrooy

2005/2006

Phil Bardsley
Wes Brown
Sylvan Ebanks-Blake
Adam Eckersley
Patrice Evra
Rio Ferdinand
Darren Fletcher
Darron Gibson
Ryan Giggs
Gabriel Heinze
Tim Howard
Ritchie Jones
Roy Keane
Lee Martin
Liam Miller
Gary Neville
John O'Shea
Ji-Sung Park
Gerard Pique
Kieran Richardson
Cristiano Ronaldo
Wayne Rooney
Giuseppe Rossi
Louis Saha
Paul Scholes
Mikael Silvestre
Alan Smith
Ole Gunnar Solskjaer
Edwin van der Sar
Ruud van Nistelrooy
Nemanja Vidic

2006/2007

Michael Barnes
Wes Brown
Michael Carrick
Chris Eagles
Patrice Evra
Dong Fangzhuo
Rio Ferdinand
Darren Fletcher
Ryan Giggs
David Gray
Gabriel Heinze
Ritchie Jones
David Jones
Tomasz Kuszczak
Henrik Larsson
Kieran Lee
Phil Marsh
Gary Neville
John O'Shea
Ji-Sung Park
Kieran Richardson
Cristiano Ronaldo
Wayne Rooney
Louis Saha
Paul Scholes
Ryan Shawcross
Mikael Silvestre
Alan Smith
Ole Gunnar Solskjaer
Edwin van der Sar
Nemanja Vidic

2007/2008

Oliveira Anderson
Phil Bardsley
Wes Brown
Fraizer Campbell
Michael Carrick
Chris Eagles
Jonny Evans
Patrice Evra
Dong Fangzhuo
Rio Ferdinand
Darren Fletcher
Ben Foster
Ryan Giggs
Owen Hargreaves
Tomasz Kuszczak
Lee Martin
Luis Nani
Gary Neville
John O'Shea
Ji-Sung Park
Gerard Pique
Cristiano Ronaldo
Wayne Rooney
Louis Saha
Paul Scholes
Mikael Silvestre
Danny Simpson
Carlos Tevez
Edwin van der Sar
Nemanja Vidic

2008/2009

Ben Amos
Oliveira Anderson
Dimitar Berbatov
Wes Brown
Fraizer Campbell
Michael Carrick
James Chester
Rafael da Silva
Fabio da Silva
Ritchie De Laet
Richard Eckersley
Jonny Evans
Patrice Evra
Rio Ferdinand
Darren Fletcher
Ben Foster
Darron Gibson
Ryan Giggs
Owen Hargreaves
Tomasz Kuszczak
Federico Macheda
Mateus Manucho
Lee Martin
Luis Nani
Gary Neville
John O'Shea
Ji Sung Park
Rodrigo Possebon
Cristiano Ronaldo
Wayne Rooney
Paul Scholes
Carlos Tevez
Zoran Tosic
Edwin van der Sar
Nemanja Vidic
Danny Welbeck

2009/2010

Oliveira Anderson
Dimitar Berbatov
Wes Brown
Michael Carrick
Rafael da Silva
Fabio da Silva
Ritchie De Laet
Mame Biram Diouf
Jonny Evans
Patrice Evra
Rio Ferdinand
Darren Fletcher
Ben Foster
Darron Gibson
Ryan Giggs
Joshua King
Tomasz Kuszczak
Federico Macheda
Luis Nani
Gary Neville
John O'Shea
Gabriel Obertan
Michael Owen
Ji-Sung Park
Wayne Rooney
Paul Scholes
Zoran Tosic
Antonio Valencia
Edwin van der Sar
Nemanja Vidic
Danny Welbeck

First Games of Every Season

Sheff Utd	2-1	Man Utd	15-08-1992
Norwich	0-2	Man Utd	15-08-1993
Man Utd	2-0	QPR	20-08-1994
Aston Villa	3-1	Man Utd	19-08-1995
Wimbledon	0-3	Man Utd	17-08-1996
Tottenham	0-2	Man Utd	10-08-1997
Man Utd	2-2	Leicester	15-08-1998
Everton	1-1	Man Utd	08-08-1999
Man Utd	2-0	Newcastle	20-08-2000
Man Utd	3-2	Fulham	19-08-2001
Man Utd	1-0	West Brom	17-08-2002
Man Utd	4-0	Bolton	16-08-2003
Chelsea	1-0	Man Utd	15-08-2004
Everton	0-2	Man Utd	13-08-2005
Man Utd	5-1	Fulham	20-08-2006
Man Utd	0-0	Reading	12-08-2007
Man Utd	1-1	Newcastle	17-08-2008
Man Utd 1	1-0	Birmingham	16-08-2009

PREMIER LEAGUE RESULTS 1992 – 2010

1992/93

Sheff Utd	2-1	Man Utd	15-08-1992
Man Utd	0-3	Everton	19-08-1992
Man Utd	1-1	Ipswich	22-08-1992
Soton	0-1	Man Utd	24-08-1992
Nottm Forest	0-2	Man Utd	29-08-1992
Man Utd	1-0	C Palace	02-09-1992
Man Utd	2-0	Leeds	06-09-1992
Everton	0-2	Man Utd	12-09-1992
Tottenham	1-1	Man Utd	19-09-1992
Man Utd	0-0	QPR	26-09-1992
Middlesbro	1-1	Man Utd	03-10-1992
Man Utd	2-2	Liverpool	18-10-1992
Blackburn	0-0	Man Utd	24-10-1992
Man Utd	0-1	Wimbledon	31-10-1992
Aston Villa	1-0	Man Utd	07-11-1992
Man Utd	3-0	Oldham	21-11-1992
Arsenal	0-1	Man Utd	28-11-1992
Man Utd	2-1	Man City	06-12-1992
Man Utd	1-0	Norwich	12-12-1992
Chelsea	1-1	Man Utd	19-12-1992
Sheff Wed	3-3	Man Utd	26-12-1992
Man Utd	5-0	Coventry	28-12-1992
Man Utd	4-1	Tottenham	09-01-1993
QPR	1-3	Man Utd	18-01-1993
Man Utd	2-0	Nottm Forest	27-01-1993
Ipswich	2-1	Man Utd	30-01-1993
Man Utd	2-1	Sheff Utd	06-02-1993
Leeds	0-0	Man Utd	08-02-1993
Man Utd	2-1	Soton	20-02-1993
Man Utd	3-0	Middlesbro	27-02-1993
Liverpool	1-2	Man Utd	06-03-1993
Oldham	1-0	Man Utd	09-03-1993
Man Utd	1-1	Aston Villa	14-03-1993
Man City	1-1	Man Utd	20-03-1993
Man Utd	0-0	Arsenal	24-03-1993
Norwich	1-3	Man Utd	05-04-1993
Man Utd	2-1	Sheff Wed	10-04-1993
Coventry	0-1	Man Utd	12-04-1993
Man Utd	3-0	Chelsea	17-04-1993
C Palace	0-2	Man Utd	21-04-1993
Man Utd	3-1	Blackburn	03-05-1993
Wimbledon	1-2	Man Utd	09-05-1993

Cup Games

UEFA Cup	Man Utd	0-0	T. Moscow	16-09-1992
League Cup	Brighton	1-1	Man Utd	23-09-1992
UEFA Cup	T. Moscow	0-0	Man Utd	29-09-1992
League Cup	Man Utd	1-0	Brighton	07-10-1992
League Cup	Aston Villa	1-0	Man Utd	28-10-1992
FA Cup	Man Utd	2-0	Bury	05-01-1993
FA Cup	Man Utd	1-0	Brighton	23-01-1993
FA Cup	Sheff Utd	2-1	Man Utd	14-02-1993

Total

Played	Won	Drawn	Lost	Points
42	24(57 %)	12 (29 %)	6 (14 %)	84

Home

Played	Won	Drawn	Lost	Points
21	14 (67 %)	5 (24 %)	2 (10 %)	47

Away

Played	Won	Drawn	Lost	Points
21	10 (48 %)	7 (33 %)	4 (19 %)	37

Biggest home win

Dec 28th 1992	United	5-0	Coventry City

Biggest home loss

Aug 19th 1992	United	0-3	Everton

Biggest away win

Aug 29th 1992	Nottingham Forest	0-2	United
Sep 12th 1992	Everton	0-2	United
Jan 18th 1993	Queens Park Rangers	1-3	United
Apr 5th 1993	Norwich City	1-3	United
Apr 2first 1993	Crystal Palace	0-2	United

Biggest away loss

Aug 15th 1992	Sheffield United	2-1	United
Nov 7th 1992	Aston Villa	1-0	United

Jan 30th 1993	Ipswich Town	2-1	United
Mar 9th 1993	Oldham Athletic	1-0	United

Highest aggregate score home

Dec 28th 1992	United	5-0	Coventry City
Jan 9th 1993	United	4-1	Tottenham Hotspur

Highest aggregate score away

Dec 26th 1992	Sheff. Wed,	3-3	United

Pos Club	Pld	W	D	L	F	A	GD	Pts
1. MANCHESTER UNITED	42	24	12	6	67	31	36	84
2. Aston Villa	42	21	11	10	57	40	17	74
3. Norwich City	42	21	9	12	61	65	-4	72
4. Blackburn Rovers	42	20	11	11	68	46	22	71
5. Queens Park Rangers	42	17	12	13	63	55	8	63
6. Liverpool	42	16	11	15	62	55	7	59
7. Sheffield Wednesday	42	15	14	13	55	51	4	59
8. Tottenham Hotspur	42	16	11	15	60	66	-6	59
9. Manchester City	42	15	12	15	56	51	5	57
10. Arsenal	42	15	11	16	40	38	2	56
11. Chelsea	42	14	14	14	51	54	-3	56
12. Wimbledon	42	14	12	16	56	55	1	54
13. Everton	42	15	8	19	53	55	-2	53
14. Sheffield United	42	14	10	18	54	53	1	52
15. Coventry City	42	13	13	16	52	57	-5	52
16. Ipswich Town	42	12	16	14	50	55	-5	52
17. Leeds United	42	12	15	15	57	62	-5	51
18. Soton	42	13	11	18	54	61	-7	50
19. Oldham Athletic	42	13	10	19	63	74	-11	49
20. Crystal Palace	42	11	16	15	48	61	-13	49
21. Middlesbrough	42	11	11	20	54	75	-21	44
22. Nottingham Forest	42	10	10	22	41	62	-21	40

1993/94

Norwich	0-2	Man Utd	15-08-1993
Man Utd	3-0	Sheff Utd	18-08-1993
Man Utd	1-1	Newcastle	21-08-1993
Aston Villa	1-2	Man Utd	23-08-1993
Soton	1-3	Man Utd	28-08-1993
Man Utd	3-0	West Ham	01-09-1993
Chelsea	1-0	Man Utd	11-09-1993
Man Utd	1-0	Arsenal	19-09-1993
Man Utd	4-2	Swindon	25-09-1993
Sheff Wed	2-3	Man Utd	02-10-1993
Man Utd	2-1	Tottenham	16-10-1993
Everton	0-1	Man Utd	23-10-1993
Man Utd	2-1	QPR	30-10-1993
Man City	2-3	Man Utd	07-11-1993
Man Utd	3-1	Wimbledon	20-11-1993
Man Utd	0-0	Ipswich	24-11-1993
Coventry	0-1	Man Utd	27-11-1993
Man Utd	2-2	Norwich	04-12-1993
Sheff Utd	0-3	Man Utd	07-12-1993
Newcastle	1-1	Man Utd	11-12-1993
Man Utd	3-1	Aston Villa	19-12-1993
Man Utd	1-1	Blackburn	26-12-1993
Oldham	2-5	Man Utd	29-12-1993
Man Utd	0-0	Leeds	01-01-1994
Liverpool	3-3	Man Utd	04-01-1994
Tottenham	0-1	Man Utd	15-01-1994
Man Utd	1-0	Everton	22-01-1994
QPR	2-3	Man Utd	05-02-1994
West Ham	2-2	Man Utd	26-02-1994
Man Utd	0-1	Chelsea	05-03-1994
Man Utd	5-0	Sheff Wed	16-03-1994
Swindon	2-2	Man Utd	19-03-1994
Arsenal	2-2	Man Utd	22-03-1994
Man Utd	1-0	Liverpool	30-03-1994
Blackburn	2-0	Man Utd	02-04-1994
Man Utd	3-2	Oldham	04-04-1994
Wimbledon	1-0	Man Utd	16-04-1994
Man Utd	2-0	Man City	23-04-1994
Leeds	0-2	Man Utd	27-04-1994
Ipswich	1-2	Man Utd	01-05-1994
Man Utd	2-0	Soton	04-05-1994
Man Utd	0-0	Coventry	08-05-1994

Cup Games

FACS	Man Utd	1-1	Arsenal	07-08-1993
European Cup	Honved	2-3	Man Utd	15-09-1993
European Cup	Man Utd	2-1	Honved	29-09-1993
League Cup	Man Utd	2-0	Stoke	06-10-1993
European Cup	Man Utd	3-3	Galatasaray	20-10-1993
League Cup	Man Utd	5-1	Leicester	27-10-1993
European Cup	Galatas'y	0-0	Man Utd	03-11-1993
League Cup	Everton	0-2	Man Utd	30-11-1993
FA Cup	Sheff Utd	0-1	Man Utd	09-01-1994
League Cup	Man Utd	2-2	Portsmouth	12-01-1994
League Cup	Portsmouth	0-1	Man Utd	26-01-1994
FA Cup	Norwich	0-2	Man Utd	30-01-1994
League Cup	Man Utd	1-0	Sheff Wed	13-02-1994
FA Cup	Wimbledon	0-3	Man Utd	20-02-1994
League Cup	Sheff Wed	1-4	Man Utd	02-03-1994
FA Cup	Man Utd	3-1	Charlton	12-03-1994
League Cup	Aston Villa	3-1	Man Utd	27-03-1994
FA Cup	Man Utd	1-1	Oldham	09-04-1994
FA Cup	Man Utd	4-1	Oldham	13-04-1994
FA Cup	Man Utd	4-0	Chelsea	14-05-1994

Total

Played	Won	Drawn	Lost	Points
42	27(64 %)	11 (26 %)	4 (10 %)	92

Home

Played	Won	Drawn	Lost	Points
21	14 (67 %)	6 (29 %)	1 (5 %)	48

Away

Played	Won	Drawn	Lost	Points
21	13 (62 %)	5 (24 %)	3 (14 %)	44

Biggest home win

Mar 16th 1994	United	5-0	Sheff. Wednesday

Biggest home loss

Mar 5th 1994	United	0-1	Chelsea

Biggest away win
| Dec 7th 1993 | Sheff. United | 0-3 | United |
| Dec 29th 1993 | Oldham Ath. | 2-5 | United |

Biggest away loss
| Apr 2nd 1994 | Blackburn R. | 2-0 | United |

Highest aggregate score home
| Sep 25th 1993 | United | 4-2 | Swindon Town |

Highest aggregate score away
| Dec 29th 1993 | Oldham Ath. | 2-5 | United |

Pos Club	Pld	W	D	L	F	A	GD	Pts
1. MANCHESTER UNITED	42	27	11	4	80	38	42	92
2. Blackburn Rovers	42	25	9	8	63	36	27	84
3. Newcastle United	42	23	8	11	82	41	41	77
4. Arsenal	42	18	17	7	53	28	25	71
5. Leeds United	42	18	16	8	65	39	26	70
6. Wimbledon	42	18	11	13	56	53	3	65
7. Sheffield Wednesday	42	16	16	10	76	54	22	64
8. Liverpool	42	17	9	16	59	55	4	60
9. Queens Park Rangers	42	16	12	14	62	61	1	60
10. Aston Villa	42	15	12	15	46	50	-4	57
11. Coventry City	42	14	14	14	43	45	-2	56
12. Norwich City	42	12	17	13	65	61	4	53
13. West Ham United	42	13	13	16	47	58	-11	52
14. Chelsea	42	13	12	17	49	53	-4	51
15. Tottenham Hotspur	42	11	12	19	54	59	-5	45
16. Manchester City	42	9	18	15	38	49	-11	45
17. Everton	42	12	8	22	42	63	-21	44
18. Soton	42	12	7	23	49	66	-17	43
19. Ipswich Town	42	9	16	17	35	58	-23	43
20. Sheffield United	42	8	18	16	42	60	-18	42
21. Oldham Athletic	42	9	13	20	42	68	-26	40
22. Swindon Town	42	5	15	22	47	100	-53	30

1994/95

Man Utd	2-0	QPR	20-08-1994
Nottm F.	1-1	Man Utd	22-08-1994
Tottenham	0-1	Man Utd	27-08-1994
Man Utd	3-0	Wimbledon	31-08-1994
Leeds	2-1	Man Utd	11-09-1994
Man Utd	2-0	Liverpool	17-09-1994
Ipswich	3-2	Man Utd	24-09-1994
Man Utd	2-0	Everton	01-10-1994
Sheff Wed	1-0	Man Utd	08-10-1994
Man Utd	1-0	West Ham	15-10-1994
Blackburn	2-4	Man Utd	23-10-1994
Man Utd	2-0	Newcastle	29-10-1994
Aston Villa	1-2	Man Utd	06-11-1994
Man Utd	5-0	Man City	10-11-1994
Man Utd	3-0	C Palace	19-11-1994
Arsenal	0-0	Man Utd	26-11-1994
Man Utd	1-0	Norwich	03-12-1994
QPR	2-3	Man Utd	10-12-1994
Man Utd	1-2	Nottm Forest	17-12-1994
Chelsea	2-3	Man Utd	26-12-1994
Man Utd	1-1	Leicester	28-12-1994
Soton	2-2	Man Utd	31-12-1994
Man Utd	2-0	Coventry	03-01-1995
Newcastle	1-1	Man Utd	15-01-1995
Man Utd	1-0	Blackburn	22-01-1995
C Palace	1-1	Man Utd	25-01-1995
Man Utd	1-0	Aston Villa	04-02-1995
Man City	0-3	Man Utd	11-02-1995
Norwich	0-2	Man Utd	22-02-1995
Everton	1-0	Man Utd	25-02-1995
Man Utd	9-0	Ipswich	04-03 1995
Wimbledon	0-1	Man Utd	07-03-1995
Man Utd	0-0	Tottenham	15-03-1995
Liverpool	2-0	Man Utd	19-03-1995
Man Utd	3-0	Arsenal	22-03-1995
Man Utd	0-0	Leeds	02-04-1995
Leicester	0-4	Man Utd	15-04-1995
Man Utd	0-0	Chelsea	17-04-1995
Coventry	2-3	Man Utd	01-05-1995
Man Utd	1-0	Sheff Wed	07-05-1995
Man Utd	2-1	Soton	10-05-1995
West Ham	1-1	Man Utd	14-05-1995

Cup Games

FA CS	Man Utd	2-0	Blackburn	14-08-1994
European Cup	Man Utd	4-2	IFK Goth'burg	14-09-1994
League Cup	Port Vale	1-2	Man Utd	21-09-1994
European Cup	Galatas'y	0-0	Man Utd	28-09-1994
League Cup	Man Utd	2-0	Port Vale	05-10-1994
European Cup	Man Utd	2-2	Barcelona	19-10-1994
League Cup	Newcastle	2-0	Man Utd	26-10-1994
European Cup	Barcelona	4-0	Man Utd	02-11-1994
European Cup	IFK Goth'bg	3-1	Man Utd	23-11-1994
European Cup	Man Utd	4-0	Galatasaray	07-12-1994
FA Cup	Sheff Utd	0-2	Man Utd	09-01-1995
FA Cup	Man Utd	5-2	Wrexham	28-01-1995
FA Cup	Man Utd	3-1	Leeds	19-02-1995
FA Cup	Man Utd	2-0	QPR	12-03-1995
FA Cup	Man Utd	2-2	C Palace	09-04-1995
FA Cup	C Palace	0-2	Man Utd	12-04-1995
FA Cup	Everton	1-0	Man Utd	20-05-1995

Total

Played	Won	Drawn	Lost	Points
42	26(62 %)	10 (24 %)	6 (14 %)	88

Home

Played	Won	Drawn	Lost	Points
21	16 (76 %)	4 (19 %)	1 (5 %)	52

Away

Played	Won	Drawn	Lost	Points
21	10 (48 %)	6 (29 %)	5 (24 %)	36

Biggest home win

Mar 4th 1995	United	9-0	Ipswich Town

Biggest home loss

Dec 17th 1994	United	1-2	Nottingham Forest

Biggest away win
Apr 15th 1995   Leicester C.   0-4   United

Biggest away loss
Mar 19th 1995   Liverpool   2-0   United

Highest aggregate score home
Mar 4th 1995   United   9-0   Ipswich Town

Highest aggregate score away
Oct 23rd 1994   Blackburn R.   2-4   United

Pos	Club	Pld	W	D	L	F	A	GD	Pts
1.	Blackburn Rovers	42	27	8	7	80	39	41	89
2.	MANCHESTER UNITED	42	26	10	6	77	28	49	88
3.	Nottingham Forest	42	22	11	9	72	43	29	77
4.	Liverpool	42	21	11	10	65	37	28	74
5.	Leeds United	42	20	13	9	59	38	21	73
6.	Newcastle United	42	20	12	10	67	47	20	72
7.	Tottenham Hotspur	42	16	14	12	66	58	8	62
8.	Queens Park Rangers	42	17	9	16	61	59	2	60
9.	Wimbledon	42	15	11	16	48	65	-17	56
10.	Soton	42	12	18	12	61	63	-2	54
11.	Chelsea	42	13	15	14	50	55	-5	54
12.	Arsenal	42	13	12	17	52	49	3	51
13.	Sheffield Wednesday	42	13	12	17	49	57	-8	51
14.	West Ham United	42	13	11	18	44	48	-4	50
15.	Everton	42	11	17	14	44	51	-7	50
16.	Coventry City	42	12	14	16	44	62	-18	50
17.	Manchester City	42	12	13	17	53	64	-11	49
18.	Aston Villa	42	11	15	16	51	56	-5	48
19.	Crystal Palace	42	11	12	19	34	49	-15	45
20.	Norwich City	42	10	13	19	37	54	-17	43
21.	Leicester City	42	6	11	25	45	80	-35	29
22.	Ipswich Town	42	7	6	29	36	93	-57	27

1995/96

Aston Villa	3-1	Man Utd	19-08-1995
Man Utd	2-1	West Ham	23-08-1995
Man Utd	3-1	Wimbledon	26-08-1995
Blackburn	1-2	Man Utd	28-08-1995
Everton	2-3	Man Utd	09-09-1995
Man Utd	3-0	Bolton	16-09-1995
Sheff Wed	0-0	Man Utd	23-09-1995
Man Utd	2-2	Liverpool	01-10-1995
Man Utd	1-0	Man City	14-10-1995
Chelsea	1-4	Man Utd	21-10-1995
Man Utd	2-0	Middlesbro	28-10-1995
Arsenal	1-0	Man Utd	04-11-1995
Man Utd	4-1	Soton	18-11-1995
Coventry	0-4	Man Utd	22-11-1995
Nottm Forest	1-1	Man Utd	27-11-1995
Man Utd	1-1	Chelsea	02-12-1995
Man Utd	2-2	Sheff Wed	09-12-1995
Liverpool	2-0	Man Utd	17-12-1995
Leeds	3-1	Man Utd	24-12-1995
Man Utd	2-0	Newcastle	27-12-1995
Man Utd	2-1	QPR	30-12-1995
Tottenham	4-1	Man Utd	01-01-1996
Man Utd	0-0	Aston Villa	13-01-1996
West Ham	0-1	Man Utd	22-01-1996
Wimbledon	2-4	Man Utd	03-02-1996
Man Utd	1-0	Blackburn	10-02-1996
Man Utd	2-0	Everton	21-02-1996
Bolton	0-6	Man Utd	25-02-1996
Newcastle	0-1	Man Utd	04-03-1996
QPR	1-1	Man Utd	16-03-1996
Man Utd	1-0	Arsenal	20-03-1996
Man Utd	1-0	Tottenham	24-03-1996
Man City	2-3	Man Utd	06-04-1996
Man Utd	1-0	Coventry	08-04-1996
Soton	3-1	Man Utd	13-04-1996
Man Utd	1-0	Leeds	17-04-1996
Man Utd	5-0	Nottm Forest	28-04-1996
Middlesbro	0-3	Man Utd	05-05-1996

Cup Games

UEFA Cup	R. Volgog'd	0-0	Man Utd	12-09-1995
UEFA Cup	Man Utd	2-2	R. Volgograd	26-09-1995
League Cup	York	1-3	Man Utd	03-10-1995
FA Cup	Man Utd	2-2	Sunderland	06-01-1996
FA Cup	Sunderland	1-2	Man Utd	16-01-1996
FA Cup	Reading	0-3	Man Utd	27-01-1996
FA Cup	Man Utd	2-1	Man City	18-02-1996
FA Cup	Man Utd	2-0	Soton	11-03-1996
FA Cup	Man Utd	2-1	Chelsea	31-03-1996
FA Cup	Man Utd	1-0	Liverpool	11-05-1996

Total

Played	Won	Drawn	Lost	Points
38	25(66 %)	7 (18 %)	6 (16 %)	82

Home

Played	Won	Drawn	Lost	Points
19	15 (79 %)	4 (21 %)	0 (0 %)	49

Away

Played	Won	Drawn	Lost	Points
19	10 (53 %)	3 (16 %)	6 (32 %)	33

Biggest home win

Apr 28th 1996	United	5-0	Nottingham Forest

Biggest home loss
Unbeaten

Biggest away win

Feb 25th 1996	Bolton W.	0-6	United

Biggest away loss

Jan first 1996	Spurs	4-1	United

Highest aggregate score home

| Nov 18th 1995 | United | 4-1 | Soton |
| Apr 28th 1996 | United | 5-0 | Nottingham Forest |

Highest aggregate score away

| Feb 3rd 1996 | Wimbledon | 2-4 | United |
| Feb 25th 1996 | Bolton W. | 0-6 | United |

Pos	Club	Pld	W	D	L	F	A	GD	Pts
1.	MANCHESTER UNITED	38	25	7	6	73	35	38	82
2.	Newcastle United	38	24	6	8	66	37	29	78
3.	Liverpool	38	20	11	7	70	34	36	71
4.	Aston Villa	38	18	9	11	52	35	17	63
5.	Arsenal	38	17	12	9	49	32	17	63
6.	Everton	38	17	10	11	64	44	20	61
7.	Blackburn Rovers	38	18	7	13	61	47	14	61
8.	Tottenham Hotspur	38	16	13	9	50	38	12	61
9.	Nottingham Forest	38	15	13	10	50	54	-4	58
10.	West Ham United	38	14	9	15	43	52	-9	51
11.	Chelsea	38	12	14	12	46	44	2	50
12.	Middlesbrough	38	11	10	17	35	50	-15	43
13.	Leeds United	38	12	7	19	40	57	-17	43
14.	Wimbledon	38	10	11	17	55	70	-15	41
15.	Sheffield Wednesday	38	10	10	18	48	61	-13	40
16.	Coventry City	38	8	14	16	42	60	-18	38
17.	Soton	38	9	11	18	34	52	-18	38
18.	Manchester City	38	9	11	18	33	58	-25	38
19.	Queens Park Rangers	38	9	6	23	38	57	-19	33
20.	Bolton Wanderers	38	8	5	25	39	71	-32	29

1996/97

Wimbledon	0-3	Man Utd	17-08-1996
Man Utd	2-2	Everton	21-08-1996
Man Utd	2-2	Blackburn	25-08-1996
Derby	1-1	Man Utd	04-09-1996
Leeds	0-4	Man Utd	07-09-1996
Man Utd	4-1	Nottm Forest	14-09-1996
Aston Villa	0-0	Man Utd	21-09-1996
Man Utd	2-0	Tottenham	29-09-1996
Man Utd	1-0	Liverpool	12-10-1996
Newcastle	5-0	Man Utd	20-10-1996
Soton	6-3	Man Utd	26-10-1996
Man Utd	1-2	Chelsea	02-11-1996
Man Utd	1-0	Arsenal	16-11-1996
Middlesbro	2-2	Man Utd	23-11-1996
Man Utd	3-1	Leicester	30-11-1996
West Ham	2-2	Man Utd	08-12-1996
Sheff Wed	1-1	Man Utd	18-12-1996
Man Utd	5-0	Sunderland	21-12-1996
Nottm Forest	0-4	Man Utd	26-12-1996
Man Utd	1-0	Leeds	28-12-1996
Man Utd	0-0	Aston Villa	01-01-1997
Tottenham	1-2	Man Utd	12-01-1997
Coventry	0-2	Man Utd	18-01-1997
Man Utd	2-1	Wimbledon	29-01-1997
Man Utd	2-1	Soton	01-02-1997
Arsenal	1-2	Man Utd	19-02-1997
Chelsea	1-1	Man Utd	22-02-1997
Man Utd	3-1	Coventry	01-03-1997
Sunderland	2-1	Man Utd	08-03-1997
Man Utd	2-0	Sheff Wed	15-03-1997
Everton	0-2	Man Utd	22-03-1997
Man Utd	2-3	Derby	05-04-1997
Blackburn	2-3	Man Utd	12-04-1997
Liverpool	1-3	Man Utd	19-04-1997
Leicester	2-2	Man Utd	03-05-1997
Man Utd	3-3	Middlesbro	05-05-1997
Man Utd	0-0	Newcastle	08-05-1997
Man Utd	2-0	West Ham	11-05-1997

Cup Games

FA CS	Man Utd	4-0	Newcastle	11-08-1996
European Cup	Juventus	1-0	Man Utd	11-09-1996
European Cup	Man Utd	2-0	Rapid Vienna	25-09-1996
European Cup	Fenerbahce	0-2	Man Utd	16-10-1996
League Cup	Man Utd	2-1	Swindon	23-10-1996
European Cup	Man Utd	0-1	Fenerbahce	30-10-1996
European Cup	Man Utd	0-1	Juventus	20-11-1996
League Cup	Leicester	2-0	Man Utd	27-11-1996
European Cup	R. Vienna	0-2	Man Utd	04-12-1996
FA Cup	Man Utd	2-0	Tottenham	05-01-1997
FA Cup	Man Utd	1-1	Wimbledon	25-01-1997
FA Cup	Wimbledon	1-0	Man Utd	04-02-1997
European Cup	Man Utd	4-0	Porto	05-03-1997
European Cup	Porto	0-0	Man Utd	19-03-1997
European Cup	B. Dortm'd	1-0	Man Utd	09-04-1997
European Cup	Man Utd	0-1	B. Dortmund	23-04-1997

Total

Played	Won	Drawn	Lost	Points
38	21(55 %)	12 (32 %)	5 (13 %)	75

Home

Played	Won	Drawn	Lost	Points
19	12 (63 %)	5 (26 %)	2 (11 %)	41

Away

Played	Won	Drawn	Lost	Points
19	9 (47 %)	7 (37 %)	3 (16 %)	34

Biggest home win

Dec 2first 1996	United	5-0	Sunderland

Biggest home loss

Nov 2nd 1996	United	1-2	Chelsea
Apr 5th 1997	United	2-3	Derby County

Biggest away win

| Sep 7th 1996 | Leeds Utd | 0-4 | United |
| Dec 26th 1996 | Notts. Forest | 0-4 | United |

Biggest away loss

| Oct 20th 1996 | Newc. Utd | 5-0 | United |

Highest aggregate score home

| May 5th 1997 | United | 3-3 | Middlesbrough |

Highest aggregate score away

| Oct 26th 1996 | Soton | 6-3 | United |

Pos Club	Pld	W	D	L	F	A	GD	Pts
1. MANCHESTER UNITED	38	21	12	5	76	44	32	75
2. Newcastle United	38	19	11	8	73	40	33	68
3. Arsenal	38	19	11	8	62	32	30	68
4. Liverpool	38	19	11	8	62	37	25	68
5. Aston Villa	38	17	10	11	47	34	13	61
6. Chelsea	38	16	11	11	58	55	3	59
7. Sheffield Wednesday	38	14	15	9	50	51	-1	57
8. Wimbledon	38	15	11	12	49	46	3	56
9. Leicester City	38	12	11	15	46	54	-8	47
10. Tottenham Hotspur	38	13	7	18	44	51	-7	46
11. Leeds United	38	11	13	14	28	38	-10	46
12. Derby County	38	11	13	14	45	58	-13	46
13. Blackburn Rovers	38	9	15	14	42	43	-1	42
14. Middlesbrough	38	10	12	16	51	60	-9	42
15. West Ham United	38	10	12	16	39	48	-9	42
16. Everton	38	10	12	16	44	57	-13	42
17. Soton	38	10	11	17	50	56	-6	41
18. Coventry City	38	9	14	15	38	54	-16	41
19. Sunderland	38	10	10	18	35	53	-18	40
20. Nottingham Forest	38	6	16	16	31	59	-28	34

1997/98

Tottenham	0-2	Man Utd	10-08-1997
Man Utd	1-0	Soton	13-08-1997
Leicester	0-0	Man Utd	23-08-1997
Everton	0-2	Man Utd	27-08-1997
Man Utd	3-0	Coventry	30-08-1997
Man Utd	2-1	West Ham	13-09-1997
Bolton	0-0	Man Utd	20-09-1997
Man Utd	2-2	Chelsea	24-09-1997
Leeds	1-0	Man Utd	27-09-1997
Man Utd	2-0	C Palace	04-10-1997
Derby	2-2	Man Utd	18-10-1997
Man Utd	7-0	Barnsley	25-10-1997
Man Utd	6-1	Sheff Wed	01-11-1997
Arsenal	3-2	Man Utd	09-11-1997
Wimbledon	2-5	Man Utd	22-11-1997
Man Utd	4-0	Blackburn	30-11-1997
Liverpool	1-3	Man Utd	06-12-1997
Man Utd	1-0	Aston Villa	15-12-1997
Newcastle	0-1	Man Utd	21-12-1997
Man Utd	2-0	Everton	26-12-1997
Coventry	3-2	Man Utd	28-12-1997
Man Utd	2-0	Tottenham	10-01-1998
Soton	1-0	Man Utd	19-01-1998
Man Utd	0-1	Leicester	31-01-1998
Man Utd	1-1	Bolton	07-02-1998
Aston Villa	0-2	Man Utd	18-02-1998
Man Utd	2-0	Derby	21-02-1998
Chelsea	0-1	Man Utd	28-02-1998
Sheff Wed	2-0	Man Utd	07-03-1998
West Ham	1-1	Man Utd	11-03-1998
Man Utd	0-1	Arsenal	14-03-1998
Man Utd	2-0	Wimbledon	28-03-1998
Blackburn	1-3	Man Utd	06-04-1998
Man Utd	1-1	Liverpool	10-04-1998
Man Utd	1-1	Newcastle	18-04-1998
C Palace	0-3	Man Utd	27-04-1998
Man Utd	3-0	Leeds	04-05-1998
Barnsley	0-2	Man Utd	10-05-1998

Cup Games

FACS	Man Utd	1-1	Chelsea	03-08-1997
European Cup	FC Kosice	0-3	Man Utd	17-09-1997
European Cup	Man Utd	3-2	Juventus	01-10-1997
League Cup	Ipswich	2-0	Man Utd	14-10-1997
European Cup	Man Utd	2-1	Feyenoord	22-10-1997
European Cup	Feyenoord	1-3	Man Utd	05-11-1997
European Cup	Man Utd	3-0	FC Kosice	27-11-1997
European Cup	Juventus	1-0	Man Utd	10-12-1997
FA Cup	Chelsea	3-5	Man Utd	04-01-1998
FA Cup	Man Utd	5-1	Walsall	24-01-1998
FA Cup	Man Utd	1-1	Barnsley	15-02-1998
FA Cup	Barnsley	3-2	Man Utd	25-02-1998
European Cup	Monaco	0-0	Man Utd	04-03-1998
European Cup	Man Utd	1-1	Monaco	18-03-1998

Total

Played	Won	Drawn	Lost	Points
38	23(61 %)	8 (21 %)	7 (18 %)	77

Home

Played	Won	Drawn	Lost	Points
19	13 (68 %)	4 (21 %)	2 (11 %)	43

Away

Played	Won	Drawn	Lost	Points
19	10 (53 %)	4 (21 %)	5 (26 %)	34

Biggest home win

Oct 25th 1997	United	7-0	Barnsley

Biggest home loss

Jan 3first 1998	United	0- 1	Leicester City
Mar 14th 1998	United	0-1	Arsenal

Biggest away win

Nov 22nd 1997	Wimbledon	2-5	United

Apr 27th 1998   C. Palace   0-3   United

Biggest away loss
Mar 7th 1998   Sheff Wed.   2-0   United

Highest aggregate score home
Oct 25th 1997   United   7-0   Barnsley
Nov first 1997   United   6-1   Sheff. Wed

Highest aggregate score away
Nov 22nd 1997   Wimbledon   2-5   United

Pos	Club	Pld	W	D	L	F	A	GD	Pts
1.	Arsenal	38	23	9	6	68	33	35	78
2.	MANCHESTER UNITED	38	23	8	7	73	26	47	77
3.	Liverpool	38	18	11	9	68	42	26	65
4.	Chelsea	38	20	3	15	71	43	28	63
5.	Leeds United	38	17	8	13	57	46	11	59
6.	Blackburn Rovers	38	16	10	12	57	52	5	58
7.	Aston Villa	38	17	6	15	49	48	1	57
8.	West Ham United	38	16	8	14	56	57	-1	56
9.	Derby County	38	16	7	15	52	49	3	55
10.	Leicester City	38	13	14	11	51	41	10	53
11.	Coventry City	38	12	16	10	46	44	2	52
12.	Soton	38	14	6	18	50	55	-5	48
13.	Newcastle United	38	11	11	16	35	44	-9	44
14.	Tottenham Hotspur	38	11	11	16	44	56	-12	44
15.	Wimbledon	38	10	14	14	34	46	-12	44
16.	Sheffield Wednesday	38	12	8	18	52	67	-15	44
17.	Everton	38	9	13	16	41	56	-15	40
18.	Bolton Wanderers	38	9	13	16	41	61	-20	40
19.	Barnsley	38	10	5	23	37	82	-45	35
20.	Crystal Palace	38	8	9	21	37	71	-34	33

1998/99

Man Utd	2-2	Leicester	15-08-1998
West Ham	0-0	Man Utd	22-08-1998
Man Utd	4-1	Charlton	09-09-1998
Man Utd	2-0	Coventry	12-09-1998
Arsenal	3-0	Man Utd	20-09-1998
Man Utd	2-0	Liverpool	24-09-1998
Soton	0-3	Man Utd	03-10-1998
Man Utd	5-1	Wimbledon	17-10-1998
Derby	1-1	Man Utd	24-10-1998
Everton	1-4	Man Utd	31-10-1998
Man Utd	0-0	Newcastle	08-11-1998
Man Utd	3-2	Blackburn	14-11-1998
Sheff Wed	3-1	Man Utd	21-11-1998
Man Utd	3-2	Leeds	29-11-1998
AstonVilla	1-1	Man Utd	05-12-1998
Tottenham	2-2	Man Utd	12-12-1998
Man Utd	1-1	Chelsea	16-12-1998
Man Utd	2-3	Middlesbro	19-12-1998
Man Utd	3-0	Nottm Forest	26-12-1998
Chelsea	0-0	Man Utd	29-12-1998
Man Utd	4-1	West Ham	10-01-1999
Leicester	2-6	Man Utd	16-01-1999
Charlton	0-1	Man Utd	31-01-1999
Man Utd	1-0	Derby	03-02-1999
Nottm Forest	1-8	Man Utd	06-02-1999
Man Utd	1-1	Arsenal	17-02-1999
Coventry	0-1	Man Utd	20-02-1999
Man Utd	2-1	Soton	27-02-1999
Newcastle	1-2	Man Utd	13-03-1999
Man Utd	3-1	Everton	21-03-1999
Wimbledon	1-1	Man Utd	03-04-1999
Man Utd	3-0	Sheff Wed	17-04-1999
Leeds	1-1	Man Utd	25-04-1999
Man Utd	2-1	Aston Villa	01-05-1999
Liverpool	2-2	Man Utd	05-05-1999
Middlesbro	0-1	Man Utd	09-05-1999
Blackburn	0-0	Man Utd	12-05-1999
Man Utd	2-1	Tottenham	16-05-1999

Cup Games

FACS	Arsenal	3-0	Man Utd	09-08-1998
European Cup	Man Utd	2-0	LKS Lodz	12-08-1998
European Cup	LKS Lodz	0-0	Man Utd	26-08-1998
European Cup	Man Utd	3-3	Barcelona	16-09-1998
European Cup	B Munich	2-2	Man Utd	30-09-1998
European Cup	Brondby	2-6	Man Utd	21-10-1998
League Cup	Man Utd	2-0	Bury	28-10-1998
European Cup	Man Utd	5-0	Brondby	04-11-1998
League Cup	Man Utd	2-1	Nottm Forest	11-11-1998
European Cup	Barcelona	3-3	Man Utd	25-11-1998
League Cup	Tottenham	3-1	Man Utd	02-12-1998
European Cup	Man Utd	1-1	B. Munich	09-12-1998
FA Cup	Man Utd	3-1	Middlesbro	03-01-1999
FA Cup	Man Utd	2-1	Liverpool	24-01-1999
FA Cup	Man Utd	1-0	Fulham	14-02-1999
European Cup	Man Utd	2-0	Inter	03-03-1999
FA Cup	Man Utd	0-0	Chelsea	07-03-1999
FA Cup	Chelsea	0-2	Man Utd	10-03-1999
European Cup	Inter	1-1	Man Utd	17-03-1999
European Cup	Man Utd	1-1	Juventus	07-04-1999
FA Cup	Man Utd	0-0	Arsenal	11-04-1999
FA Cup	Arsenal	1-2	Man Utd	14-04-1999
European Cup	Juventus	2-3	Man Utd	21-04-1999
FA Cup	Man Utd	2-0	Newcastle	22-05-1999
European Cup	B Munich	1-2	Man Utd	26-05-1999

Total

Played	Won	Drawn	Lost	Points
38	22(58 %)	13 (34 %)	3 (8 %)	79

Home

Played	Won	Drawn	Lost	Points
19	14 (74 %)	4 (21 %)	1 (5 %)	46

Away

Played	Won	Drawn	Lost	Points
19	8 (42 %)	9 (47 %)	2 (11 %)	33

Biggest home win

Oct 17th 1998	United	5-1	Wimbledon

Biggest home loss
Dec 19th 1998   United   2-3   Middlesbrough

Biggest away win
Feb 6th 1999   Notts Forest 1-8   United

Biggest away loss
Sep 20th 1998   Arsenal   3-0   United

Highest aggregate score home
Oct 17th 1998   United   5-1   Wimbledon

Highest aggregate score away
Feb 6th 1999   Notts Forest 1-8   United

Pos	Club	Pld	W	D	L	F	A	GD	Pts
1.	MANCHESTER UNITED	38	22	13	3	80	37	43	79
2.	Arsenal	38	22	12	4	59	17	42	78
3.	Chelsea	38	20	15	3	57	30	27	75
4.	Leeds United	38	18	13	7	62	34	28	67
5.	West Ham United	38	16	9	13	46	53	-7	57
6.	Aston Villa	38	15	10	13	51	46	5	55
7.	Liverpool	38	15	9	14	68	49	19	54
8.	Derby County	38	13	13	12	40	45	-5	52
9.	Middlesbrough	38	12	15	11	48	54	-6	51
10.	Leicester City	38	12	13	13	40	46	-6	49
11.	Tottenham Hotspur	38	11	14	13	47	50	-3	47
12.	Sheffield Wednesday	38	13	7	18	41	42	-1	46
13.	Newcastle United	38	11	13	14	48	54	-6	46
14.	Everton	38	11	10	17	42	47	-5	43
15.	Coventry City	38	11	9	18	39	51	-12	42
16.	Wimbledon	38	10	12	16	40	63	-23	42
17.	Soton	38	11	8	19	37	64	-27	41
18.	Charlton Athletic	38	8	12	18	41	56	-15	36
19.	Blackburn Rovers	38	7	14	17	38	52	-14	35
20.	Nottingham Forest	38	7	9	22	35	69	-34	30

1999/00

Everton	1-1	Man Utd	08-08-1999
Man Utd	4-0	Sheff Wed	11-08-1999
Man Utd	2-0	Leeds	14-08-1999
Arsenal	1-2	Man Utd	22-08-1999
Coventry	1-2	Man Utd	25-08-1999
Man Utd	5-1	Newcastle	30-08-1999
Liverpool	2-3	Man Utd	11-09-1999
Man Utd	1-1	Wimbledon	18-09-1999
Man Utd	3-3	Soton	25-09-1999
Chelsea	5-0	Man Utd	03-10-1999
Man Utd	4-1	Watford	16-10-1999
Tottenham	3-1	Man Utd	23-10-1999
Man Utd	3-0	Aston Villa	30-10-1999
Man Utd	2-0	Leicester	06-11-1999
Derby	1-2	Man Utd	20-11-1999
Man Utd	5-1	Everton	04-12-1999
West Ham	2-4	Man Utd	18-12-1999
Man Utd	4-0	Bradford	26-12-1999
Sunderland	2-2	Man Utd	28-12-1999
Man Utd	1-1	Arsenal	24-01-2000
Man Utd	1-0	Middlesbro	29-01-2000
Sheff Wed	0-1	Man Utd	02-02-2000
Man Utd	3-2	Coventry	05-02-2000
Newcastle	3-0	Man Utd	12-02-2000
Leeds	0-1	Man Utd	20-02-2000
Wimbledon	2-2	Man Utd	26-02-2000
Man Utd	1-1	Liverpool	04-03-2000
Man Utd	3-1	Derby	11-03-2000
Leicester	0-2	Man Utd	18-03-2000
Bradford	0-4	Man Utd	25-03-2000
Man Utd	7-1	West Ham	01-04-2000
Middlesbro	3-4	Man Utd	10-04-2000
Man Utd	4-0	Sunderland	15-04-2000
Soton	1-3	Man Utd	22-04-2000
Man Utd	3-2	Chelsea	24-04-2000
Watford	2-3	Man Utd	29-04-2000
Man Utd	3-1	Tottenham	06-05-2000
Aston Villa	0-1	Man Utd	14-05-2000

Cup Games

FACS	Arsenal	2-1	Man Utd	01-08-1999
European SC	Lazio	1-0	Man Utd	27-08-1999
European Cup	Man Utd	0-0	Dyn. Zagreb	14-09-1999
European Cup	Sturm Graz	0-3	Man Utd	22-09-1999
European Cup	Man Utd	2-1	Marseille	29-09-1999
League Cup	Aston Villa	3-0	Man Utd	13-10-1999
European Cup	Marseille	1-0	Man Utd	19-10-1999
European Cup	D. Zagreb	1-2	Man Utd	27-10-1999
European Cup	Man Utd	2-1	Sturm Graz	02-11-1999
European Cup	Fiorentina	2-0	Man Utd	23-11-1999
IC Cup	Man Utd	1-0	Palmeiras	30-11-1999
European Cup	Man Utd	3-0	Valencia	08-12-1999
FIFA Club	Necaxa	1-1	Man Utd	06-01-2000
FIFA Club	Man Utd	1-3	Vasco	08-01-2000
FIFA Club	Man Utd	2-0	S. Melbourne	11-01-2000
European Cup	Man Utd	2-0	Bordeaux	01-03-2000
European Cup	Bordeaux	1-2	Man Utd	07-03-2000
European Cup	Man Utd	3-1	Fiorentina	15-03-2000
European Cup	Valencia	0-0	Man Utd	21-03-2000
European Cup	R. Madrid	0-0	Man Utd	04-04-2000
European Cup	Man Utd	2-3	Real Madrid	19-04-2000

Total

Played	Won	Drawn	Lost	Points
38	28(74 %)	7 (18 %)	3 (8 %)	91

Home

Played	Won	Drawn	Lost	Points
19	15 (79 %)	4 (21 %)	0 (0 %)	49

Away

Played	Won	Drawn	Lost	Points
19	13 (68 %)	3 (16 %)	3 (16 %)	42

Biggest home win

Apr first 2000	United	7-1	West Ham United

Biggest home loss

Unbeaten

Biggest away win
Mar 25th 2000   Bradford C.   0-4   United

Biggest away loss
Oct 3rd 1999   Chelsea   5-0   United

Highest aggregate score home
Apr first 2000   United   7-1   West Ham United

Highest aggregate score away
Apr 10th 2000   Middlesbrough   3-4   United

Pos	Club	Pld	W	D	L	F	A	GD	Pts
1.	MANCHESTER UNITED	38	28	7	3	97	45	52	91
2.	Arsenal	38	22	7	9	73	43	30	73
3.	Leeds United	38	21	6	11	58	43	15	69
4.	Liverpool	38	19	10	9	51	30	21	67
5.	Chelsea	38	18	11	9	53	34	19	65
6.	Aston Villa	38	15	13	10	46	35	11	58
7.	Sunderland	38	16	10	12	57	56	1	58
8.	Leicester City	38	16	7	15	55	55	0	55
9.	West Ham United	38	15	10	13	52	53	-1	55
10.	Tottenham Hotspur	38	15	8	15	57	49	8	53
11.	Newcastle United	38	14	10	14	63	54	9	52
12.	Middlesbrough	38	14	10	14	46	52	-6	52
13.	Everton	38	12	14	12	59	49	10	50
14.	Coventry City	38	12	8	18	47	54	-7	44
15.	Soton	38	12	8	18	45	62	-17	44
16.	Derby County	38	9	11	18	44	57	-13	38
17.	Bradford City	38	9	9	20	38	68	-30	36
18.	Wimbledon	38	7	12	19	46	74	-28	33
19.	Sheffield Wednesday	38	8	7	23	38	70	-32	31
20.	Watford	38	6	6	26	35	77	-42	24

2000/01

Man Utd	2-0	Newcastle	20-08-2000
Ipswich	1-1	Man Utd	22-08-2000
West Ham	2-2	Man Utd	26-08-2000
Man Utd	6-0	Bradford	05-09-2000
Man Utd	3-0	Sunderland	09-09-2000
Everton	1-3	Man Utd	16-09-2000
Man Utd	3-3	Chelsea	23-09-2000
Arsenal	1-0	Man Utd	01-10-2000
Leicester	0-3	Man Utd	14-10-2000
Man Utd	3-0	Leeds	21-10-2000
Man Utd	5-0	Soton	28-10-2000
Coventry	1-2	Man Utd	04-11-2000
Man Utd	2-1	Middlesbro	11-11-2000
Man City	0-1	Man Utd	18-11-2000
Derby	0-3	Man Utd	25-11-2000
Man Utd	2-0	Tottenham	02-12-2000
Charlton	3-3	Man Utd	09-12-2000
Man Utd	0-1	Liverpool	17-12-2000
Man Utd	2-0	Ipswich	23-12-2000
Aston Villa	0-1	Man Utd	26-12-2000
Newcastle	1-1	Man Utd	30-12-2000
Man Utd	3-1	West Ham	01-01-2001
Bradford	0-3	Man Utd	13-01-2001
Man Utd	2-0	Aston Villa	20-01-2001
Sunderland	0-1	Man Utd	31-01-2001
Man Utd	1-0	Everton	03-02-2001
Chelsea	1-1	Man Utd	10-02-2001
Man Utd	6-1	Arsenal	25-02-2001
Leeds	1-1	Man Utd	03-03-2001
Man Utd	2-0	Leicester	17-03-2001
Liverpool	2-0	Man Utd	31-03-2001
Man Utd	2-1	Charlton	10-04-2001
Man Utd	4-2	Coventry	14-04-2001
Man Utd	1-1	Man City	21-04-2001
Middlesbro	0-2	Man Utd	28-04-2001
Man Utd	0-1	Derby	05-05-2001
Soton	2-1	Man Utd	13-05-2001
Tottenham	3-1	Man Utd	19-05-2001

Cup Games

FACS	Chelsea	2-0	Man Utd	13-08-2000
European Cup	Man Utd	5-1	Anderlecht	13-09-2000
European Cup	D. Kiev	0-0	Man Utd	19-09-2000
European Cup	PSV Eindh'n	3-1	Man Utd	26-09-2000
European Cup	Man Utd	3-1	PSV	18-10-2000
European Cup	Anderlecht	2-1	Man Utd	24-10-2000
League Cup	Watford	0-3	Man Utd	31-10-2000
European Cup	Man Utd	1-0	D. Kiev	08-11-2000
European Cup	Man Utd	3-1	Panathinaikos	21-11-2000
League Cup	Sunderland	2-1	Man Utd	28-11-2000
European Cup	Sturm Graz	0-2	Man Utd	06-12-2000
FA Cup	Fulham	1-2	Man Utd	07-01-2001
FA Cup	Man Utd	0-1	West Ham	28-01-2001
European Cup	Valencia	0-0	Man Utd	14-02-2001
European Cup	Man Utd	1-1	Valencia	20-02-2001
European Cup	Panath'kos	1-1	Man Utd	07-03-2001
European Cup	Man Utd	3-0	Sturm Graz	13-03-2001
European Cup	Man Utd	0-1	B Munich	03-04-2001
European Cup	B. Munich	2-1	Man Utd	18-04-2001

Total

Played	Won	Drawn	Lost	Points
38	24(63 %)	8 (21 %)	6 (16 %)	80

Home

Played	Won	Drawn	Lost	Points
19	15 (79 %)	2 (11 %)	2 (11 %)	47

Away

Played	Won	Drawn	Lost	Points
19	9 (47 %)	6 (32 %)	4 (21 %)	33

Biggest home win

Sep 5th 2000	United	6-0	Bradford City

Biggest home loss

Dec 17th 2000	United	0-1	Liverpool
May 5th 2001	United	0-1	Derby County

Biggest away win

Oct 14th 2000	Leicester City	0-3	United
Nov 25th 2000	Derby Co.	0-3	United
Jan 13th 2001	Bradford C.	0-3	United

Biggest away loss

| Mar 3first 2001 | Liverpool | 2-0 | United |
| May 19th 2001 | Tottenham H. | 3-1 | United |

Highest aggregate score home

| Feb 25th 2001 | United | 6-1 | Arsenal |

Highest aggregate score away

| Dec 9th 2000 | Charlton Ath. | 3-3 | United |

Pos	Club	Pld	W	D	L	F	A	GD	Pts
1.	MANCHESTER UNITED	38	24	8	6	79	31	48	80
2.	Arsenal	38	20	10	8	63	38	25	70
3.	Liverpool	38	20	9	9	71	39	32	69
4.	Leeds United	38	20	8	10	64	43	21	68
5.	Ipswich Town	38	20	6	12	57	42	15	66
6.	Chelsea	38	17	10	11	68	45	23	61
7.	Sunderland	38	15	12	11	46	41	5	57
8.	Aston Villa	38	13	15	10	46	43	3	54
9.	Charlton Athletic	38	14	10	14	50	57	-7	52
10.	Soton	38	14	10	14	40	48	-8	52
11.	Newcastle United	38	14	9	15	44	50	-6	51
12.	Tottenham Hotspur	38	13	10	15	47	54	-7	49
13.	Leicester City	38	14	6	18	39	51	-12	48
14.	Middlesbrough	38	9	15	14	44	44	0	42
15.	West Ham United	38	10	12	16	45	50	-5	42
16.	Everton	38	11	9	18	45	59	-14	42
17.	Derby County	38	10	12	16	37	59	-22	42
18.	Manchester City	38	8	10	20	41	65	-24	34
19.	Coventry City	38	8	10	20	36	63	-27	34
20.	Bradford City	38	5	11	22	30	70	-40	26

2001/02

Man Utd	3-2	Fulham	19-08-2001
Blackburn	2-2	Man Utd	22-08-2001
Aston Villa	1-1	Man Utd	26-08-2001
Man Utd	4-1	Everton	08-09-2001
Newcastle	4-3	Man Utd	15-09-2001
Man Utd	4-0	Ipswich	22-09-2001
Tottenham	3-5	Man Utd	29-09-2001
Sunderland	1-3	Man Utd	13-10-2001
Man Utd	1-2	Bolton	20-10-2001
Man Utd	1-1	Leeds	27-10-2001
Liverpool	3-1	Man Utd	04-11-2001
Man Utd	2-0	Leicester	17-11-2001
Arsenal	3-1	Man Utd	25-11-2001
Man Utd	0-3	Chelsea	01-12-2001
Man Utd	0-1	West Ham	08-12-2001
Man Utd	5-0	Derby	12-12-2001
Middlesbro	0-1	Man Utd	15-12-2001
Man Utd	6-1	Soton	22-12-2001
Everton	0-2	Man Utd	26-12-2001
Fulham	2-3	Man Utd	30-12-2001
Man Utd	3-1	Newcastle	02-01-2002
Soton	1-3	Man Utd	13-01-2002
Man Utd	2-1	Blackburn	19-01-2002
Man Utd	0-1	Liverpool	22-01-2002
Bolton	0-4	Man Utd	29-01-2002
Man Utd	4-1	Sunderland	02-02-2002
Charlton	0-2	Man Utd	10-02-2002
Man Utd	1-0	Aston Villa	23-02-2002
Derby	2-2	Man Utd	03-03-2002
Man Utd	4-0	Tottenham	06-03-2002
West Ham	3-5	Man Utd	16-03-2002
Man Utd	0-1	Middlesbro	23-03-2002
Leeds	3-4	Man Utd	30-03-2002
Leicester	0-1	Man Utd	06-04-2002
Chelsea	0-3	Man Utd	20-04-2002
Ipswich	0-1	Man Utd	27-04-2002
Man Utd	0-1	Arsenal	08-05-2002
Man Utd	0-0	Charlton	11-05-2002

Cup Games

FACS	Liverpool	2-1	Man Utd	12-08-2001
European Cup	Man Utd	1-0	Lille	18-09-2001
European Cup	Deportivo	2-1	Man Utd	25-09-2001
European Cup	Olympiakos	0-2	Man Utd	10-10-2001
European Cup	Man Utd	2-3	Deportivo	17-10-2001
European Cup	Man Utd	3-0	Olympiakos	23-10-2001
European Cup	Lille	1-1	Man Utd	31-10-2001
League Cup	Arsenal	4-0	Man Utd	05-11-2001
European Cup	B. Munich	1-1	Man Utd	20-11-2001
European Cup	Man Utd	3-0	Boavista	05-12-2001
FA Cup	Aston Villa	2-3	Man Utd	06-01-2002
FA Cup	Middlesbro	2-0	Man Utd	26-01-2002
European Cup	Nantes	1-1	Man Utd	20-02-2002
European Cup	Man Utd	5-1	Nantes	26-02-2002
European Cup	Man Utd	0-0	B. Munich	13-03-2002
European Cup	Boavista	0-3	Man Utd	19-03-2002
European Cup	Deportivo	0-2	Man Utd	02-04-2002
European Cup	Man Utd	3-2	Deportivo	10-04-2002
European Cup	Man Utd	2-2	B. Leverkusen	24-04-2002
European Cup	B. Leverk'n	1-1	Man Utd	30-04-2002

Total

Played	Won	Drawn	Lost	Points
38	24(63 %)	5 (13 %)	9 (24 %)	77

Home

Played	Won	Drawn	Lost	Points
19	11 (58 %)	? (11 %)	6 (32 %)	35

Away

Played	Won	Drawn	Lost	Points
19	13 (68 %)	3 (16 %)	3 (16 %)	42

Biggest home win

Dec 12th 2001	United	5-0	Derby County
Dec 22nd 2001	United	6-1	Soton

Biggest home loss
Dec first 2001   United   0-3   Chelsea

Biggest away win
Jan 29th 2002   Bolton W.   0-4   United

Biggest away loss
Nov 4th 2001   Liverpool   3-1   United
Nov 25th 2001   Arsenal   3-1   United

Highest aggregate score home
Dec 22nd 2001   United   6- 1   Soton

Highest aggregate score away
Sep 29th 2001   Tottenham H.   3-5   United
Mar 16th 2002   West Ham U   3-5   United

Pos	Club	Pld	W	D	L	F	A	GD	Pts
1.	Arsenal	38	26	9	3	79	36	43	87
2.	Liverpool	38	24	8	6	67	30	37	80
3.	MANCHESTER UNITED	38	24	5	9	87	45	42	77
4.	Newcastle United	38	21	8	9	74	52	22	71
5.	Leeds United	38	18	12	8	53	37	16	66
6.	Chelsea	38	17	13	8	66	38	28	64
7.	West Ham United	38	15	8	15	48	57	-9	53
8.	Aston Villa	38	12	14	12	46	47	-1	50
9.	Tottenham Hotspur	38	14	8	16	49	53	-4	50
10.	Blackburn Rovers	38	12	10	16	55	51	4	46
11.	Soton	38	12	9	17	46	54	-8	45
12.	Middlesbrough	38	12	9	17	35	47	-12	45
13.	Fulham	38	10	14	14	36	44	-8	44
14.	Charlton Athletic	38	10	14	14	38	49	-11	44
15.	Everton	38	11	10	17	45	57	-12	43
16.	Bolton Wanderers	38	9	13	16	44	62	-18	40
17.	Sunderland	38	10	10	18	29	51	-22	40
18.	Ipswich Town	38	9	9	20	41	64	-23	36
19.	Derby County	38	8	6	24	33	63	-30	30
20.	Leicester City	38	5	13	20	30	64	-34	28

2002/03

Man Utd	1-0	West Brom	17-08-2002
Chelsea	2-2	Man Utd	23-08-2002
Sunderland	1-1	Man Utd	31-08-2002
Man Utd	1-0	Middlesbro	03-09-2002
Man Utd	0-1	Bolton	11-09-2002
Leeds	1-0	Man Utd	14-09-2002
Man Utd	1-0	Tottenham	21-09-2002
Charlton	1-3	Man Utd	28-09-2002
Man Utd	3-0	Everton	07-10-2002
Fulham	1-1	Man Utd	19-10-2002
Man Utd	1-1	Aston Villa	26-10-2002
Man Utd	2-1	Soton	02-11-2002
Man City	3-1	Man Utd	09-11-2002
West Ham	1-1	Man Utd	17-11-2002
Man Utd	5-3	Newcastle	23-11-2002
Liverpool	1-2	Man Utd	01-12-2002
Man Utd	2-0	Arsenal	07-12-2002
Man Utd	3-0	West Ham	14-12-2002
Blackburn	1-0	Man Utd	22-12-2002
Middlesbro	3-1	Man Utd	26-12-2002
Man Utd	2-0	Birmingham	28-12-2002
Man Utd	2-1	Sunderland	01-01-2003
West Brom	1-3	Man Utd	11-01-2003
Man Utd	2-1	Chelsea	18-01-2003
Soton	0-2	Man Utd	01-02-2003
Birmingham	0-1	Man Utd	04-02-2003
Man Utd	1-1	Man City	09-02-2003
Bolton	1-1	Man Utd	22-02-2003
Man Utd	2-1	Leeds	05-03-2003
Aston Villa	0-1	Man Utd	15-03-2003
Man Utd	3-0	Fulham	22-03-2003
Man Utd	4-0	Liverpool	05-04-2003
Newcastle	2-6	Man Utd	12-04-2003
Arsenal	2-2	Man Utd	16-04-2003
Man Utd	3-1	Blackburn	19-04-2003
Tottenham	0-2	Man Utd	27-04-2003
Man Utd	4-1	Charlton	03-05-2003
Everton	1-2	Man Utd	11-05-2003

Cup Games

European Cup	Zalaers'g	1-0	Man Utd	14-08-2002
European Cup	Man Utd	5-0	Zalaegerszeg	27-08-2002
European Cup	Man Utd	5-2	M. Haifa	18-09-2002
European Cup	B. Leverk'n	1-2	Man Utd	24-09-2002
European Cup	Man Utd	4-0	Olympiakos	01-10-2002
European Cup	Olympiakos	2-3	Man Utd	23-10-2002
European Cup	M. Haifa	3-0	Man Utd	29-10-2002
League Cup	Man Utd	2-0	Leicester	05-11-2002
European Cup	Man Utd	2-0	B. Leverkusen	13-11-2002
European Cup	Basle	1-3	Man Utd	26-11-2002
League Cup	Burnley	0-2	Man Utd	03-12-2002
European Cup	Man Utd	2-0	Deportivo	11-12-2002
League Cup	Man Utd	1-0	Chelsea	17-12-2002
FA Cup	Man Utd	4-1	Portsmouth	04-01-2003
League Cup	Man Utd	1-1	Blackburn	07-01-2003
League Cup	Blackburn	1-3	Man Utd	22-01-2003
FA Cup	Man Utd	6-0	West Ham	26-01-2003
FA Cup	Man Utd	0-2	Arsenal	15-02-2003
European Cup	Man Utd	2-1	Juventus	19-02-2003
European Cup	Juventus	0-3	Man Utd	25-02-2003
League Cup	Liverpool	2-0	Man Utd	02-03-2003
European Cup	Man Utd	1-1	Basle	12-03-2003
European Cup	Deportivo	2-0	Man Utd	18-03-2003
European Cup	Real Madrid	3-1	Man Utd	08-04-2003
European Cup	Man Utd	4-3	Real Madrid	23-04-2003

Total

Played	Won	Drawn	Lost	Points
38	25(66 %)	8 (21 %)	5 (13 %)	83

Home

Played	Won	Drawn	Lost	Points
19	16 (84 %)	2 (11 %)	1 (5 %)	50

Away

Played	Won	Drawn	Lost	Points
19	9 (47 %)	6 (32 %)	4 (21 %)	33

Biggest home win
Apr 5th 2003   United   4-0   Liverpool

Biggest home loss
Sep 11th 2002   United   0-1   Bolton Wanderers

Biggest away win
Apr 12th 2003   Newcastle U.   2-6   United

Biggest away loss
Nov 9th 2002   Man City   3-1   United
Dec 26th 2002   Middlesbro   3-1   United

Highest aggregate score home
Nov 23rd 2002   United   5-3   Newcastle United

Highest aggregate score away
Apr 12th 2003   Newcastle U   2-6   United

Pos	Club	Pld	W	D	L	F	A	GD	Pts
1.	MANCHESTER UNITED	38	25	8	5	74	34	40	83
2.	Arsenal	38	23	9	6	85	42	43	78
3.	Newcastle United	38	21	6	11	63	48	15	69
4.	Chelsea	38	19	10	9	68	38	30	67
5.	Liverpool	38	18	10	10	61	41	20	64
6.	Blackburn Rovers	38	16	12	10	52	43	9	60
7.	Everton	38	17	8	13	48	48	0	59
8.	Soton	38	13	13	12	43	46	-3	52
9.	Manchester City	38	15	6	17	47	54	-7	51
10.	Tottenham Hotspur	38	14	8	16	51	62	-11	50
11.	Middlesbrough	38	13	10	15	48	44	4	49
12.	Charlton Athletic	38	14	7	17	45	56	-11	49
13.	Birmingham City	38	13	9	16	41	49	-8	48
14.	Fulham	38	13	9	16	41	50	-9	48
15.	Leeds United	38	14	5	19	58	57	1	47
16.	Aston Villa	38	12	9	17	42	47	-5	45
17.	Bolton Wanderers	38	10	14	14	40	51	-11	44
18.	West Ham United	38	10	12	16	42	59	-17	42
19.	West Bromwich Albion	38	6	8	24	29	65	-36	26
20.	Sunderland	38	4	7	27	21	65	-44	19

2003/04

Man Utd	4-0	Bolton	16-08-2003
Newcastle	1-2	Man Utd	23-08-2003
Man Utd	1-0	Wolves	27-08-2003
Soton	1-0	Man Utd	31-08-2003
Charlton	0-2	Man Utd	13-09-2003
Man Utd	0-0	Arsenal	21-09-2003
Leicester	1-4	Man Utd	27-09-2003
Man Utd	3-0	Birmingham	04-10-2003
Leeds	0-1	Man Utd	18-10-2003
Man Utd	1-3	Fulham	25-10-2003
Man Utd	3-0	Portsmouth	01-11-2003
Liverpool	1-2	Man Utd	09-11-2003
Man Utd	2-1	Blackburn	22-11-2003
Chelsea	1-0	Man Utd	30-11-2003
Man Utd	4-0	Aston Villa	06-12-2003
Man Utd	3-1	Man City	13-12-2003
Tottenham	1-2	Man Utd	21-12-2003
Man Utd	3-2	Everton	26-12-2003
Middlesbro	0-1	Man Utd	28-12-2003
Bolton	1-2	Man Utd	07-01-2004
Man Utd	0-0	Newcastle	11-01-2004
Wolves	1-0	Man Utd	17-01-2004
Man Utd	3-2	Soton	31-01-2004
Everton	3-4	Man Utd	07-02-2004
Man Utd	2-3	Middlesbro	11-02-2004
Man Utd	1-1	Leeds	21-02-2004
Fulham	1-1	Man Utd	28-02-2004
Man City	4-1	Man Utd	14-03-2004
Man Utd	3-0	Tottenham	20-03-2004
Arsenal	1-1	Man Utd	28-03-2004
Birmingham	1-2	Man Utd	10-04-2004
Man Utd	1-0	Leicester	13-04-2004
Portsmouth	1-0	Man Utd	17-04-2004
Man Utd	2-0	Charlton	20-04-2004
Man Utd	0-1	Liverpool	24-04-2004
Blackburn	1-0	Man Utd	01-05-2004
Man Utd	1-1	Chelsea	08-05-2004
Aston Villa	0-2	Man Utd	15-05-2004

Cup Games

FACS	Man Utd	1-1	Arsenal		10-08-2003
European Cup	Man Utd	5-0	Panathinaikos		16-09-2003
European Cup	Stuttgart	2-1	Man Utd		01-10-2003
European Cup	Rangers	0-1	Man Utd		22-10-2003
League Cup	Leeds	2-3	Man Utd		28-10-2003
European Cup	Man Utd	3-0	Rangers		04-11-2003
European Cup	Pan'kos	0-1	Man Utd		26-11-2003
League Cup	West Brom	2-0	Man Utd		03-12-2003
European Cup	Man Utd	2-0	Stuttgart		09-12-2003
FA Cup	Aston Villa	1-2	Man Utd		04-01-2004
FA Cup	North'ton	0-3	Man Utd		25-01-2004
FA Cup	Man Utd	4-2	Man City		14-02-2004
European Cup	Porto	2-1	Man Utd		25-02-2004
FA Cup	Man Utd	2-1	Fulham		06-03-2004
European Cup	Man Utd	1-1	Porto		09-03-2004
FA Cup	Arsenal	0-1	Man Utd		03-04-2004
FA Cup	Man Utd	3-0	Millwall		22-05-2004

Total

Played	Won	Drawn	Lost	Points
38	23(61 %)	6 (16 %)	9 (24 %)	75

Home

Played	Won	Drawn	Lost	Points
19	12 (63 %)	4 (21 %)	3 (16 %)	40

Away

Played	Won	Drawn	Lost	Points
19	11 (58 %)	2 (11 %)	6 (32 %)	35

Biggest home win

Aug 16th 2003	United	4-0	Bolton Wanderers
Dec 6th 2003	United	4-0	Aston Villa

Biggest home loss

Oct 25th 2003	United	1-3	Fulham

Biggest away win
Sep 27th 2003   Leicester C.   1-4   United

Biggest away loss
Mar 14th 2004   Man City   4-1   United

Highest aggregate score home
Dec 26th 2003   United   3-2   Everton
Jan 3first 2004 United   3-2   Soton
Feb 11th 2004   United   2-3   Middlesbrough

Highest aggregate score away
Feb 7th 2004   Everton   3-4   United

Pos Club	Pld	W	D	L	F	A	GD	Pts
1. Arsenal	38	26	12	0	73	26	47	90
2. Chelsea	38	24	7	7	67	30	37	79
3. MANCHESTER UNITED	38	23	6	9	64	35	29	75
4. Liverpool	38	16	12	10	55	37	18	60
5. Newcastle United	38	13	17	8	52	40	12	56
6. Aston Villa	38	15	11	12	48	44	4	56
7. Charlton Athletic	38	14	11	13	51	51	0	53
8. Bolton Wanderers	38	14	11	13	48	56	-8	53
9. Fulham	38	14	10	14	52	46	6	52
10. Birmingham City	38	12	14	12	43	48	-5	50
11. Middlesbrough	38	13	9	16	44	52	-8	48
12. Soton	38	12	11	15	44	45	-1	47
13. Portsmouth	38	12	9	17	47	54	-7	45
14. Tottenham Hotspur	38	13	6	19	47	57	-10	45
15. Blackburn Rovers	38	12	8	18	51	59	-8	44
16. Manchester City	38	9	14	15	55	54	1	41
17. Everton	38	9	12	17	45	57	-12	39
18. Leicester City	38	6	15	17	48	65	-17	33
19. Leeds United	38	8	9	21	40	79	-39	33
20. Wolverhampton Wanderers	38	7	12	19	38	77	-39	33

2004/05

Chelsea	1-0	Man Utd	15-08-2004
Man Utd	2-1	Norwich	21-08-2004
Blackburn	1-1	Man Utd	28-08-2004
Man Utd	0-0	Everton	30-08-2004
Bolton	2-2	Man Utd	11-09-2004
Man Utd	2-1	Liverpool	20-09-2004
Tottenham	0-1	Man Utd	25-09-2004
Man Utd	1-1	Middlesbro	03-10-2004
Birmingham	0-0	Man Utd	16-10-2004
Man Utd	2-0	Arsenal	24-10-2004
Portsmouth	2-0	Man Utd	30-10-2004
Man Utd	0-0	Man City	07-11-2004
Newcastle	1-3	Man Utd	14-11-2004
Man Utd	2-0	Charlton	20-11-2004
West Brom	0-3	Man Utd	27-11-2004
Man Utd	3-0	Soton	04-12-2004
Fulham	1-1	Man Utd	13-12-2004
Man Utd	5-2	C Palace	18-12-2004
Man Utd	2-0	Bolton	26-12-2004
Aston Villa	0-1	Man Utd	28-12-2004
Middlesbro	0-2	Man Utd	01-01-2005
Man Utd	0-0	Tottenham	04-01-2005
Liverpool	0-1	Man Utd	15-01-2005
Man Utd	3-1	Aston Villa	22-01-2005
Arsenal	2-4	Man Utd	01-02-2005
Man Utd	2-0	Birmingham	05-02-2005
Man City	0-2	Man Utd	13-02-2005
Man Utd	2-1	Portsmouth	26-02-2005
C Palace	0 0	Man Utd	05-03-2005
Man Utd	1-0	Fulham	19-03-2005
Man Utd	0-0	Blackburn	02-04-2005
Norwich	2-0	Man Utd	09-04-2005
Everton	1-0	Man Utd	20-04-2005
Man Utd	2-1	Newcastle	24-04-2005
Charlton	0-4	Man Utd	01-05-2005
Man Utd	1-1	West Brom	07-05-2005
Man Utd	1-3	Chelsea	10-05-2005
Soton	1-2	Man Utd	15-05-2005

Cup Games

FACS	Arsenal	3-1	Man Utd	08-08-2004
European Cup	Din. Buch'st	1-2	Man Utd	11-08-2004
European Cup	Man Utd	3-0	D. Bucharest	25-08-2004
European Cup	Lyon	2-2	Man Utd	15-09-2004
European Cup	Man Utd	6-2	Fenerbahce	28-09-2004
European Cup	Sp. Prague	0-0	Man Utd	19-10-2004
League Cup	Crewe	0-3	Man Utd	26-10-2004
European Cup	Man Utd	4-1	Sparta Prague	03-11-2004
League Cup	Man Utd	2-0	C Palace	10-11-2004
European Cup	Man Utd	2-1	Lyon	23-11-2004
League Cup	Man Utd	1-0	Arsenal	01-12-2004
European Cup	Fenerbahce	3-0	Man Utd	08-12-2004
FA Cup	Man Utd	0-0	Exeter	08-01-2005
League Cup	Chelsea	0-0	Man Utd	12-01-2005
FA Cup	Exeter	0-2	Man Utd	19-01-2005
League Cup	Man Utd	1-2	Chelsea	26-01-2005
FA Cup	Man Utd	3-0	Middlesbro	29-01-2005
FA Cup	Everton	0-2	Man Utd	19-02-2005
European Cup	Man Utd	0-1	Milan	23-02-2005
European Cup	Milan	1-0	Man Utd	08-03-2005
FA Cup	Soton	0-4	Man Utd	12-03-2005
FA Cup	Newcastle	1-4	Man Utd	17-04-2005
FA Cup	Arsenal	0-0	Man Utd	21-05-2005

(Lost 5-4 on pens)

Total

Played	Won	Drawn	Lost	Points
38	22(58 %)	11 (29 %)	5 (13 %)	77

Home

Played	Won	Drawn	Lost	Points
19	12 (63 %)	6 (32 %)	1 (5 %)	42

Away

Played	Won	Drawn	Lost	Points
19	10 (53 %)	5 (26 %)	4 (21 %)	35

Biggest home win

Dec 4th 2004	United	3-0	Soton

STATISTICS 1992-2010

Dec 18th 2004   United   5-2   Crystal Palace

Biggest home loss
May 10th 2005   United   1-3   Chelsea

Biggest away win
May first 2005   Charlton Ath   0-4   United

Biggest away loss
Oct 30th 2004   Portsmouth   2-0   United
Apr 9th 2005   Norwich City   2-0   United

Highest aggregate score home
Dec 18th 2004   United   5-2   Crystal Palace

Highest aggregate score away
Feb first 2005   Arsenal   2-4   United

Pos	Club	Pld	W	D	L	F	A	GD	Pts
1.	Chelsea	38	29	8	1	72	15	57	95
2.	Arsenal	38	25	8	5	87	36	51	83
3.	MANCHESTER UNITED	38	22	11	5	58	26	32	77
4.	Everton	38	18	7	13	45	46	-1	61
5.	Liverpool	38	17	7	14	52	41	11	58
6.	Bolton Wanderers	38	16	10	12	49	44	5	58
7.	Middlesbrough	38	14	13	11	53	46	7	55
8.	Manchester City	38	13	13	12	47	39	8	52
9.	Tottenham Hotspur	38	14	10	14	47	41	6	52
10.	Aston Villa	38	12	11	15	45	52	-7	47
11.	Charlton Athletic	38	12	10	16	42	58	-16	46
12.	Birmingham City	38	11	12	15	40	46	-6	45
13.	Fulham	38	12	8	18	52	60	-8	44
14.	Newcastle United	38	10	14	14	47	57	-10	44
15.	Blackburn Rovers	38	9	15	14	32	43	-11	42
16.	Portsmouth	38	10	9	19	43	59	-16	39
17.	West Bromwich Albion	38	6	16	16	36	61	-25	34
18.	Crystal Palace	38	7	12	19	41	62	-21	33
19.	Norwich City	38	7	12	19	42	77	-35	33
20.	Soton	38	6	14	18	45	66	-21	32

2005/06

Everton	0-2	Man Utd	13-08-2005
Man Utd	1-0	Aston Villa	20-08-2005
Newcastle	0-2	Man Utd	28-08-2005
Man Utd	1-1	Man City	10-09-2005
Liverpool	0-0	Man Utd	18-09-2005
Man Utd	1-2	Blackburn	24-09-2005
Fulham	2-3	Man Utd	01-10-2005
Sunderland	1-3	Man Utd	15-10-2005
Man Utd	1-1	Tottenham	22-10-2005
Middlesbro	4-1	Man Utd	29-10-2005
Man Utd	1-0	Chelsea	06-11-2005
Charlton	1-3	Man Utd	19-11-2005
West Ham	1-2	Man Utd	27-11-2005
Man Utd	3-0	Portsmouth	03-12-2005
Man Utd	1-1	Everton	11-12-2005
Man Utd	4-0	Wigan	14-12-2005
Aston Villa	0-2	Man Utd	17-12-2005
Man Utd	3-0	West Brom	26-12-2005
Birmingham	2-2	Man Utd	28-12-2005
Man Utd	4-1	Bolton	31-12-2005
Arsenal	0-0	Man Utd	03-01-2006
Man City	3-1	Man Utd	14-01-2006
Man Utd	1-0	Liverpool	22-01-2006
Blackburn	4-3	Man Utd	01-02-2006
Man Utd	4-2	Fulham	04-02-2006
Portsmouth	1-3	Man Utd	11-02-2006
Wigan	1-2	Man Utd	06-03-2006
Man Utd	2-0	Newcastle	12-03-2006
West Brom	1-2	Man Utd	18-03-2006
Man Utd	3-0	Birmingham	26-03-2006
Man Utd	1-0	West Ham	29-03-2006
Bolton	1-2	Man Utd	01-04-2006
Man Utd	2-0	Arsenal	09-04-2006
Man Utd	0-0	Sunderland	14-04-2006
Tottenham	1-2	Man Utd	17-04-2006
Chelsea	3-0	Man Utd	29-04-2006
Man Utd	0-0	Middlesbro	01-05-2006
Man Utd	4-0	Charlton	07-05-2006

Cup Games

European Cup	Man Utd	3-0	Debrecen	09-08-2005
European Cup	Debrecen	0-3	Man Utd	24-08-2005
European Cup	Villarreal	0-0	Man Utd	14-09-2005
European Cup	Man Utd	2-1	Benfica	27-09-2005
European Cup	Man Utd	0-0	Lille	18-10-2005
League Cup	Man Utd	4-1	Barnet	26-10-2005
European Cup	Lille	1-0	Man Utd	02-11-2005
European Cup	Man Utd	0-0	Villarreal	22-11-2005
League Cup	Man Utd	3-1	West Brom	30-11-2005
European Cup	Benfica	2-1	Man Utd	07-12-2005
League Cup	Birmingham	1-3	Man Utd	20-12-2005
FA Cup	Burton	0-0	Man Utd	08-01-2006
League Cup	Blackburn	1-1	Man Utd	11-01-2006
FA Cup	Man Utd	5-0	Burton	18-01-2006
League Cup	Man Utd	2-1	Blackburn	25-01-2006
FA Cup	Wolves	0-3	Man Utd	29-01-2006
FA Cup	Liverpool	1-0	Man Utd	18-02-2006
League Cup	Man Utd	4-0	Wigan	26-02-2006

Total

Played	Won	Drawn	Lost	Points
38	25(66 %)	8 (21 %)	5 (13 %)	83

Home

Played	Won	Drawn	Lost	Points
19	13 (68 %)	5 (26 %)	1 (5 %)	44

Away

Played	Won	Drawn	Lost	Points
19	12 (63 %)	3 (16 %)	4 (21 %)	39

Biggest home win

Dec 14th 2005	United	4-0	Wigan Athletic
May 7th 2006	United	4-0	Charlton Athletic

Biggest home loss

Sep 24th 2005	United	1-2	Blackburn Rovers

211

Biggest away win

Aug 13th 2005	Everton	0-2	United
Aug 28th 2005	United	0-2	United
Oct 15th 2005	Sunderland	1-3	United
Nov 19th 2005	Charlton Ath	1-3	United
Dec 17th 2005	Aston Villa	0-2	United
Feb 11th 2006	Portsmouth	1-3	United

Biggest away loss

| Oct 29th 2005 | Middlesbro | 4-1 | United |
| Apr 29th 2006 | Chelsea | 3-0 | United |

Highest aggregate score home

| Feb 4th 2006 | United | 4-2 | Fulham |

Highest aggregate score away

| Feb first 2006 | Blackburn R. | 4-3 | United |

Pos	Club	Pld	W	D	L	F	A	GD	Pts
1.	Chelsea	38	29	4	5	72	22	50	91
2.	Manchester United	38	25	8	5	72	34	38	83
3.	Liverpool	38	25	7	6	57	25	32	82
4.	Arsenal	38	20	7	11	68	31	37	67
5.	Tottenham Hotspur	38	18	11	9	53	38	15	65
6.	Blackburn Rovers	38	19	6	13	51	42	9	63
7.	Newcastle United	38	17	7	14	47	42	5	58
8.	Bolton Wanderers	38	15	11	12	49	41	8	56
9.	West Ham United	38	16	7	15	52	55	-3	55
10.	Wigan Athletic	38	15	6	17	45	52	-7	51
11.	Everton	38	14	8	16	34	49	-15	50
12.	Fulham	38	14	6	18	48	58	-10	48
13.	Charlton Athletic	38	13	8	17	41	55	-14	47
14.	Middlesbrough	38	12	9	17	48	58	-10	45
15.	Manchester City	38	13	4	21	43	48	-5	43
16.	Aston Villa	38	10	12	16	42	55	-13	42
17.	Portsmouth	38	10	8	20	37	62	-25	38
18.	Birmingham City	38	8	10	20	28	50	-22	34
19.	West Bromwich Albion	38	7	9	22	31	58	-27	30
20.	Sunderland	38	3	6	29	26	69	-43	15

2006/07

Man Utd	5-1	Fulham	20-08-2006
Charlton	0-3	Man Utd	23-08-2006
Watford	1-2	Man Utd	26-08-2006
Man Utd	1-0	Tottenham	09-09-2006
Man Utd	0-1	Arsenal	17-09-2006
Reading	1-1	Man Utd	23-09-2006
Man Utd	2-0	Newcastle	01-10-2006
Wigan	1-3	Man Utd	14-10-2006
Man Utd	2-0	Liverpool	22-10-2006
Bolton	0-4	Man Utd	28-10-2006
Man Utd	3-0	Portsmouth	04-11-2006
Blackburn	0-1	Man Utd	11-11-2006
Sheff Utd	1-2	Man Utd	18-11-2006
Man Utd	1-1	Chelsea	26-11-2006
Man Utd	3-0	Everton	29-11-2006
Middlesbro	1-2	Man Utd	02-12-2006
Man Utd	3-1	Man City	09-12-2006
West Ham	1-0	Man Utd	17-12-2006
Aston Villa	0-3	Man Utd	23-12-2006
Man Utd	3-1	Wigan	26-12-2006
Man Utd	3-2	Reading	30-12-2006
Newcastle	2-2	Man Utd	01-01-2007
Man Utd	3-1	Aston Villa	13-01-2007
Arsenal	2-1	Man Utd	21-01-2007
Man Utd	4-0	Watford	31-01-2007
Tottenham	0-4	Man Utd	04-02-2007
Man Utd	2-0	Charlton	10-02-2007
Fulham	1-2	Man Utd	24-02-2007
Liverpool	0-1	Man Utd	03-03-2007
Man Utd	4-1	Bolton	17-03-2007
Man Utd	4-1	Blackburn	31-03-2007
Portsmouth	2-1	Man Utd	07-04-2007
Man Utd	2-0	Sheff Utd	17-04-2007
Man Utd	1-1	Middlesbro	21-04-2007
Everton	2-4	Man Utd	28-04-2007
Man City	0-1	Man Utd	05-05-2007
Chelsea	0-0	Man Utd	09-05-2007
Man Utd	0-1	West Ham	13-05-2007

Cup Games

European Cup	Man Utd	3-2	Celtic	13-09-2006
European Cup	Benfica	0-1	Man Utd	26-09-2006
European Cup	Man Utd	3-0	FC Cop'hagen	17-10-2006
League Cup	Crewe	1-2	Man Utd	25-10-2006
European Cup	FC Cop'gen	1-0	Man Utd	01-11-2006
League Cup	Southend	1-0	Man Utd	07-11-2006
European Cup	Celtic	1-0	Man Utd	21-11-2006
European Cup	Man Utd	3-1	Benfica	06-12-2006
FA Cup	Man Utd	2-1	Aston Villa	07-01-2007
FA Cup	Man Utd	2-1	Portsmouth	27-01-2007
FA Cup	Man Utd	1-1	Reading	17-02-2007
European Cup	Lille	0-1	Man Utd	20-02-2007
FA Cup	Reading	2-3	Man Utd	27-02-2007
European Cup	Man Utd	1-0	Lille	07-03-2007
FA Cup	Middlesbro	2-2	Man Utd	10-03-2007
FA Cup	Man Utd	1-0	Middlesbro	19-03-2007
European Cup	AS Roma	2-1	Man Utd	04-04-2007
European Cup	Man Utd	7-1	AS Roma	10-04-2007
FA Cup	Watford	1-4	Man Utd	14-04-2007
European Cup	Man Utd	3-2	Milan	24-04-2007
European Cup	Milan	3-0	Man Utd	02-05-2007
FA Cup	Chelsea	1-0	Man Utd	19-05-2007

Total

Played	Won	Drawn	Lost	Points
38	28(74 %)	5 (13 %)	5 (13 %)	89

Home

Played	Won	Drawn	Lost	Points
19	15 (79 %)	2 (11 %)	2 (11 %)	47

Away

Played	Won	Drawn	Lost	Points
19	13 (68 %)	3 (16 %)	3 (16 %)	42

Biggest home win

Aug 20th 2006	United	5-1	Fulham
Jan 3first 2007	United	4-0	Watford

Biggest home loss
Sep 17th 2006	United	0-1	Arsenal
May 13th 2007	United	0-1	West Ham United

Biggest away win
Oct 28th 2006	Bolton W	0-4	United
Feb 4th 2007	Tottenham H	0-4	United

Biggest away loss
Dec 17th 2006	West Ham U	1-0	United
Jan 2first 2007	Arsenal	2-1	United
Apr 7th 2007	Portsmouth	2-1	United

Highest aggregate score home
Aug 20th 2006	United	5-1	Fulham

Highest aggregate score away
Apr 28th 2007	Everton	2-4	United

Pos	Club	Pld	W	D	L	F	A	GD	Pts
1.	Manchester United	38	28	5	5	83	27	56	89
2.	Chelsea	38	24	11	3	64	24	40	83
3.	Liverpool	38	20	8	10	57	27	30	68
4.	Arsenal	38	19	11	8	63	35	28	68
5.	Tottenham Hotspur	38	17	9	12	57	54	3	60
6.	Everton	38	15	13	10	52	36	16	58
7.	Bolton Wanderers	38	16	8	14	47	52	-5	56
8.	Reading	38	16	7	15	52	47	5	55
9.	Portsmouth	38	14	12	12	45	42	3	54
10.	Blackburn Rovers	38	15	7	16	52	54	-2	52
11.	Aston Villa	38	11	17	10	43	41	2	50
12.	Middlesbrough	38	12	10	16	44	49	-5	46
13.	Newcastle United	38	11	10	17	38	47	-9	43
14.	Manchester City	38	11	9	18	29	44	-15	42
15.	West Ham United	38	12	5	21	35	59	-24	41
16.	Fulham	38	8	15	15	38	60	-22	39
17.	Wigan Athletic	38	10	8	20	37	59	-22	38
18.	Sheffield United	38	10	8	20	32	55	-23	38
19.	Charlton Athletic	38	8	10	20	34	60	-26	34
20.	Watford	38	5	13	20	29	59	-30	28

2007/08

Man Utd	0-0	Reading	12-08-2007
Portsmouth	1-1	Man Utd	15-08-2007
Man City	1-0	Man Utd	19-08-2007
Man Utd	1-0	Tottenham	26-08-2007
Man Utd	1-0	Sunderland	01-09-2007
Everton	0-1	Man Utd	15-09-2007
Man Utd	2-0	Chelsea	23-09-2007
Birmingham	0-1	Man Utd	29-09-2007
Man Utd	4-0	Wigan	06-10-2007
Aston Villa	1-4	Man Utd	20-10-2007
Man Utd	4-1	Middlesbro	27-10-2007
Arsenal	2-2	Man Utd	03-11-2007
Man Utd	2-0	Blackburn	11-11-2007
Bolton	1-0	Man Utd	24-11-2007
Man Utd	2-0	Fulham	03-12-2007
Man Utd	4-1	Derby	08-12-2007
Liverpool	0-1	Man Utd	16-12-2007
Man Utd	2-1	Everton	23-12-2007
Sunderland	0-4	Man Utd	26-12-2007
West Ham	2-1	Man Utd	29-12-2007
Man Utd	1-0	Birmingham	01-01-2008
Man Utd	6-0	Newcastle	12-01-2008
Reading	0-2	Man Utd	19-01-2008
Man Utd	2-0	Portsmouth	30-01-2008
Tottenham	1-1	Man Utd	02-02-2008
Man Utd	1-2	Man City	10-02-2008
Newcastle	1-5	Man Utd	23-02-2008
Fulham	0-3	Man Utd	01-03-2008
Derby	0-1	Man Utd	15-03-2008
Man Utd	2-0	Bolton	19-03-2008
Man Utd	3-0	Liverpool	23-03-2008
Man Utd	4-0	Aston Villa	29-03-2008
Middlesbro	2-2	Man Utd	06-04-2008
Man Utd	2-1	Arsenal	13-04-2008
Blackburn	1-1	Man Utd	19-04-2008
Chelsea	2-1	Man Utd	26-04-2008
Man Utd	4-1	West Ham	03-05-2008
Wigan	0-2	Man Utd	11-05-2008

Cup Games

FACS	Chelsea	1-1	Man Utd	05-08-2007
European Cup	Sp. Lisbon	0-1	Man Utd	19-09-2007
League Cup	Man Utd	0-2	Coventry	26-09-2007
European Cup	Man Utd	1-0	Roma	02-10-2007
European Cup	D. Kiev	2-4	Man Utd	23-10-2007
European Cup	Man Utd	4-0	D. Kiev	07-11-2007
European Cup	Man Utd	2-1	S. Lisbon	27-11-2007
European Cup	Roma	1-1	Man Utd	12-12-2007
FA Cup	Aston Villa	0-2	Man Utd	05-01-2008
FA Cup	Man Utd	3-1	Tottenham	27-01-2008
FA Cup	Man Utd	4-0	Arsenal	16-02-2008
European Cup	Lyon	1-1	Man Utd	20-02-2008
European Cup	Man Utd	1-0	Lyon	04-03-2008
FA Cup	Man Utd	0-1	Portsmouth	08-03-2008
European Cup	Roma	0-2	Man Utd	01-04-2008
European Cup	Man Utd	1-0	Roma	09-04-2008
European Cup	Barcelona	0-0	Man Utd	23-04-2008
European Cup	Man Utd	1-0	Barcelona	29-04-2008
European Cup	Man Utd	1-1	Chelsea	21-05-2008

won 6-5 on pens

Total

Played	Won	Drawn	Lost	Points
38	27(71 %)	6 (16 %)	5 (13 %)	87

Home

Played	Won	Drawn	Lost	Points
19	17 (89 %)	1 (5 %)	1 (5 %)	52

Away

Played	Won	Drawn	Lost	Points
19	10 (53 %)	5 (26 %)	4 (21 %)	35

Biggest home win

Jan 12th 2008	United	6-0	Newcastle United

Biggest home loss

Feb 10th 2008	United	1-2	Manchester City

Biggest away win

| Dec 26th 2007 | Sunderland | 0-4 | United |
| Feb 23rd 2008 | Newcastle U | 1-5 | United |

Biggest away loss

Aug 19th 2007	Man City	1-0	United
Nov 24th 2007	Bolton W	1-0	United
Dec 29th 2007	West Ham U	2-1	United
Apr 26th 2008	Chelsea	2-1	United

Highest aggregate score home

| Jan 12th 2008 | United | 6-0 | Newcastle United |

Highest aggregate score away

| Feb 23rd 2008 | Newcastle U | 1-5 | United |

Pos	Club	Pld	W	D	L	F	A	GD	Pts
1.	MANCHESTER UNITED	38	27	6	5	80	22	58	87
2.	Chelsea	38	25	10	3	65	26	39	85
3.	Arsenal	38	24	11	3	74	31	43	83
4.	Liverpool	38	21	13	4	67	28	39	76
5.	Everton	38	19	8	11	55	33	22	65
6.	Aston Villa	38	16	12	10	71	51	20	60
7.	Blackburn Rovers	38	15	13	10	50	48	2	58
8.	Portsmouth	38	16	9	13	48	40	8	57
9.	Manchester City	38	15	10	13	45	53	-8	55
10.	West Ham United	38	13	10	15	42	50	-8	49
11.	Tottenham Hotspur	38	11	13	14	66	61	5	46
12.	Newcastle United	38	11	10	17	45	65	-20	43
13.	Middlesbrough	38	10	12	16	43	53	-10	42
14.	Wigan Athletic	38	10	10	18	34	51	-17	40
15.	Sunderland	38	11	6	21	36	59	-23	39
16.	Bolton Wanderers	38	9	10	19	36	54	-18	37
17.	Fulham	38	8	12	18	38	60	-22	36
18.	Reading	38	10	6	22	41	66	-25	36
19.	Birmingham City	38	8	11	19	46	62	-16	35
20.	Derby County	38	1	8	29	20	89	-69	11

2008/09

Man Utd	1-1	Newcastle	17-08-2008
Portsmouth	0-1	Man Utd	25-08-2008
Liverpool	2-1	Man Utd	13-09-2008
Chelsea	1-1	Man Utd	21-09-2008
Man Utd	2-0	Bolton	27-09-2008
Blackburn	0-2	Man Utd	04-10-2008
Man Utd	4-0	West Brom	18-10-2008
Everton	1-1	Man Utd	25-10-2008
Man Utd	2-0	West Ham	29-10-2008
Man Utd	4-3	Hull	01-11-2008
Arsenal	2-1	Man Utd	08-11-2008
Man Utd	5-0	Stoke	15-11-2008
Aston Villa	0-0	Man Utd	22-11-2008
Man City	0-1	Man Utd	30-11-2008
Man Utd	1-0	Sunderland	06-12-2008
Tottenham	0-0	Man Utd	13-12-2008
Stoke	0-1	Man Utd	26-12-2008
Man Utd	1-0	Middlesbro	29-12-2008
Man Utd	3-0	Chelsea	11-01-2009
Man Utd	1-0	Wigan	14-01-2009
Bolton	0-1	Man Utd	17-01-2009
West Brom	0-5	Man Utd	27-01-2009
Man Utd	1-0	Everton	31-01-2009
West Ham	0-1	Man Utd	08-02-2009
Man Utd	3-0	Fulham	18-02-2009
Man Utd	2-1	Blackburn	21-02-2009
Newcastle	1-2	Man Utd	04-03-2009
Man Utd	1-4	Liverpool	14-03-2009
Fulham	2-0	Man Utd	21-03-2009
Man Utd	3-2	Aston Villa	05-04-2009
Sunderland	1-2	Man Utd	11-04-2009
Man Utd	2-0	Portsmouth	22-04-2009
Man Utd	5-2	Tottenham	25-04-2009
Middlesbro	0-2	Man Utd	02-05-2009
Man Utd	2-0	Man City	10-05-2009
Wigan	1-2	Man Utd	13-05-2009
Man Utd	0-0	Arsenal	16-05-2009
Hull	0-1	Man Utd	24-05-2009

Cup Games

FACS	Man Utd	0-0	Portsmouth	10-08-2008
European SC	Man Utd	1-2	Zenit	29-08-2008
European Cup	Man Utd	0-0	Villarreal	17-09-2008
League Cup	Man Utd	3-1	Middlesbro	23-09-2008
European Cup	Aalborg	0-3	Man Utd	30-09-2008
European Cup	Man Utd	3-0	Celtic	21-10-2008
European Cup	Celtic	1-1	Man Utd	05-11-2008
League Cup	Man Utd	1-0	QPR	11-11-2008
European Cup	Villarreal	0-0	Man Utd	25-11-2008
League Cup	Man Utd	5-3	Blackburn	03-12-2008
European Cup	Man Utd	2-2	Aalborg	10-12-2008
FIFA Club	G. Osaka	3-5	Man Utd	18-12-2008
FIFA Club	Man Utd	1-0	LDU Quito	21-12-2008
FA Cup	Sot'on	0-3	Man Utd	04-01-2009
League Cup	Derby	1-0	Man Utd	07-01-2009
League Cup	Man Utd	4-2	Derby	20-01-2009
FA Cup	Man Utd	2-1	Tottenham	24-01-2009
FA Cup	Derby	1-4	Man Utd	15-02-2009
European Cup	Inter	0-0	Man Utd	24-02-2009
League Cup	Man Utd	0-0	Tottenham	01-03-2009
FA Cup	Fulham	0-4	Man Utd	07-03-2009
European Cup	Man Utd	2-0	Inter	11-03-2009
European Cup	Man Utd	2-2	Porto	07-04-2009
European Cup	Porto	0-1	Man Utd	15-04-2009
FA Cup	Man Utd	0-0	Everton	19-04-2009
European Cup	Man Utd	1-0	Arsenal	29-04-2009
European Cup	Arsenal	1-3	Man Utd	05-05-2009
European Cup	Barcelona	2-0	Man Utd	27-05-2009

Total

Played	Won	Drawn	Lost	Points
38	28(74 %)	6 (16 %)	4 (11 %)	90

Home

Played	Won	Drawn	Lost	Points
19	16 (84 %)	2 (11 %)	1 (5 %)	50

Away

Played	Won	Drawn	Lost	Points
19	12 (63 %)	4 (21 %)	3 (16 %)	40

Biggest home win
Nov 15th 2008   United   5-0   Stoke City

Biggest home loss
Mar 14th 2009   United   1-4   Liverpool

Biggest away win
Jan 27th 2009   WBA   0-5   United

Biggest away loss
Mar 2first 2009   Fulham   2-0   United

Highest aggregate score home
Nov first 2008   United   4-3   Hull City
Apr 25th 2009   United   5-2   Tottenham Hotspur

Highest aggregate score away
Jan 27th 2009   WBA   0-5   United

Pos	Club	PLD	W	D	L	F	A	GD	Pts
1.	MANCHESTER UNITED	38	28	6	4	68	24	44	90
2.	Liverpool	38	25	11	2	77	27	50	86
3.	Chelsea	38	25	8	5	68	24	44	83
4.	Arsenal	38	20	12	6	68	37	31	72
5.	Everton	38	17	12	9	55	37	18	63
6.	Aston Villa	38	17	11	10	54	48	6	62
7.	Fulham	38	14	11	13	39	34	5	53
8.	Tottenham Hotspur	38	14	9	15	45	45	0	51
9.	West Ham United	38	14	9	15	42	45	-3	51
10.	Manchester City	38	15	5	18	58	50	8	50
11.	Wigan Athletic	38	12	9	17	34	45	-11	45
12.	Stoke City	38	12	9	17	38	55	-17	45
13.	Bolton Wanderers	38	11	8	19	41	53	-12	41
14.	Portsmouth	38	10	11	17	38	57	-19	41
15.	Blackburn Rovers	38	10	11	17	40	60	-20	41
16.	Sunderland	38	9	9	20	34	54	-20	36
17.	Hull City	38	8	11	19	39	64	-25	35
18.	Newcastle United	38	7	13	18	40	59	-19	34
19.	Middlesbrough	38	7	11	20	28	57	-29	32
20.	West Bromwich Albion	38	8	8	22	36	67	-31	32

2009/10

Man Utd	1-0	Birmingham	16-08-2009
Burnley	1-0	Man Utd	19-08-2009
Wigan	0-5	Man Utd	22-08-2009
Man Utd	2-1	Arsenal	29-08-2009
Tottenham	1-3	Man Utd	12-09-2009
Man Utd	4-3	Man City	20-09-2009
Stoke	0-2	Man Utd	26-09-2009
Man Utd	2-2	Sunderland	03-10-2009
Man Utd	2-1	Bolton	17-10-2009
Liverpool	2-0	Man Utd	25-10-2009
Man Utd	2-0	Blackburn	31-10-2009
Chelsea	1-0	Man Utd	08-11-2009
Man Utd	3-0	Everton	21-11-2009
Portsmouth	1-4	Man Utd	28-11-2009
West Ham	0-4	Man Utd	05-12-2009
Man Utd	0-1	Aston Villa	12-12-2009
Man Utd	3-0	Wolves	15-12-2009
Fulham	3-0	Man Utd	19-12-2009
Hull	1-3	Man Utd	27-12-2009
Man Utd	5-0	Wigan	30-12-2009
Birmingham	1-1	Man Utd	09-01-2010
Man Utd	3-0	Burnley	16-01-2010
Man Utd	4-0	Hull	23-01-2010
Arsenal	1-3	Man Utd	31-01-2010
Man Utd	5-0	Portsmouth	06-02-2010
Aston Villa	1-1	Man Utd	10-02-2010
Everton	3-1	Man Utd	20-02-2010
Man Utd	3-0	West Ham	23-02-2010
Wolves	0-1	Man Utd	06-03-2010
Man Utd	3-0	Fulham	14-03-2010
Man Utd	2-1	Liverpool	21-03-2010
Bolton	0-4	Man Utd	27-03-2010
Man Utd	1-2	Chelsea	03-04-2010
Blackburn	0-0	Man Utd	11-04-2010
Man City	0-1	Man Utd	17-04-2010
Man Utd	3-1	Tottenham	24-04-2010
Sunderland	0-1	Man Utd	02-05-2010
Man Utd	4-0	Stoke	09-05-2010

Cup Games

FA CS	Chelsea	2-2	Man Utd	09-08-2009
European Cup	Besiktas	0-1	Man Utd	15-09-2009
League Cup	Man Utd	1-0	Wolves	23-09-2009
European Cup	Man Utd	2-1	Wolfsburg	30-09-2009
European Cup	CSKA Mosc.	0-1	Man Utd	21-10-2009
League Cup	Barnsley	0-2	Man Utd	27-10-2009
European Cup	Man Utd	3-3	CSKA Mosc.	03-11-2009
European Cup	Man Utd	0-1	Besiktas	25-11-2009
League Cup	Man Utd	2-0	Tottenham	01-12-2009
European Cup	Wolfsburg	1-3	Man Utd	08-12-2009
FA Cup	Man Utd	0-1	Leeds	03-01-2010
League Cup	Man City	2-1	Man Utd	19-01-2010
League Cup	Man Utd	3-1	Man City	27-01-2010
European Cup	Milan	2-3	Man Utd	16-02-2010
League Cup	Aston Villa	1-2	Man Utd	28-02-2010
European Cup	Man Utd	4-0	Milan	10-03-2010
European Cup	B. Munich	2-1	Man Utd	30-03-2010
European Cup	Man Utd	3-2	B. Munich	07-04-2010

Total

Played	Won	Drawn	Lost	Points
38	27 (71 %)	4 (11 %)	7 (18 %)	85

Home

Played	Won	Drawn	Lost	Points
19	16 (84 %)	1 (5 %)	2 (11 %)	49

Away

Played	Won	Drawn	Lost	Points
19	11 (58 %)	3 (16 %)	5 (26 %)	36

Biggest home win

Dec 30th 2009	United	5-0	Wigan Athletic
Feb 6th 2010	United	5-0	Portsmouth

Biggest home loss

| Dec 12th 2009 | United | 0-1 | Aston Villa |
| Apr 3rd 2010 | United | 1-2 | Chelsea |

Biggest away win

| Aug 22nd 2009 | Wigan Ath | 0-5 | United |

Biggest away loss

| Dec 19th 2009 | Fulham | 3-0 | United |

Highest aggregate score home

| Sep 20th 2009 | United | 4-3 | Manchester City |

Highest aggregate score away

| Aug 22nd 2009 | Wigan Ath | 0-5 | United |
| Nov 28th 2009 | Portsmouth | 1-4 | United |

	Club	Pld	W	D	L	F	A	GD	Pts
1	Chelsea	38	27	5	6	103	32	71	86
2	MANCHESTER UNITED	38	27	4	7	86	28	58	85
3	Arsenal	38	23	6	9	83	41	42	75
4	Tottenham Hotspur	38	21	7	10	67	41	26	70
5	Manchester City	38	18	13	7	73	45	28	67
6	Aston Villa	38	17	13	8	52	39	13	64
7	Liverpool	38	18	9	11	61	35	26	63
8	Everton	38	16	13	9	60	49	11	61
9	Birmingham City	38	13	11	14	38	47	-9	50
10	Blackburn Rovers	38	13	11	14	41	55	-14	50
11	Stoke City	38	11	14	13	34	48	-14	47
12	Fulham	38	12	10	16	39	46	-7	46
13	Sunderland	38	11	11	16	48	56	-8	44
14	Bolton	38	10	9	19	42	67	-25	39
15	Wolverhampton	38	9	11	18	32	56	-24	38
16	Wigan Athletic	38	9	9	20	37	79	-42	36
17	West Ham United	38	8	11	19	47	66	-19	35
18	Burnley	38	8	6	24	42	82	-40	30
19	Hull City	38	6	12	20	34	75	-41	30
20	Portsmouth	38	7	7	24	34	66	-32	18

Portsmouth deducted 10 points

For All of Premiership Seasons ...

Total

Played	Won	Drawn	Lost	Points
696	449(65 %)	147 (21 %)	100 (14 %)	1494

Home

Played	Won	Drawn	Lost	Points
348	256 (74 %)	63 (18 %)	29 (8 %)	831

Away

Played	Won	Drawn	Lost	Points
348	193 (55 %)	84 (24 %)	71 (20 %)	663

Biggest home win

Mar 4th 1995	United	9-0	Ipswich Town

Biggest home loss

Aug 19th 1992	United	0-3	Everton
Dec first 2001	United	0-3	Chelsea
Mar 14th 2009	United	1-4	Liverpool

Biggest away win

Feb 6th 1999	Notts Forest	1-8	United

Biggest away loss

Oct 20th 1996	Newcastle U	5-0	United
Oct 3rd 1999	Chelsea	5-0	United

Highest aggregate score home

Mar 4th 1995	United	9-0	Ipswich Town

Highest aggregate score away

Oct 26th 1996	Soton	6-3	United
Feb 6th 1999	Notts Forest	1-8	United

MANCHESTER UNITED HONOURS

FOOTBALL LEAGUE CHAMPIONS (18)

1908, 1911, 1952, 1956 ,1957, 1965, 1967, 1993, 1994, 1996,
1997, 1999, 2000, 2001, 2003, 2007, 2008, 2009

FA CUP (11)

1909, 1948, 1963, 1977, 1983, 1985, 1990, 1994, 1996, 1999,
2004

FOOTBALL LEAGUE CUP (4)

1992, 2006, 2009, 2010

FA CHARITY / COMMUNITY SHIELD (17)

1908, 1911, 1952, 1956, 1957, 1965, 1967, 1977, 1983, 1990,
1993, 1994, 1996, 1997, 2003, 2007, 2008

EUROPEAN CUP (3)

1968, 1999, 2008

INTERCONTINENTAL CUP (1)

1999

FIFA CLUB WORLD CUP (1)

2008

UEFA SUPER CUP (1)

1991

EUROPEAN CUP WINNERS' CUP (1)

1991

THE MANCHESTER DERBY

HEAD TO HEAD

	Utd wins	draws	City wins
LEAGUE	57	48	37
FA CUP	4	0	2
LGE CUP	2	1	3
OTHER	1	0	0
TOTAL	**64**	**49**	**42**

League matches unless stated

2009/2010
Premier League	City	0-1	United	17-04-2010
League Cup	United	3-1	City	27-01-2010
League Cup	City	2-1	United	19-01-2010
Premier League	United	4-3	City	20-09-2009

2008/2009
Premier League	United	2-0	City	10-05-2009
Premier League	City	0 1	United	30-11-2008

2007/2008
Premier League	United	1-2	City	10-02-2008
Premier League	City	1-0	United	19-08-2007

2006/2007
Premier League	City	0-1	United	05-05-2007
Premier League	United	3-1	City	09-12-2006

2005/2006

Premier League	City	3-1	United	14-01-2006
Premier League	United	1-1	City	10-09-2005

2004/2005

Premier League	City	0-2	United	13-02-2005
Premier League	United	0-0	City	07-11-2004

2003/2004

Premier League	City	4-1	United	14-03-2004
FA Cup	United	4-2	City	14-02-2004
Premier League	United	3-1	City	13-12-2003

2002/2003

Premier League	United	1-1	City	09-02-2003
Premier League	City	3-1	United	09-11-2002

2000/2001

Premier League	United	1-1	City	21-04-2001
Premier League	City	0-1	United	18-11-2000

1995/1996

Premier League	City	2-3	United	06-04-1996
FA Cup	United	2-1	City	18-02-1996
Premier League	United	1-0	City	14-10-1995

1994/1995

Premier League	City	0-3	United	11-02-1995
Premier League	United	5-0	City	10-11-1994

1993/1994

Premier League	United	2-0	City	23-04-1994
Premier League	City	2-3	United	07-11-1993

1992/1993

Premier League	City	1-1	United	20-03-1993
Premier League	United	2-1	City	06-12-1992

1991/1992

Division One	United	1-1	City	07-04-1992
Division One	City	0-0	United	16-11-1991

1990/1991

Division One	United	1-0	City	04-05-1991
Division One	City	3-3	United	27-10-1990

1989/1990

Division One	United	1-1	City	03-02-1990
Division One	City	5-1	United	23-09-1989

1986/1987

Division One	United	2-0	City	07-03-1987
FA Cup	United	1-0	City	10-01-1987
Division 1 (old)	City	1-1	United	26-10-1986

1985/1986

Division One	United	2-2	City	22-03-1986
Division One	City	0-3	United	14-09-1985

1982/1983

Division One	City	1-2	United	05-03-1983
Division One	United	2-2	City	23-10-1982

1981/1982

Division One	United	1-1	City	27-02-1982
Division One	City	0-0	United	10-10-1981

1980/1981

Division One	City	1-0	United	21-02-1981
Division One	United	2-2	City	27-09-1980

1979/1980

Division One	United	1-0	City	22-03-1980
Division One	City	2-0	United	10-11-1979

1978/1979

Division One	City	0-3	United	10-02-1979
Division One	United	1-0	City	30-09-1978

1977/1978

Division One	United	2-2	City	15-03-1978
Division One	City	3-1	United	10-09-1977

1976/1977

Division One	United	3-1	City	05-03-1977
Division One	City	1-3	United	25-09-1976

1975/1976

Division One	United	2-0	City	04-05-1976
Division One	City	2-2	United	27-09-1975
League Cup	City	4-0	United	12-11-1975

1974/1975

League Cup	United	1-0	City	27-04-74

1973/1974

Division One	United	0-1	City	27-04-1974
Division One	City	0-0	United	13-03-1974

1972/1973

Division One	United	0-0	City	21-04-1973
Division One	City	3-0	United	18-11-1972

1971/1972

Division One	United	1- 3	City	12-04-1972
Division One	City	3-3	United	06-11-1971

1970/1971

| Division One | City | 3-4 | United | 05-05-1971 |
| Division One | United | 1-4 | City | 12-12-1970 |

1969/1970

Division One	United	1-2	City	28-03-1970
FA Cup	United	3-0	City	24-01-1970
League Cup	United	2-2	City	17-12-1969
League Cup	City	2-1	United	03-12-1969
Division One	City	4-0	United	15-11-1969

1968/1969

| Division One | United | 0-1 | City | 08-03-1969 |
| Division One | City | 0-0 | United | 17-08-1968 |

1967/1968

| Division One | United | 1-3 | City | 27-03-1968 |
| Division One | City | 1-2 | United | 30-09-1967 |

1966/1967

| Division One | City | 1-1 | United | 21-01-1967 |
| Division One | United | 1-0 | City | 17-09-1966 |

1962/1963

| Division One | City | 1-1 | United | 15-05-1963 |
| Division One | United | 2-3 | City | 15-09-1962 |

1961/1962

| Division One | City | 0-2 | United | 10-02-1962 |
| Division One | United | 3-2 | City | 23-09-1961 |

1960/1961

| Division One | City | 1-3 | United | 04-03-1961 |
| Division One | United | 5-1 | City | 31-12-1960 |

1959/1960

Division One	United	0-0	City	06-02-1960
Division One	City	3-0	United	19-09-1959

1958/1959

Division One	United	4-1	City	14-02-1959
Division One	City	1-1	United	27-09-1958

1957/1958

Division One	City	2-2	United	28-12-1957
Division One	United	4-1	City	31-08-1957

1956/1957

Division One	City	2-4	United	02-02-1957
FACS	City	0-1	United	24-10-1956
Division One	United	2-0	City	22-09-1956

1955/1956

Division One	United	2-1	City	31-12-1955
Division One	City	1-0	United	03-09-1955

1954/1955

Division One	United	0-5	City	12-02-1955
FA Cup	City	2-0	United	29-01-1955
Division One	City	3-2	United	25-09-1954

1953/1954

Division One	United	1-1	City	16-01-1954
Division One	City	2-0	United	05-09-1953

1952/1953

Division One	United	1-1	City	03-01-1953
Division One	City	2-1	United	30-08-1952

1951/1952
| Division One | United | 1-1 | City | 19-01-1952 |
| Division One | City | 1-2 | United | 15-09-1951 |

1949/1950
| Division One | City | 1-2 | United | 31-12-1949 |
| Division One | United | 2-1 | City | 03-09-1949 |

1948/1949
| Division One | United | 0-0 | City | 22-01-1949 |
| Division One | City | 0-0 | United | 11-09-1948 |

1947/1948
| Division One | United | 1-1 | City | 07-04-1948 |
| Division One | City | 0-0 | United | 20-09-1947 |

1936/1937
| Division One | City | 1-0 | United | 09-01-1937 |
| Division One | United | 3-2 | City | 12-09-1936 |

1930/1931
| Division One | United | 1-3 | City | 07-02-1931 |
| Division One | City | 4-1 | United | 04-10-1930 |

1929/1930
| Division One | City | 0-1 | United | 08-02-1930 |
| Division One | United | 1-3 | City | 05-10-1929 |

1928/1929
| Division One | United | 1-2 | City | 05-01-1929 |
| Division One | City | 2-2 | United | 01-09-1928 |

1925/1926
FA Cup	City	3-0	United	21-03-1926
Division One	United	1-6	City	23-01-1926
Division One	City	1-1	United	12-09-1925

233

1921/1922

Division One	United	3-1	City	29-10-1921
Division One	City	4-1	United	22-10-1921

1920/1921

Division One	City	3-0	United	27-11-1920
Division One	United	1-1	City	20-11-1920

1919/1920

Division One	United	1-0	City	18-10-1919
Division One	City	3-3	United	11-10-1919

1914/1915

Division One	City	1-1	United	02-01-1915
Division One	United	0-0	City	05-09-1914

1913/1914

Division One	United	0-1	City	11-04-1914
Division One	City	0-2	United	06-12-1913

1912/1913

Division One	City	0-2	United	28-12-1912
Division One	United	0-1	City	07-09-1912

1911/1912

Division One	United	0-0	City	30-12-1911
Division One	City	0-0	United	02-09-1911

1910/1911

Division One	City	1-1	United	21-01-1911
Division One	United	2-1	City	17-09-1910

1908/1909

Division One	United	3-1	City	23-01-1909
Division One	City	1-2	United	19-09-1908

1907/1908

| Division One | City | 0-0 | United | 18-04-1908 |
| Division One | United | 3-1 | City | 21-12-1907 |

1906/1907

| Division One | United | 1-1 | City | 06-04-1907 |
| Division One | City | 3-0 | United | 01-12-1906 |

1902/1903

| Division Two | City | 0-2 | United | 10-04-1903 |
| Division Two | United | 1-1 | City | 25-12-1902 |

1898/1899

| Division Two | City | 4-0 | United | 26-12-1898 |
| Division Two | United | 3-0 | City | 10-09-1898 |

1897/1898

| Division Two | City | 0-1 | United | 25-12-1897 |
| Division Two | United | 1-1 | City | 16-10-1897 |

1896/1897

| Division Two | United | 2-1 | City | 25-12-1896 |
| Division Two | City | 0-0 | United | 03-10-1896 |

1895/1896

| Division Two | City | 2-1 | United | 07-12-1895 |
| Division Two | United | 1-1 | City | 05-10-1895 |

1894/1895

| Division Two | United | 4-1 | City | 05-01-1895 |
| Division Two | City | 2-5 | United | 03-11-1894 |

SOME FANS MEMORIES

The Manchester derby on 20-09-2009 which was at Old Trafford, I believe it was the greatest Manchester derby of all time. When Michael Owen scored a clinical, tremendous goal and MANCHESTER UNITED defeated MANCHESTER CITY by 4-3.

I cannot forget it till death.

Imbesat Xaidi, 21, Karachi, Pakistan.

I remember being in the fantastic Old Trafford for the Manchester derby, I will never forget that moment the legend of ryan giggs picked out Michael owen inside the area and he places it into the bottom corner! What a moment, that's what football is all about! I also remember back in the 2008-2009 season a game against aston villa when it was all square with 1 minute to go and debutant Federico Macheda curled a stunner into the corner, which I feel won us the league, the stand was shaking with the celebrations,

One Love One United! I look forward to much more successful trophy winning seasons ahead and watching our youngsters shine!

Also Sir Alex Ferguson is a living legend and deserves a statue next to sir matt busby's outside the best place on earth.

Glenn Roberts, 16, Hutton, Preston.

It was end of season 96/97 I was 9 years old. Manchester United was doing an open top parade around manchester to show off the premier league trophy as well as the charity shield. I remember being so excited to go and see the players because i was in love with Solskjaer from the day he signed for manchester united. Me, my mum Elaine, my auntie and cousin was in the car, we got there before the bus arrived, the police had blocked all the roads off so no-one was able to get down, for a unknown reason a policeman let us through and to this day I can not understand how we managed it, Manchester United fans was lined down both sides of the street cheering and shouting because they seen a car coming towards them, as we got closer to them and they realised we was not anybody famous all the fans faces were a picture. eventually after getting to the end of the road we managed to get the car parked up and watch my heroes coming home. A classic moment.

I also will also remember why I respect and admire Sir Alex as much as I do, I was 6 years old and my mum (Elaine Williams) took me to The Cliff to watch United train. It was pouring down with rain but i didnt want to leave. Both me and my mum were soaking wet when sir alex pulled out of the car park in his car. He put down his window pointed at me and signalled for me to come over, I was nervous but built up the courage to go over with my mum. He took out a piece of paper from his car signed his autograph and gave it to me before leaving.

Natalie Williams, 22 Clayton, Manchester

First, I knew about Manchester united when after World Cup 2006. I was really in love with Cristiano Ronaldo and Wayne Rooney, so I began to support manchester united. Game by game were so amazing, United were champions. I love Rooney, Ronaldo, Giggs, Neville, Evra, Ji-sung, van Der Sar, Sir Fergie and the others. I'm still supporting United although Ronaldo left Manchester United. Unfortunately, we failed to get the championship on 2008 and 2010. But I always appreciate them to get treble champions...Come on my red army... GLORY GLORY MANUTD !!

Julia Hartanty, 18 jakarta, Indonesia

I was 11 years old and went to the Champions League Final 1999 with my dad, I was sitting six rows behind the goal in the united end, the most amazing night in my life, unforgettable.

Marc Leighfield, 21 Moffat Dumfriesshire Scotland

THE MANCHESTER UNITED PREMIER YEARS

I have 2 outstanding memories, the first is from the 1998-99 Champions League Final. I always watch football with my mum. 89 minutes played and she said 'getting to the final is a really good achievement.' I replied ' its not over yet. Never say never.' Seconds later Teddy Sheringham scored. I jumped across the room and we where celebrating so loud that we missed Ole's winner. My second comes from the 2009-10 season. Me, my mum and my dad were watching the first manchester derby. I had been released from hospital after having my appendix removed. As a city fan my dad was beginning to gloat being happy with the draw. Michael Owen scored the winner I jumped up to celebrate and burst my stiches.

Darren Wilkie,   20,   York,   North Yorkshire

The great years for me were the 80's and 90's, working for SPS Security at Old Trafford during the years when Eric Cantona was there. I practically lived there, one day I came face to face with Eric, it was awesome. Mid 90's things started to change at Old Trafford, now the atmosphere has changed so much it's like a different set of fans. We used to sing loud and proud and wave a flag, now it's just small groups of around 4 or 5 clapping in certain parts of Old Trafford, happy clappers, just hope they don't have those horns this season, it's really sad how it is all changing.

1999, what a season, what it must have been like to have been a fan of MUFC in Barcelona for the final, when Ole put the goal in the Germans net. I jumped so high in the pub, I completely forgot there was a large extractor fan on the ceiling immediately above where I was sat. Broke my hand, but I still partied for quite a while.

Phil Alexander, 42 Cheshire

My memory in last season was the Sunderland game, the score was 1-2 we were sitting at the stretford End.. we went out 1 minute from the full time so we can catch the tram..while we were walking next to the musuem United scored and everyone including us were running around Old Trafford celebrating as we scored.

Majid Al Ahmedi, 25, UAE

The 1999 champions league semi final 2nd leg v juventus 2-0 down early in the game looked like the dream was over then Roy Keane gets booked which meant he would miss the final if we qualified. He took it on himself to get the team through to the final, he played like a man on mission to get the game back on track he pulled one back with a bullet of a header Yorke scored the second and then Cole got the winner. we won 4-3 on aggregate and the rest is history...

Lee Williams 33 wolverhampton

"Beckham into Sheringham and Solskjaer has won it! Manchester United have reached the Promised Land."

Every United fan in the world must remember these epic words and if they are like me, they still get chills!

What makes this even more special for me is that I was 10 and it was the first football match I had ever seen in my life. What an introduction to the beautiful game! As Sir. Alex would say "Football - bloody hell." I've been a Manchester United ever since.

Dawn Rosales 20 Trinidad and Tobago

My favourite memory was 1999, champions league final when united was a goal down and we bounced back to win the title.

Kwabena Sarfo Boamey, 20, Kumasi,Ghana

Best memory for me would be United V Arsenal 1999 Fa cup semi final, Schemiechel penalty save and Giggsy's goal.. My favourite match ever!

Rob Shipton, 18, Whitland

I am Natie, from London, age 25, I was 14 when United won the treble and remember watching it with my neighbours and we were so upset but suddenly in 2 mins united won it and we was all dancing round the house!

Natie Grossnass, 25, London

Well the Champions League win against Bayern Munich and Chelsea are the top for me and the wins against arsenal in the champions league at the emirates with the Ronaldo goals, and finally the Paul Scholes goal against City in the last minute

Rebecca Lucy Darrington   21   Romford Essex

Cantona's goal away at Newcastle sticks in my mind and the game away at Chelsea which was really high scoring, I loved both recent European cup wins of course, my fave player of all time is Paul Scholes, his passing and shooting, I just love to watch him. I loved Rooneys goal v Villa in the carling cup final 2010 also to win us the game.

Michael Reeman, 28, Birmingham

MY BEST PREMIER XI

SCHMEICHEL

G.NEVILLE   BRUCE   FERDINAND   IRWIN

RONALDO   SCHOLES   KEANE   GIGGS

CANTONA   ROONEY

BACK FROM THE BRINK
by Justin Blundell
The Untold story of Manchester United in the Depression Years 1919-32

If Manchester United revelled in innocent childhood during the Edwardian era, winning two league titles and an FA Cup within 9 years of the club's establishment, it endured a painful adolescence as the inter-war years saw it absent from the honours lists. In this amusing, irreverent and fascinating account, Justin Blundell traces the events of the club's lost youth between the end of the Great War and the worldwide economic crisis that almost scuppered the club yet ushered in a new era under James Gibson.

SPECIAL OFFER: £8

Blundell's punchy account deserves to stand alongside the many volumes written about the post-war glory years - it tells the story of how United survived the Depression Years and came back from the brink.

OLD TRAFFORD
BY IAIN MCCARTNEY
FOREWORD BY PADDY CRERAND

February 2010 saw the Centenary of Manchester United's first game at Old Trafford. To celebrate this auspicious occasion Iain McCartney has updated his original 1996 book on the stadium with new pictures of the last 100 years.

Calling on the vast photographic resources of avid Manchester United collectors and enthusiasts, what emerges is a fascinating history of the first super stadium of English football. It also traces the history of United via its home ground.

SPECIAL OFFER: £10

Now the stadium, a vast arena holding over 75,000 seats, is worth over £200m. Not bad for a patch of land once given over to cattle grazing.

From Goal line to Touch-line
My Career with Manchester United
by Jack Crompton

Jack Crompton is one of the surviving members of Manchester United's swashbuckling 1948 FA Cup winning side and the first to pen his autobiography. Jack served the club as goalkeeper, trainer and caretaker manager for over 9 years playing a major part in the triumphs of the immediate post-war years and witnessed the rise of the Busby Babes first hand before leaving for a coaching role with Luton Town in 1956.

Now a sprightly octagenarian, Jack is in a unique position to discuss the considerable changes in the game during his lifetime and look back on a seven decade long association with Manchester United.

SPECIAL OFFER £12

THE COMPLETE ERIC CANTONA
BY DARREN PHILLIPS
ISBN: 1901746585 - £10.95 - PAPERBACK

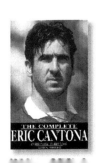

ERIC CANTONA'S CAREER at Old Trafford lasted only 5 years but its lasting impact is still being felt today. During that comparatively small span, Cantona's dedication and self-confidence enabled a club to emerge from over a quarter of a century of failure and self-doubt. THE COMPLETE ERIC CANTONA details every game Eric played for Manchester United, Leeds United and the French national team as well as potted summaries of his career in France. Darren Phillips has painstakingly researched his remarkable career in France, England and in the French national team. The Complete Eric Cantona sheds new light on a football career that altered the dynamics of English football

SPECIAL OFFER: £8

THE STORY OF THE GREEN & GOLD
by Charbel Boujaude
Newton Heath 1878-1902

THE GREEN AND GOLD campaign launched recently by Manchester United fans against the club's owners, the Glazer family, took its inspiration from the colours of the original Newton Heath club from which United emerged in 1902. This book attempts to explain the characters and history of that club.

Unfortunately, Heath's financial health took a turn for the worse following a ruinous court case. The debts dragged the club slowly but surely toward bankruptcy and a date with destiny. By 1902 a decade of Second Division anonymity, ever-decreasing quality on the field and mounting debts forced the club to the brink and, eventually, via Harry Stafford's famous dog, the salvation of local brewing magnate John Henry Davies and the formation of Manchester United.

SPECIAL OFFER £7

THE VILLA PREMIER YEARS 1992-2010
A Fan's View From A Fan
By Steve Brookes
128PP - Paperback - £8.95

Looking back over 18 seasons in the Premier League, Aston Villa fanatic Steve Brookes chooses his favourites players and most memorable moments. From Paul 'God' McGrath to James Milner, Steve's favaourites in Claret and Blue are assessed and rated for their commitment to the cause.

'The Villa Premier Years' contains Steve's subjective assessment of his favourites, along with profiles of the owners and managers who have presided over affairs at Villa Park. But with a steady partnership of manager and owner at the helm, it seems those troubled times are over.

SPECIAL OFFER: £8

18 TIMES AND THAT'S A FACT!
BY JUSTIN BLUNDELL
400PP - PAPERBACK - £10.95

This was the season when Sir Alex Ferguson's long-held wish to 'knock Liverpool off their f**king perch' was made flesh. A season so successful that even European Cup Final defeat to Barcelona couldn't fully diminish the club's achievements. Justin Blundell tells the story of United's triumphs in a punchy, rabidly red-eyed review of every single match and goal.

Written with an eye for the humour and pomoposity surrounding the modern game, Justin Blundell brings the matches, goals and managerial spats back to life in an entertaining, minute-by-minute guide to the matches that really mattered. "18 times" is a book for everyone who lives and breathes United, not just on match day but every single day.

EMPIRE PUBLICATIONS

Dear Reader,

If you have read this far it's probably safe to say you've enjoyed the boo We are an independent Mancunian publisher specialising in books on the spor music and history of our great city.

If you would like to receive regular updates on our titles you can join o mailing list by email: **enquiries@empire-uk.com**, by sending your details t **Empire Publications, 1 Newton St., Manchester M1 1HW** or by calli 0161 872 4721.

We also update our website regularly: **www.empire-uk.com** with o latest title information.

Cheers

Ashley Shaw
Editor

COMPLETIST'S DELIGHT - THE FULL EMPIRE BACK LIST

ISBN	TITLE	AUTHOR	PRICE	STATUS†
1901746003	SF Barnes: His Life and Times	A Searle	£14.95	IP
1901746011	Chasing Glory	R Grillo	£7.95	IP
190174602X	Three Curries and a Shish Kebab	R Bott	£7.99	IP
1901746038	Seasons to Remember	D Kirkley`	£6.95	IP
1901746046	Cups For Cock-Ups+	A Shaw	£8.99	OOP
1901746054	Glory Denied	R Grillo	£8.95	IP
1901746062	Standing the Test of Time	B Alley	£16.95	IP
1901746070	The Encyclopaedia of Scottish Cricket	D Potter	£9.99	IP
1901746089	The Silent Cry	J MacPhee	£7.99	OOP
1901746097	The Amazing Sports Quiz Book	F Brockett	£6.99	IP
1901746100	I'm Not God, I'm Just a Referee	R Entwistle	£7.99	OOP
1901746119	The League Cricket Annual Review 2000	ed. S. Fish	£6.99	IP
1901746143	Roger Byrne - Captain of the Busby Babes	I McCartney	£16.95	OOP
1901746151	The IT Manager's Handbook	D Miller	£24.99	IP
190174616X	Blue Tomorrow	M Meehan	£9.99	IP
1901746178	Atkinson for England	G James	£5.99	IP
1901746186	Think Cricket	C Bazalgette	£6.00	IP
1901746194	The League Cricket Annual Review 2001	ed. S. Fish	£7.99	IP
1901746208	Jock McAvoy - Fighting Legend *	B Hughes	£9.95	IP
1901746216	The Tommy Taylor Story*	B Hughes	£8.99	OOP
1901746224	Willie Pep*+	B Hughes	£9.95	OOP
1901746232	For King & Country*+	B Hughes	£9.95	OOP
1901746240	Three In A Row	P Windridge	£7.99	IP
1901746259	Viollet - Life of a legendary goalscorer+PB	R Cavanagh	£16.95	OOP
1901746267	Starmaker	B Hughes	£16.95	IP
1901746283	Morrissey's Manchester	P Gatenby	£5.99	IP
1901746313	Sir Alex, United & Me	A Pacino	£8.99	IP
1901746321	Bobby Murdoch, Different Class	D Potter	£10.99	OOP
190174633X	Goodison Maestros	D Hayes	£5.99	OOP
1901746348	Anfield Maestros	D Hayes	£5.99	OOP
1901746364	Out of the Void	B Yates	£9.99	IP
1901746356	The King - Denis Law, hero of the…	B Hughes	£17.95	OOP
1901746372	The Two Faces of Lee Harvey Oswald	G B Fleming	£8.99	IP
1901746380	My Blue Heaven	D Friend	£10.99	IP
1901746399	Viollet - life of a legendary goalscorer	B Hughes	£11.99	IP
1901746402	Quiz Setting Made Easy	J Dawson	£7.99	IP
1901746410	The Insider's Guide to Manchester United	J Doherty	£20	IP
1901746437	Catch a Falling Star	N Young	£17.95	IP
1901746453	Birth of the Babes	T Whelan	£12.95	OOP
190174647X	Back from the Brink	J Blundell	£10.95	IP
1901746488	The Real Jason Robinson	D Swanton	£17.95	IP
1901746496	This Simple Game	K Barnes	£14.95	IP
1901746518	The Complete George Best	D Phillips	£10.95	IP
1901746526	From Goalline to Touch line	J Crompton	£16.95	IP
1901746534	Sully	A Sullivan	£8.95	IP
901746542	Memories…	P Hince	£10.95	IP
1901746550	Reminiscences of Manchester	L Hayes	£12.95	IP
1901746569	Morrissey's Manchester - 2nd Ed.	P Gatenby	£8.95	IP
901746577	The Story of the Green & Gold	C Boujaoude	£10.95	IP
901746585	The Complete Eric Cantona	D Phillips	£10.95	IP
901746593	18 Times	J Blundell	£9.95	IP
901746 607	Old Trafford - 100 Years at the Theatre of Dreams	I McCartney	£12.95	IP
901746615	Remember Me	K C Kanjilal	£7.95	IP
901746623	The Villa Premier Years	S Brookes	£8.95	IP
901746631	Broken Youth	K Woods	£8.95	IP

Originally published by Collyhurst & Moston Lads Club + Out of print PB Superceded by Paperback edition
In Print/Out Of Print/To Be Published (date)